A Woman Speaks

A Woman Speaks

The Lectures,
Seminars, and Interviews of

ANAÏS NIN

edited with an introduction

by

Evelyn J. Hinz

THE **SWALLOW PRESS** ᴵɴᴄ.

CHICAGO

Published by
The Swallow Press Incorporated
1139 South Wabash Avenue
Chicago, Illinois 60605

First Edition
    Second printing, 1976

Library of Congress Catalog Card Number: 75-15111
ISBN 0-8040-0693-8

Jacket photo by Donna Emerson

Contents

Introduction

Anaïs Nin is fond of reminding her audiences that as a child she was so shy that literally she could not speak to anyone outside her immediate family. Observing her silence, a visiting relative once sympathized with her mother for having borne an abnormal child. The typical response to this anecdote is incredulous laughter, for Anaïs Nin is one of the most fluent, engaging, and spontaneous speakers of our time. She is a woman who calmly commands audiences in the thousands, and one who is equally adept at turning the briefest encounter with a stranger into a memorable dialogue; it is difficult to imagine that even "once upon a time" such an uninhibited and articulate personality should have found communicating difficult.

In view of her present ease, Anaïs Nin knows that the description of what she was like as a child will be difficult to accept and so will occasion laughter; indeed, she relates the episode in such a way that one is compelled to laugh. Nin also knows, however, how much we need to believe that such a triumph over handicaps is possible and how much our admiration for an accomplished person can be discouraging rather than encouraging to our own aspirations if we are not reminded of the struggles that preceded that success. Finally, she also knows that the tendency to cling to the idea that the person who exhibits remarkable qualities was invariably born with exceptional talents and advantages may be an inverted way of rationalizing one's own passivity and mediocrity.

So, far from passing off her early reticence as a joke, Nin's tactic is to turn the incredulity and admiration of her listeners back upon them in the form of a challenge. She goes on to explain how it was that she overcame her shyness and came to be able to communicate so well: it was through the process of keeping her diary in which she struggled to discover her identity and to perfect her ability to articulate what she thought and felt. What it took, in other words, was a determination to find a way out and a willingness to work for one's dreams. So that the secret of success, she emphatically concludes, is not necessarily a matter of exceptional talent; rather it is a matter of exceptional stubbornness. We are not exceptional in our beginnings; we become exceptional by refusing to accept the obstacles which destiny has placed before us.

When publication of the *Diary* first brought requests that she speak in person, Nin was hesitant. "I didn't know at first why you wanted to see me," she observed to a university audience in March, 1973; "I felt everything was in the work and I didn't know why we needed to talk together." She was concerned that the desire to see and hear her might reflect a spurious curiosity about her personal life or a faddish response to publicity, a desire to get in on the latest thing without having to do any homework. What she had to offer, what she wanted to be credited with and remembered for were the struggles she had gone through in her determination to perfect herself as an artist, as a woman, and as an integrated human being, and the complete story of these struggles she had told and published in her *Diary*. Why, then, did people still insist upon seeing her in person?

As she gradually came to understand, the need reflected an apprehensiveness about the reality of the life portrayed in the *Diary*, a concern that possibly the woman with whose struggles one had identified and in whose convictions one wanted to share was not real but a fictional creation, a fear lest this apparently painstaking record of an individual's search for viable truths might be discovered to be partially or totally a masterful fabrication. The need to see her, the writer of the *Diary*, was a need to be reassured that such a life was possible because such a person was real.

As Nin explained to an audience in October, 1972, it was her awareness of this general disillusionment, the "painful discovery of our loss of faith" in the integrity of our public leaders and artists, together with the loss of faith in the reality of the creative will, which motivated her to come forward and speak in person. Having read the story of her life as she had told it, having watched how she created and shaped that life, her readers "needed to be sure that there was an integrity between the writer and the *Diary*, that the *Diary* was not an invention—that it was not image-making in the false, fraudulent sense. They needed to know that. They needed to hear my voice. The needed for me to be there." The reason that Nin finally decided to answer the demand for her appearance in person, then, was through her own example to combat the skepticism on the part of the modern individual toward the possibility of achieving and exercising personal integrity and then to demonstrate the possibility of retaining that integrity when functioning in a public capacity.

Aside from her words themselves, there are three major ways in which an address by Anaïs Nin operates to reassure the audience that there is a continuity between what she has written and who she is. One is the simple matter of her physical presence itself, in the sense that there is a perfect correlation between the kind of woman which the *Diary* leads one to expect and the woman who rises to her feet or walks to the center of the stage in response to the words of the Master of Ceremonies. "Ladies and gentleman, may I present Anaïs Nin." It is not a question of likeness to photographs one may have seen but rather of correspondence between her appearance and gestures and the style and substance of her writing. There are in her movements the same fluidity and grace, there is in her manner the same balance of gaiety and intimacy, there is in her eyes and smile the same quality of tenderness and honesty which characterizes the way she relates her experiences in the *Diary*. As one watches her approach the microphone one never has the feeling that here is the author coming out from *behind* the hard covers of her book but rather that here is the woman herself stepping out from *between* its pages. It's quite as if one were sitting and reading the *Diary* and suddenly looked up to see the image one had formed become real. Possibly it is more this thrill of recognition than any excitement simply over seeing her in person that sweeps her audiences to their feet when she appears.

Then she begins to speak, and again it is the voice one expects: a youthful voice—high, pure, melodious, something like that of a boy soprano; a cultured voice—with a French accent contouring the harsher English consonants and giving her words a magical quality; a tremulous voice—warm, unhurried, and haunting. Her first words themselves, or words that she typically utters at the outset, are: "Can you all hear me? can you hear me in the back?" If there are answers of "no," she waits until the necessary acoustical adjustments have been made, or if it is a small room and the arrangements are to have her seated, she offers to solve the problem herself by standing—her usual position in large assemblies and which she frequently maintains for as long as two hours at a time. Whatever the situation, she is concerned to make certain that every person is able to hear her, because it is to the individual and not to the mass that she addresses herself.

The issues which Nin treats in her lectures are characteristically contemporary ones—the status of women, racial injustice, space-age technology and its relation to art, trends in art and psychology, alienation—in some ways issues with which she does not deal in the *Diary,* or at least not directly. But her method is to approach these subjects in terms of the discoveries she has made and recorded in the *Diary,* and thus one is never given the impression that in the face of contemporary reality Nin has come to think differently or that the convictions expressed in the *Diary* are impractical and relevant only to artificial situations. Furthermore, often her practice is to take a theme or situation from the *Diary* and then to analyze and expand upon it until its relevance to the contemporary scene becomes evident. So that the general impression her lecture generates is that of a rhythmic interchange: back from the present to the *Diary,* forward from the *Diary* to the present. And in this way the *Diary* is revealed to be not only a living document but a perpetually open and ongoing book.

Frequently also Nin includes in her address a reading of a portion of the *Diary,* and typically this reading functions as the conclusion to her lecture. So that, just as she comes out of the *Diary* to speak in person, having spoken, having reassured her audience that the woman who is speaking to them is the same woman who spoke from the *Diary,* she then withdraws back again into its pages, leaving her audience with the *Diary* in place of her physical presence, leaving them with the place where she may always be found and from which she will always continue to speak.

A final way in which Nin's lectures serve to reassure the audience is through the question-and-answer period with which they characteristically end. The usual procedure is for her to speak *to* her audience for from thirty minutes to an hour and then, though she also extends this invitation frequently throughout her lecture, to invite her audience to speak *with* her. "I don't like this to be just a one-sided thing, I speaking to you," she explains; "I would like you now to talk with me, ask me any questions you may have, about what I have said, about the diaries, about anything at all." If by chance no questions are immediately forthcoming, Nin does not take this opportunity, as so many would, to depart; instead she goes on speaking for awhile and then issues the invitation again. Thus one never has the feeling that she volunteers to answer questions simply because it is part of the contract, but rather that she is genuinely interested in hearing from her audience and in speaking together. Similarly, she sets no time limit on the answering of questions, staying until everyone has had the opportunity to speak.

Depending upon the nature of the question, Nin's answers may range from a simple "yes" or "no" to a lengthy consideration or explanation of the issue, from an uncompromising "I don't believe that" to a compassionate "I understand." But whatever the question, in answering, her chief concern is first that she has understood the question correctly and second that the person asking the question understands her answer. Although the questions she is asked are frequently deliberate and rehearsed, her answers never are. Similarly, though she will, in the best pedagogical manner, repeat a question asked of her in order to make certain that her entire audience has heard what is being asked, she does not then treat it as an anonymous question but rather directs her answer back to the specific questioner. In this way, despite the fact that literally the situation is one of a crowd on the one side and Anaïs Nin alone facing them on the other, each individual comes away with the impression that there has been a personal and intimate conversation with Anaïs Nin.

This association with the personal and the intimate, finally, is according to Nin the source of woman's strength and humanity, and thus her lectures are ultimately important for their demonstration of what it means to be a woman. When Anaïs Nin speaks it is a woman who speaks; whatever her subject, she approaches it from a feminine point of view and expresses herself in a distinctly feminine idiom; thus her lectures represent not only the capabilities of women in the arts or as public figures, they also exemplify the power and range of the authentically feminine voice and vision. We have many women today who are not afraid to speak their minds; we need more like Anaïs Nin who are not afraid to speak from their hearts, who are proud to be women and are concerned with articulating what womanhood means—for themselves, for other women, and for men. We need to read the *Diary*, we need to listen to Anaïs Nin.

* * *

For every person who has been able to hear and talk to Anaïs Nin a thousand would like to, a million need to, and only a relative few will ever now be able to. Consequently the purpose of this edition of the lectures, seminars, and interviews of Anaïs Nin is to provide the next best thing: an edited reproduction of Nin's public voice as others have heard it, giving many more the opportunity to participate imaginatively and to experience her presence at least indirectly. This being the objective, wherever necessary, humanistic principles have outweighed academic rules. This is not an edition designed to "preserve" Nin's spoken words for future scholars but to make her words immediately and ultimately available to the widest possible audience. My aim throughout has been to generate for the reader the *effect* which Nin's addresses have upon her listeners; my goal has been to transcribe her presence rather than simply to record her words.

At the same time this is not a popularized edition of Nin's lectures, for if to be true to the spirit of Anaïs Nin involves being concerned with the needs of the public, it also involves the recognition that communication is an art, and that art is for all times. Hence this is not a haphazard collection and uncritical transcription of everything at hand but rather a carefully researched edition prepared in accordance with the following principles.

The edition consists of edited excerpts selected from three basic sources: public lectures Nin delivered, seminars she conducted together with material from less formal gatherings in which she participated, and broadcast or private interviews she has granted. The period covered is roughly seven years—from 1966 when the first volume of her *Diary* was published to late 1973, the year in which she was probably most active as a public speaker. Nin had, of course, given lectures prior to 1966, just as she did not stop making public appearances in 1973. But for the purposes of this edition some arbitrary limits had to be set, and for the above reasons, plus my discussion earlier of the role of the response to the *Diary* in determining Nin's decision to become a public person, these dates seem sufficiently justifiable.

Even so, because of Nin's enormous output, not everything within this period could be included, and hence further selectivity became necessary. Now the alternate method to the one which I have adopted would have been to choose representative lectures and to reproduce them in their entirety, but the problem with such a procedure as I came to see it was that too much that was important would have to be left out—i.e., an important passage from a lecture which could not be included because others were on the whole more representative—while one lecture which it was important to include for its representativeness on one account might also contain sections which were repetitive of other lectures specifically chosen for their representativeness in that area. Consequently my practice was to choose representative passages from the entire range of lectures and then to arrange these in such a way as to reflect the structure of a characteristic lecture, in this way attempting to provide total coverage in terms of content and at the same time suggesting Nin's lecture style. Each chapter, with the exception of the first, is concerned with one of Nin's major themes and is composed of lecture and question-and-answer sections, since, as I noted, Nin's practice is first to speak and then to invite questions. The first chapter consists of the complete text of a commencement address Nin delivered, the last consists mainly of questions and answers, and thus the general format of the edition is also designed to reflect the structure of an individual lecture, or, in other words, the edition may be read as one large composite address.

Specifically my procedure was as follows: first to audit all the available tapes of her lectures, seminars, and interviews with a view to isolating her representative themes and defining her style; next, working from transcripts, to compare respective treatments of a similar theme to decide which was most characteristic; and then finally to arrange the chosen excerpts in accordance with the present format.

Each excerpt used is coded in the following manner: with the example as 73-A, the numerals refer to the year (1973) in which the address was given, the letter to the relative chronological position within that year. More complete information regarding dates and also the place and nature of the individual addresses is provided in the Table of Tape Codes which follows. Hopefully this method will prove convenient for those who are interested in the historical context of a given lecture, or in Nin's development, for example, and yet prevent bibliographical details from standing in the way of those who want to read with the illusion that they are listening to Nin in person.

In regard to transcribing and editing the respective excerpts, my aim was similarly to reproduce Nin's words and phrases as faithfully as possible but also to reproduce for the reader the impression which Nin's lectures make on the listener. Recognizing that occasionally direct transcription does not necessarily produce for the reader the same impression which the spoken words do for the listener, I have frequently deleted such things as repetitious phrases, false starts, sentence fragments—although none that would in any way serve to qualify a given passage. Major deletions, of course, are signified by ellipses, and all of these were made either because the deleted material itself was to be reproduced in another chapter or place or because a better expression of the same idea was to be found in a different lecture. Finally, again in the interests of keeping the text clear of editorial apparatus and at the same time in the awareness that unspecific references to certain persons or books might puzzle the reader and interrupt his response, names and titles have sometimes been silently inserted.

In editing the words of others, particularly the questions addressed to Nin, a rigorous use of paraphrase and condensation had to be employed. For as Nin herself quipped in response to one question which went on and on: "That's not a question, that's a lecture!" In selecting questions, my rule again was to choose the most representative ones, and then to decide on the basis of both the question and the answer into which chapter they should be placed. I should also mention that excerpts from interviews are typically placed in the question-and-answer sections, but that occasionally when the interview question was extremely general Nin's answer was excerpted and placed in a lecture section.

Whatever changes have been made in the process of editing the material for this edition have been approved by Anaïs Nin, and consequently it should be regarded as a totally authorized reproduction. And furthermore, as one feels called upon to observe in the Age of Watergate, whatever else may be missing, no expletives of substance have been deleted.

Evelyn Hinz
Winnepeg, Manitoba

Table of Tape Codes

I
A New Center
of Gravity

As I was coming to you today I was thinking: what would I most like to be given on a day like today? What do we seem to lack most, what do we seem to be hungriest for? And I felt it was *faith.*

As we evolved into a new consciousness and clarity and clairvoyance, seeing through certain dogmas and certain hypocrisies and certain traditions that we didn't want, there came with this lucidity also a fear and a great loneliness and a loss of faith. I hope this will only be temporary, because when we begin to have a new vision of the world, together with that new vision we have to have the courage to do away with the old way of looking at things. So what I would like to give you today is the one faith that has supported and has meant so much to me all through my life.

It was a faith that at the beginning was tabooed in the American culture. It was a faith that there is one place where we can work for perfection, for evolution, for growth, for the cessation of hostilities, for the end of prejudices. It was the faith that we must turn to ourselves as a creative piece of work—not only in the arts but in the creation of our lives.

What I wanted to give you today was a new center of gravity, because we have tried to live too much within the group and with

1

the notion of the millions, with the sense of the too many, of the outer forces, the external world. Great pressures have been put on us, and some of us, not having something to equalize it in our inner life, collapsed under the weight and felt despair, depression, frustration, and therefore became angry people. And an angry and unhappy man is dangerous to society. As Otto Rank said one time in a book called *Will to Happiness:* "A happy man is an addition to society, an unhappy man is a great danger."

What I wanted to do is to displace the axis from thinking in terms of the many, which we thought was virtuous and unselfish, to thinking in terms, first of all, of making the perfect individual who could receive with sensitivity the messages and the signals of other people's distress; who could consider other human beings as human beings and transcend matters of race and religion and tradition and whatever background, whatever ideas were given to us, unquestioned by us. Today we have questioned everything, but we have also entered into some negative rebellion—against rather than for.

Now the will to create, or creative will, which pursues the artist and haunts the artist, I found to be applicable to our individual life, to our personal life, as it is to a work of art. That is, we do have a will, a possibility, and a potential to change ourselves, and doing that is not an egocentric or turned-in activity. It is an activity that ultimately affects, influences, and transforms an entire community. So I feel the great changes in the world will come from a great change in our consciousness. We have become more aware; we must not despair.

We are more aware of the obstacles, we are more aware of the falsities that we have to peel away. R. D. Laing, an English psychologist, put it this way in *Politics of Experience*: "We all live in the hope that authentic meetings between human beings can still occur. Psychotherapy consists in the tearing away of all that stands between us—the props, masks, roles, lies, anxieties, projections, and introjections—in short, all the carry-overs from the past, the transference and counter-transference, that we use by habit and collusion, wittingly or unwittingly, as our currency for relationships."

Now all this may seem to belong to the purely personal world, but it's the same principle that would apply to countries and to other races. If we perfected our ability for relationship to the near, if we really understood and saw the people near us, we would also be able to understand the people far away whom we wage war against instead.

I want to give you a center of gravity in your own soul, an axis in an unstable world, and a core so that you will build a one-celled world with a creative will—the world as we would like it. I have no faith in exchanges of systems, because systems are corruptible, and until we have worked for the uncorruptible human being, we will not have an uncorruptible system. Systems are corruptible but not the creative self, not the self and not the world that is created on a human basis. The personal and the human and the intimate give us a compassion and an insight into others' motives and ways of acting. They eliminate the guilt which is associated with the feeling of individual responsibility. For the minute we take personal responsibility for everything that happens, we also become aware that we can create an individual world and a beautiful world.

There is a new consciousness, an awareness that we have to equalize the inner and the outer worlds, and for this we have to have what the Thai people call "the house of the spirit." For every house that they build they build a little miniature replica to be inhabited by the spirits. I think we need that. We need the sanctuary, we need a place of meditation, we need the inner core with which to watch events, understand them, relive them. We need to have a new kind of religion without dogma, a new kind of nationalism without fanaticism, a new synthesis of character.

The real meaning of the word "educate" is "to lead the way out," and sometimes the artist has been able to do that unconsciously. He doesn't despair. He doesn't say, as our pragmatic culture has said, that the world is the way it is, unchangeable, nothing can be altered. Instead, the artist has always said: "Although the world is like this, if I don't like it, I can change it." And he has changed it. He's changed our music, he's changed our painting. He's changed our theatre, he's changed our point of view in the novel. He changes every day. And it is because he believes that life is changeable, that it can be metamorphosed, and that it can be conquered, that he allies himself much more with the hero. The hero is the one who believes that he can conquer. But today we seem to have stopped believing that we can conquer. We have repudiated the idea of the hero.

We need this individuality to resist the contagion of negative states, and if there is anything I have observed in my visits to the colleges it was this combination of romantic and marvelous emotional openness to life, and occasionally this shadow underneath, a negative kind of rebellion—not liking what *is,* but never thinking about what must be done with this world to make it what you want it to be, nor even the strength of the creative will which says that one can make what is not there. And I'm not speaking only of the artist, because this starts from the making of a house to everything that we do in our lives. We need to see that the barriers are not there, that they are created by pragmatic reality and they are meant to be defeated by us.

The disease of our time is this loss of faith, because the individual was made to feel so helpless and was so imbued with the idea of an unchanging reality, that his mind was filled with negativity. It is because we abdicated personal responsibility and personal orientation that we became passive in the face of destiny. We were overwhelmed by the great spaces opened by science and were overwhelmed by the machine, whereas everything could fall under our dominion and be a part of a creation. Without this individual resistance, this individual core and axis, we are subject to group sickness, we are subject to collective neurosis. For neurosis, after all, is only a word for negativity.

So I want to create faith in you. There is a realm in which you are all-powerful, in which you are the captain of your soul. And ultimately this cell that you work at connects with millions of other cells. You project your inner reality into the external. But first you have to make your psychic core a reality.

I'm going to read you a letter I wrote to a young writer who felt that if he gave away a story he would have nothing left—very similar to the way Truman Capote sold his dreams for ten dollars and then missed them and asked for them back. This young writer was questioning why I felt friendship toward him or listened to him. And I said: "I like to live always at the beginnings of life, not its end. We all lose some of our faith under the oppression of vain leaders, insane history, pathological cruelties of daily life. I am by nature always beginning and believing and so I find your company more fruitful than some of the other people who have asserted their opinions and beliefs and knowledge as the ultimate verity and have fallen into rigid patterns. Curiosity, risk, exploration are forgotten by some of us. You have not yet discovered that you have a lot to give, and that the more you give the more riches you will find in yourself. It amazes me that you feel that each time you write a story you give away one of your dreams and you feel the poorer for it. But then you have not thought that this dream is planted in others, others begin to live it too, it is shared, it is the beginning of friendship and love. How is this world made which you enjoy, the friends around me that you love? They came because I first gave away my stories. They came to respond and to replenish the source. They heard the calling of the *Under a Glass Bell* stories, calling for the fiesta, and they arrived with their own stories. You must not fear or hold back, count or be a miser with your thoughts and your feelings. It is also true that creation comes from an overflow, so you have to learn to intake, to imbibe, to receive, to nourish yourself, and not be afraid of fullness. The fullness is like a tidal wave which then carries you, sweeps you into experience and into writing. Permit yourself to flow and overflow. Allow for the rise in temperature and all the expansions and intensifications. Something is always born of excess. Great art was born of great terror, great loneliness, great inhibitions, instabilities, and it always balances them. If it seems to you that I move in a world of certitudes, you must benefit from the great priviledge of youth, which is that you move in a world of mysteries. But both must be ruled by faith." (71-A)

II
Refusal to Despair

I think we are living now in a period which in some ways resembles the time of the plague. It sounds like a very exaggerated image, but we are confronted every day with despair and horror. There is the nightmare of the war and the fear of the bomb, but you know as well as I all the events that cause our universal anxiety. So the feeling I wanted to give you tonight is that during these events, during these happenings, it is as important for us to step out of history as it is for us to live within it. We have to step out of it in order to find the strength with which to participate in it, with which to live in it, and with which to achieve what I was finally able to achieve in the later diaries, which is a *refusal to despair*. This has meant creativity on the one hand and relationship on the other—the obsession with establishing intimate contact, with friendship, with every form of relationship to man, woman, child, to people close to us and to people in other countries.

It's not only the artist who talks about creativity. We can begin to create in a desert of life, we can begin to create with those that we live with, we can begin to create as children do—immediately writing poems or painting when they can hardly hold a brush or a pen. This creativity is a constant interaction between our life

6

and the struggle with larger issues such as history, whose victim we can become. And in order not to be victimized by it we also have to learn to live apart from it. It's not escape, it's having a place that we return to in order to regain our strength, in order to regain our values, in order not to be shattered by events. (73-C)

It's almost like the man who goes to the bottom of the ocean and takes with him some oxygen to equalize the pressure. I'm talking about equalizing the pressure between outer actions and events which are shattering and devastating to us and then the place where we recompose and reconstruct ourselves, where we finally achieve what Jung called the second birth. The second birth we are entirely responsible for; it's a self-creation. This second birth is the one that *you* can make, and the discovery of that to me was always a great relief. As long as we expect the changes to come only from the outside or from action outside or from political systems, then we are bound to feel helpless, to feel sometimes that reality is bigger and stronger than we are. But if suddenly we begin to feel that there is one person *we* can change, simultaneously we change many people around us. And as a writer I suddenly discovered the enormous radius of influence that one person can have.

So when we make this interior change we do affect the external world. Now everybody separated that and said: there is *either* rushing virtuously to live a collective life *or else* there is this selfish introspection and concern with your own development. But the two are completely interdependent, they are completely intera. 'ive; and the more you have this response to life, the more you have a source to respond with, then of course the more enrichment you pass around you. Why we made a dichotomy between those two— saying that the two wouldn't enrich each other—I don't know. Because whatever the individual does for himself and by himself is something that ultimately flows back again like a river into the collective unconscious. So if we are disappointed today in the external changes it's because not enough of us have worked at raising a better quality of human being: one who is more aware, more able to evaluate, judge others, judge the characters of our leaders. (72-M)

That is the kind of responsibility I think we have to take. For example, when I got hysterical over the assassination of Dr. King, what I felt was guilt, a kind of total guilt. Though I am incapable of such an act of hostility, still I felt it came from all our hostilities. I wrote at the end of one diary about war. When war came in '39, I said: "I have never been responsible for an act of war and yet I am now involved in this thing that has happened to the whole world." And even then I felt that this was an aggregate of all our hostilities, and that's why I fight hostility. (72-D)

We have to work upon ourselves because, as Loren Eisley said, every time we come to terms with hostility within ourselves we are creating the possibility of someday not having war. In other words, I'm putting back into the self the responsibility for the collective life. If each one of us took very seriously the fact that every little act, every little word we utter, every injury we do to another human being is really what is projected into larger issues; if we could once begin to think of it that way, then each one of us, like a small cell, would do the work of creating a human self, a kind of self who wouldn't have ghettos, a kind of self that wouldn't go to war. Then we could begin to have the cell which would influence an enormous amount of cells around you. I don't think we can measure the radius of the personal influence of one person, within the home, outside of the home, in the neighborhood, and finally in national affairs.

We never connected those two; we always thought we had to approach the larger issues directly; we never thought we could transform the larger issues by transforming ourselves. If first of all every individual had taught himself lucidity about character, the knowledge of psychological disturbances in depth, and had learned to go inside of himself, he could learn to perceive the workings of others, he would be able to choose better leaders. He would be able to do whatever it is that he does in his profession far better if he had this added lucidity, this clairvoyance that the

recognition of other people's subtlety and complexity gives. (73-E)
As recently as a few weeks ago, I was reading a book called
Future Shock—which gave *me* a shock! Because it implied that
because of technology and our world's accelerated rhythm, we
were doomed not to relate to each other. Because things were happening so fast and we were moving from town to town and we
were uprooted and we were transients, we didn't have time really
for relation. What shocked me was the concept that technology
should dictate to us what our human relations should be and decide that because our life has been accelerated we have no time
for relationship. This is the unfortunate consequence of the false
concept we had about *contact*. And what helped us to distort the
sense of contact was the media, which gave us the illusion that
we were in touch with all the world and everything that was happening in the world. The media fabricate personalities and offer
as false a vision of the world as we can possibly have. Although
sometimes it serves us, most of the time it deceives us. So, ultimately it comes back to the way we conceive of human beings or
events or history or wars or other nations or other races; only from
some kind of evaluation from within, not from the media, do we
really come to an understanding of others. The media give us a
false sense of communication and of contact. (73-G)
We talk about media and we talk about new sensitive tapes and
we think about all kinds of ways of recording, but we never think
of our bodies and our mind and our hearts as receptors. And that
can only happen when we develop a sensitivity, when we get rid
of the defenses which I call the calluses of the soul. R. D. Laing
has a beautiful long paragraph explaining that while we all have
a hope of authentic encounters and relationships taking place, they
will not take place until we unmask ourselves, until we get rid of
the persona, until we get rid of the defenses, the projections and
introjections. He mentions all the interferences; and the diary revealed to me, when I finally opened it up to you, what those interferences were. They were mostly fear, fear of other human beings
—which I suddenly lost the moment that I published the diaries.

So the gamble proved to me that if we gamble in depth, if we offer the deep and the genuine part of ourselves, then it's not destructible. We cannot be destroyed. (73-I)

Alvin Toffler also says in *Future Shock* that the students who are turning toward astrology, toward mysticism, toward the East, toward anything of the spirit, are *dropping out* of technology. I say: "No, they are trying to find a source of strength and a center so that technology doesn't enslave us, so that we are the captains of our own lives." So I don't agree with him at all. The turning toward other things is really an attempt to create a self which can then survive in the air in which we live. He lays great stress on what he calls the acceleration of our lives, and he argues that this is ruining the possibility of contact, of friendships. But I was able to disprove that this year because I took an unusually heavy load of lectures. I couldn't say no; I said yes, yes, yes and I went all over the country. Finally it became very accelerated. I saw so many people, and they passed by so quickly. Yet in spite of that, seeing thousands of people, I was able to select friends and make friendships in those few minutes of passing. So it isn't necessary for us to be victims of accelerated living or of transience or of moving away. It is a question of how deep the contact is when the contact is made. (73-B)

I always had the wish to commune with others, despite the fact that during childhood, what I call my bridge to the world was broken by the desertion of the father, a situation which usually instills a great deal of mistrust. Traumas create this mistrust of human beings, because a human being can hurt you, can desert you, can betray you. Yet I still say that it's a million times better to risk being deserted or betrayed than to withdraw into a fortress of alienation, shut the door and break the contact with others. Because then we really die. That is death. That is emotional death. It is mistrust that makes us do that, mistrust and fear of pain, which I expressed in the diary very often. As a child of eleven, I said I never wanted to love again because whatever you love you lose—I was thinking of my Spanish grandmother whom I would never see again. So I learned that mistrust was the root of the separation between human beings.

I struggled all my life—now with the women's studies, with the women's movement, with men—to involve everyone in this connection, this contact which comes out of feeling for others. For though I experienced mistrust, I did not let that make me insensitive. Yet what *Future Shock* says, specifically almost, is that we are bound to become insensitive; that since we receive too much information, are battered by too many events, and are confronted with the whole universe, the best thing to do and the thing we will ultimately do is to shut off the source of feeling. That's why it's a dangerous book, I think. It's a shocking book because it is accepting what technology might do to us instead of saying we have to struggle against this tendency, against the dehumanization and loss of contact occasioned by the acceleration of life or the fact that we move about so much. (73-G)

I read a remarkable statement the other day about Aldous Huxley who, toward the end of his life when he was invited to speak at Berkeley, said; "I expect that you think I will talk about very scholarly things and give you the sum of all my life's knowledge." And he went on and on about what he knew people expected of him. But then he said: "Tonight I only feel like coming to ask you to be a little kinder to each other." (72-G)

This warmth is something we all need, we need nourishment, we need encouragement. Our culture, however, made us ashamed of paying compliments, of saying beautiful things to other people. We were not supposed to. A compliment was a falsity in itself to the Puritan. You never said anything complimentary. Now the Latin races encourage compliments. They believe that if someone looks beautiful today one should say it. Why do we eliminate that? Why should we consider it false to give each other the nourishing encouragement which sustains us, which is the obverse of destructive criticism, of hostility? (72-D)

Messages are conveyed by the eyes, sometimes by no words at all. It is no excuse to say that technology has accelerated our life to the point where we pass others without noticing them, without contacting, or without a real meeting. A real meeting can take place in one instant. But how does that come about? How do we reach a moment when in one instant we can communicate with another human being? (73-F)

The most beautiful metaphor I know for this connecting with others I discovered when I was invited to Stanford by the electrical engineers to talk about the integrated circuits. I couldn't understand first of all why I was invited. I didn't know anything about integrated circuits. I tried to read the book by the professor who invited me and finally had to ask my friends for explanations. When I got there I was shown through the laboratory and finally talked with the fifteen electrical engineers who do electronic circuits. They showed me the drawings on the walls, the large drawings that they start with and which become smaller and smaller. And then I understood that as a metaphor this was really a wonderful thing. Of course when the artist is ignorant of science then he turns science into a metaphor. And I always said that the artist today will use the images of science, that he will use all the marvelous metaphors of science when he really begins to understand them. So I began to understand the integrated circuit, and I began to think of it as an image of our psychic problem, which was really to find all these fine, terribly delicate connections with other human beings.

Now these circuits are damaged very often in childhood and we don't receive anything. These circuits very often are damaged by the culture or they become insensitive to stimuli. There is also in *Future Shock* the theory that, as a result of technology, we are receiving too many messages, too much information which we cannot cope with, too much devastating news of everything that is happening in the world, and that the way human beings protect themselves from too much emotional receptivity is by trying not to feel at all. And Toffler points out the dangers, just as the psychologists have, of what corresponds to the physical shock in the face of an accident or a sudden death or a sudden tragedy: the body ceases in a sense to be really alive or conscious, and this condition, known as psychic shock, is the way we protect ourselves when we see, for instance, the war in Vietnam on television. The way we have learned to protect ourselves is *not to feel*, which is a terrible danger because then we really become sub-human or non-human and are as far away from our real connection with other human beings as we possibly can be. So we have to fight these dangerous elements in technology which come with an expanded universe and the illusion the media give us of being in touch with everything simply because we are given so much to *see*. You can only be in touch by feeling.

So the integrated circuit is really for the human being quite different from the scientific integrated circuit. It is really the channel of feeling that has to be kept open. Now how do we do that when we want to protect ourselves from feeling too much or from being devastated or being disintegrated by experience? Well, my suggestion was that you build up a sufficient inner spiritual resistance —what I call "the spirit house." We must not close off the circuits, the emotional circuits. That's not the way. Because then we become arid and we really die, psychically. So all those words we used so carelessly before, such as alienation, dropping out, all those words really had a very fatal meaning. Because it is really a kind of death to separate from others, to separate from what is happening in the world, to separate from feeling. (73-E)

I think if we came back to the concept of a small and intimate universe and then realized that what we call the communal life or mass movements are really aggregates of individuals and that the more marvelous, the more developed, the more expanded, the deeper, the more poetic, the more free the individual is, then the mass, the larger movements, would take on a different character. We would not be subjected then to the will or to the distorted power-thoughts of other people. Somehow we felt that the best thing for the community was to abdicate our individuality, not to think for ourselves or to examine ourselves, never realizing that what we could bring to the group and what we brought to the communal life was really the summary of our own self-development, our own growth, and that the more we bring something that *we* have already worked out to the collective life, the more we bring to this mass movement. If we brought something besides our problems or our difficulties or the unsolved parts of our lives, then these tremendously large movements would have another character. They would not serve for war and they wouldn't serve for separations between races and they wouldn't divide us. We wouldn't have so much hostility as we have in our society, a frightening amount of hostility. It's almost a blind hostility that doesn't even know where it comes from, blind anger which strikes out at others and blames others always for whatever trouble we find ourselves in. (73-C)

To me war is a multiplication of our own hostilities, and possibly we are beginning to realize that. For example, when I went to Germany, invited to the Book Fair, I went with a tight heart because so many of my friends are Jews, and I felt very full of hatred of Germany. But on the radio they had a philosopher, who is now the head of the government of the new Germany, saying that we had to combat hostility, individually, every one of us, if we didn't want a war again. *He was saying that, over the radio.* That was my first inkling that possibly there was a new Germany —this consciousness of what hostility or of what passivity toward the leader could lead to. (72-D)

So we can't go on just marching and expecting the change to come always from outside. We tried and we saw that some external changes could be made: the abortion laws, women's rights. There are some changes that can be effected from the outside. But the greatest and most important change must be inner; we must change ourselves as human beings. Because we have really caused minor wars and minor types of violence right amongst ourselves, within our immediate and personal situations: in the family, in relationships, in school, and through our hostility towards the stranger. I experienced that very strongly when I first came to America. The foreigner was an outsider. This feeling belongs to the American culture, and until recently (now I've been adopted) they always used to say "Paris-born Anaïs Nin"—as they say "Russian-born Nabokov" or "Polish-born Kozinski." That is a way of saying that you are an outsider. (73-I)

Then the anger about blaming society for the situation in which we find ourselves—blaming, say, man for the situation in which woman finds herself. I don't believe in that because I believe very much our double responsibility, that we engage ourselves in destructive relationships, that we have a part of the responsibility, unconsciously. When I engaged in a destructive relationship with Gonzalo, there was a part of me that was living through him—the rebel—which I refused to live out myself. I wasn't a victim of anything. There was something going on there which happened to be a destructive alliance. But there was also a positive thing; he was showing me how destructive explosions were, how destructive that kind of rebellion was, the kind of rebellion he manifested. So that I was learning, I was experiencing, I was testing that through another person.

I'll tell you one thing I do feel. I feel we do have a surplus of hostility, of undirected hostility, because we refuse to take part of the responsibility for the things we find ourselves caught in, and that we despair because we only live on the external part of history. If we are going to live in history then we are going to have despair; if we find absolutely no nourishing, no revitalizing, no recharging power in ourselves, then we're going to be bitter and we are always going to be shifting the blame either to society or to the other—or on man, as some women are doing at the moment. You see this makes us feel helpless. If we are helpless, we are angry and if we are angry, we're violent. (72-D)

I came to realize that our need and hunger for closeness, after the terrible period of alienation, occurred because we always blamed alienation on every possible cause except the right one. We were alienated from *ourselves*. How could we love, how could we give, how could we trust, how could we share what we didn't have to give? If we did not spend some time in creating ourselves in depth and power, with what were we going to relate to others? (72-G)

And of course when you're interested in growth, you're interested in the growth of those around you. They are absolutely interdependent. You grow only insofar as people around you are also growing and expanding and becoming freer. It is something that is interactive, something that you give to each other.

It isn't something that you accomplish alone. What you accomplish alone and what you have to do first of all is to *exist*, to *be*, so that you can be then a friend or a lover or a mother or a child. In other words, what our culture was saying was something so illogical, so impossible. It was saying: "Don't concern yourself with yourself. Be generous, be active in the world, give yourself to causes and all that *without a self!*" What can you give when there is no self, when you have no sensitivity, no receptivity, no warmth, nothing to contact others *with*? And this error grew and grew. (73-G)

In our twenties we have conflicts. We think everything is either-or, black or white; we are caught between them and we lose all our energy in the conflicts. My answer, later on in maturity, was to do them all. Not to exclude any, not to make a choice. I wanted to be a woman, I wanted to be an artist, I wanted to be everything. And I took everything in, and the more you take in the more strength you find waiting to accomplish things and to expand your life, instead of the other (which is what we have been taught to do) which is to look for structure and to fear change, *above all to fear change*. Now I didn't fear change, and that is another thing I learned from psychology, that we evolve. We don't need revolutions provided we evolve, provided we are constantly open to new experience, provided we are open to other human beings and what they have to give us. (72-L)

There is a beautiful book, entitled *Out of Africa*, by Isak Dinesen, who had a coffee farm and lived a long time with the Africans. Natural disasters played a central role in the court of justice of the Africans and were used as evidence, whether in the case of an accident or a deliberate act like murder. This is a totally different idea of justice, absolutely different from ours, and she had a very difficult time trying to see things as the Africans saw them. But she conceded that it was part of their culture and it was sincere. It was their concept of justice, and it had to be carried out. She didn't try to impose white justice on the African village. The recognition of other cultures and other forms of thought, knowing when to yield, I think is part of our gift for relationship. There is a time when yielding is not conceding but acceptance of the other's existence and also of the motivation for what he does. (72-D)

This is a good night to talk about the source of strength which we need when the outer changes fail us. Before, when I talked about that, people said I was referring to the Ivory Tower, to a great concern and obsession with art and a turning away from action. But I never meant that. I meant that they were interrelated and that when we can't act in the outside or the outside doesn't change and we want to break our heads against the things that we can't change, then it is time just simply to move back to the center of ourselves. I discovered this source of strength in the way all of us discover a source of strength, which is during the first traumatic experiences, the first handicaps, the first difficulties. Coming from what the social welfare calls the broken home, being uprooted, knowing what poverty is, coming to a country whose language I didn't know—all these things taught me simply to put my roots in the self. As I said, I became "a lady with transportable roots." This is very important to all of us because our culture gave us a false impression of the value of living completely in history, completely objectively, completely outside in what was happening—that there was something almost evil about subjectivity. . . . So I like to have this image of a place where you construct some source of strength, some way of resisting outer pressures. And I didn't mean the Ivory Tower. I often say if you write me a letter to the Ivory Tower, I won't answer.

I started with a conviction which I've never had to retract: that all of us can be hurt or in trouble. I had another conviction, which came from Baudelaire, that in all of us there is a man, a woman, and child—which solves all the question of militancy! In all of us there is a man, a woman, and a child, and the child is usually an orphan. So we have a tremendous task to do: we have to take care of this orphan in ourselves and in others; we have to act out our creativity in every moment of our life. And I remember doing something which was considered very silly at the time. When war was imminent in '39, I was living on a houseboat. I hadn't finished painting and fixing it and so I was still working on it while my friends were collapsing and saying: "The war is coming. Why are you painting and fixing the boat?" I said: "Well, I'm only doing it to sustain my own defiance of catastrophe." It was really a spiritual thing. I had to do that to maintain myself from collapsing—as they were collapsing *in my boat*! It was just a challenge. You see, I knew the war was coming. It wasn't lack of a sense of reality, it wasn't schizophrenia. I knew perfectly well what was coming. But I wanted to make a gesture which strengthened *me*, which strengthened this capacity to endure catastrophe. (72-M)

This is why I have been able to speak, for instance at City College in Los Angeles, which is almost entirely Black. They are the most underprivileged students that you could possibly imagine, their backgrounds are so very difficult. But they understood when I spoke. They had a student paper, and all the paper said was: the world is falling apart. That was their image of the world—that it was hopeless. They had lost faith in any social change, and the only thing they did understand was that I asked them to put their stability in themselves. They understood that, the search, in an unstable world, for a place of stability and clarity and faith. Some place to recover their faith. Because they feel that the external is immovable. (71-B)

Walter Lippmann said that "the discontent that is shocking the world cannot be dealt with by politics only, or on the periphery of life, but must touch the central and intimate places of personal life. What has been wrecked cannot be restored by some new political gadget." This has been the substance of all my talks this year. (73-E)

*   *   *

Q. You speak about the great acceleration in awareness in the present decade. Why do you think this has happened in the past

˜tːn or fifteen years rather than in the fifties?

A. N. Well, it's such a complex combination of things that I don't think I can define it. It's partly technological, partly the media, partly the expansion of the universe by science. It's a combination of many elements. It's the intensive learning, intensive research which is accessible to more people. Mostly technology has accelerated the rhythm, but then we have gone along with that and have also condensed forms of learning and have quickened most every process. Also we have worked in groups to do research; women have worked in groups for their awareness as they call it, for the raising of consciousness. There are so many factors that I don't think it can be defined in one answer.

If you read *Future Shock,* of course, you are given all the outer reasons; but psychologists will give all the inner reasons for the acceleration. The interpretation of symbols and the interpretation of myths have become increasingly disseminated. We are much more aware of our acts as we do them. You see there were people who were not aware that our acts are symbolic, that even shaking hands is a symbolic act. A female student once said to me: "Symbolism is romantic. It is part of the romantic movement. We have nothing to do with it in the modern world." And then when I offered to shake hands with her, she refused to do so. I said: "Well, you're being symbolic now." You see everything we do has that kind of meaning.

But I think we can combat the destructive or negative aspects of acceleration, and there are also some good aspects. We can travel more quickly to another country; we ought to be able to connect with other countries more quickly also. So we can combat the negative aspects of it by the emphasis on the intimate. If we balanced our technological knowledge with a greater sense of nearness to other people then we wouldn't have this terrible nostalgia, the feeling that the world is getting vaster and we are becoming lonelier. (73-E)

Q. When you speak of transcending, do you mean finding a higher meaning?

A. N. No, I'm talking about transparency. That we suddenly see our human life, our daily life not in plain, homely, burdensome terms, as we sometimes see it, but as having a significance, as having a beauty, as having a purpose. So we see it as part of the whole, we see it as part of the country, as part of the community or part of history; so we see beyond the daily chores and duties that are demanded of us. That's what I mean by transcending. It's just simply the transparency which shows us that life has a meaning. And if it has a meaning then we can live in it with greater equanimity.

Q. Is the meaning there or is it something you make?

A. N. It's there, the meaning is there, but we sometimes don't see it. In fact when I came from Europe I remember I read in the early part of American literature of the "transcendentalists." And since I always adhered to my own interpretation of that, I thought: "This is wonderful, these are the people who see the spiritual meaning or the psychic meaning behind our lives. Emerson's people." And I was quite amazed to find that the whole literature was not transcendental—it was just the opposite—because I thought that that was the road that American literature was going to take. I took that word very literally and they didn't quite mean that. But if you believe in this transparency, which is what the creative personality does, you realize that everything you do really has a meaning—the gesture you make or the something that you give— that the whole thing has a ritualistic significance which then makes us bear the homely part of it. Not escape from it, no. But acceptance of it.

Q. Is it then a refusal to accept the way things are, a rejection of their ordinary meaning?

A. N. No, that's not quite right. There's no rejection. It's simply an interpretation. I think, for example, that if women were content, say in some creative aspect of their lives, they would then regard what we call the chores as something of a means to an end.

I regard the things that I do in the house as simply a part of the larger pattern of life which is satisfying to me. So that I don't mind the things that accompany it. It's that you see the chores as part of a whole pattern, and if the creative part of your life is fulfilling then you do the things that are part of your work, just as I had the chores of doing the printing when I was printing the books. Something like that. (72-G)

Q. You emphasize knowing yourself, the personal life, and relationships, and I get the feeling that you mean that's the only way to effect change.

A. N. No, no that's not what I said. I said just the opposite. I said that in order to effect outer changes we had to have this personal change take place within us. Because otherwise our effectiveness, our strength, our faith are shattered by the outer happenings. I didn't say that we didn't continue to work at the outer changes. All evening I have been saying just the opposite.

Q. Could you say something about how to effect outer changes?

A. N. Oh that's what I do not go into; one person cannot cover two areas. I mean I'm talking about the psychological change which can affect the outer change, and you want me to talk about how to work to effect a political change. I'm not a political specialist. I know exactly in what realm I have some wisdom, and I don't think you can be a specialist in both fields. I have worked at political movements, I have belonged to movements against war, and I've worked for the women's movement. I've worked for McGovern. I worked to change abortion laws. But that doesn't mean I consider myself very skillful in that particular form of expression. Each one of us has a skill, and we can apply that skill. Of course I mean I work at outer changes, but what I don't want it to do is to make me feel completely hopeless as some students have felt the past few years after the disappointment in McCarthy. They said it was absolutely useless to do anything, and then they have *gone in*. But they have gone in for a different reason. *I go in to come out.* (72-M)

Q. You suggest that if each individual looked into himself and found his real self this would therefore generally make a better world. But what if the individual looks within and finds that the core is corrupted and simple and evil. Or worse yet, if you discovered you weren't an artichoke but an onion, after all?

A. N. Well, I think a person like that wouldn't bother with the inner journey anyway. I mean he would go into action. That's what we call the criminal; he takes his anger out on society or hurts others in some way. I don't think that he would bother to confront himself. I think that is the characteristic of the person who is corrupt and angry. Such people don't want to think that they themselves are responsible for themselves. They want to be able to blame society or something else.

Q. But what if you found that there was nothing there—that your reality or existence consisted in the layers of the onion?

A. N. I have never found that. I have never found an empty person. I have never found a life without meaning, if you really look for the meaning of it. That is the danger of saying that we won't look in, because that is how we reached the point where we felt that life didn't have any significance. You see we repudiated so many forms of therapy. I mean so many of us today have repudiated philosophy or or religion or whatever pattern held us together before. We repudiated everything. We even repudiated the therapy of art. So there was nothing left for us really than to look into the self, and those who do so discover that every life has significance because life has significance. We were severely damaged by people who said that life was irrational and didn't mean anything anyway. But as soon as we begin to look, we do find the pattern, and we do find the person. I have never met what you would call an entirely empty person.

Q. But an onion isn't *empty*. The reality *is* its layers. This is what I mean.

A. N. I always found the opposite. That whoever made the effort found there was always a richness, almost like whoever wishes to mine the earth. There is always something, you see. The men who study dreams have gone into the most unlikely places to find interesting dreams; the men who have studied the effects of certain drugs and all that have gone to the most unlikely people. Like Ira Progoff, the psychoanalyst, who has gone with his *Intensive Journal* to people who couldn't read or couldn't write in Harlem and has found them making fabulous dreams and fabulous fantasies. So I'm apt to believe that there is more there than meets the eye, and that the effort we haven't made is really to mine this, because we don't really believe in it. I find people extraordinarily interesting the minute they are really willing to dig for this part of themselves—which they usually cover up. (73-E)

Q. In the fourth *Diary* you speak about anger being negative, and about your being passive. Could you speak more about your attitude toward anger?

A. N. The anger between my parents is what caused the great breakup of our family, and so I began to have an image of anger as a destructive force. Now this was a traumatic personal image of anger, and I didn't want to have any part of it. I mean I became non-violent and passivist. I wanted things to be settled without anger. Both my parents were very explosive, and when the family explosion came, the whole family fell apart. So this was personal.

I had to fight my way out of that because there are times when anger is right and just and can be used. Anger can be an energizing thing that will make you act. What I was very cautious about was irrational anger, anger that didn't have a good motivation. I wanted to know the motivation of anger. I wanted to know what to do with it. I didn't want to live with it; I didn't want it to be a toxic. So when I was angry at something—for example when I first came back to America and nobody would publish me—instead of getting angry and then bitter and turning in, I bought a press and published a book. This is what I meant by converting. So I was no longer angry or bitter because I was able to act. . . . like Ray Bradbury. He said he woke up one morning, meditating. He'd read an article that made him very angry about the South and the Blacks. So he sat down and wrote a short story, which became very famous, in which all the Black people left the South and left the whites to their own chaos. And then he wasn't angry anymore. He had really done something, he had written a story about it which was very good. So that's my feeling about anger. I didn't want undirected, lashing-out, volcanic anger, which doesn't know what it's doing. (72-G)

Q. But don't you think sometimes anger is a gift to someone?

A. N. I think justified angers are. But first we have to know what we are angry about. I think blind anger is destructive. Anger can be effective when we know what we are angry about. I was angry about what happened to the Black people because I always loved them. I was angry when Dr. King was assassinated; I was hysterically angry, I was absolutely hysterical, violently angry that such a thing should happen. So that there were times when my anger got away from me. But in general I didn't think that it constructed anything; rather, it just hurt *me*. It's like the man who, when the airlines killed his dog, went and blew up the airline I don't think that that is a satisfactory solution to anger and violence. You have to understand what it is about.

If I got angry about the American publishers' attitude toward the commercial value of my work, what good would it have done for twenty years to be angry at them? Simply embittered. So that's simply an example of saying: "Very well, I am angry; so I will commit an independent act."

Q. But don't you think if you take too much responsibility and don't express your anger you will become blocked?

A. N. Yes, that's absolutely true. That's why psychology has been helpful to us, by saying: you *were* angry about that, and your passivity or your training or your controls were bad for you. You see, Rank said: "Be careful, don't make understanding a philosophy of life because then you'll never act." However, there is a danger in this. In a culture which really endangered, diminished, and threatened our sense of relationship, fighting became a substitute. We didn't have a reality of the other person's presence, and I think that the vicious part of our culture became that—having no contact. The only contact we had became a negative one, which was to fight, and then you felt that this person was real. I really did sense this desperateness in American relationships, in American writers, particularly coming from another culture where there was more diplomacy going on. Once when I talked about the art of relationship, I got a very violent reaction from people who thought I was suggesting artificiality. What I meant was that relationship is a craft, something to work at, it's a science. But the idea that relationships would really require this kind of creative effort was obnoxious to many people. (72-D)

Q. You said earlier that we have to learn to transform, transpose, and transcend historical events. I was wondering exactly what you meant by that?

A. N. I can only give you a definition of the word "trans." "Trans" means a changing, and for me it is something like the alchemist changing dross into gold. It's a process that can be done by the spirit, by creativity, by the creative will. That is, let's suppose that you are poisoned by someone's hostility, and instead of being able to work, this toxic is working in you. You examine this and you find the cause of it and you ward it off. You begin by analyzing the hostility and by asking yourself: why does this other person behave in this way? what are the human reasons? And finding these enables you to forgive and understand, and ultimately to rise above the immediate and personal implications of the situation. You emerge undamaged. That's what I mean by transforming. It's the psychological transposition.

I can't go into explaining how you transpose the events of the world or history except that it's very important for us to keep our sensitivity. We ought to be able to measure that and not go through the spiritual shock which some of us have experienced by watching, say, the Vietnamese war more than we can take and then becoming callous and ceasing to feel. By learning to transpose, I found that I can take so much and then I have to do something creative so that I can retain my sensitivity. *Not* become *indifferent.* That's one of the dangers of our culture, that through the media we receive psychic shocks, and then we become callous and then we stop feeling. In order to avoid that we have to learn this kind of transcendence. This is not indifference; it's far from it. It's knowing how much you will respond to emotionally and how much you want to preserve of your responsiveness. (72-M)

Q. Do you ever hope that there will be a more humane society, or will the situation always be the individual against repressive structures?

A. N. The only utopia I believe in is the one I hope someday we can have when we have recognized the importance of assuming personal responsibility. A day when we will tackle our prejudices, hostilities, and angers in such a way that they will not be projected onto the collective. To me the war is an aggregate of all our individual hostilities and prejudices, and I still see the majority as a lot of individuals who have projected the destructive part of themselves. My only utopia is the hope that if we have prejudices, we can deal with them and stop them. If we have a hostility we can find out what it means and convert it to something else, convert it to energy. Then we *might* have a more humane society. There is a possibility of that. But it will depend on our quality. (71-B)

Q. What is the future of the bourgeois family?

A. N. I don't think I'm equipped to answer that. I think we're a little off center; I don't think we're speaking quite on the same wave length. I don't see a generalization like a bourgeois family. There isn't any bourgeois family; there is a family that seems to live by bourgeois patterns. But then you look underneath, and there is no bourgeois family. There are only individuals. (73-H)

Q. May I ask your opinion on John Cage and the chance musicians who feel that in nature nothing is planned, everything just happens, and that if you plan to create anything it's false?

A. N. The question of John Cage is completely outside of my knowledge and I wouldn't discuss that. But the concept of a happening and chance I do not believe, because I think every chance and every happening comes from someone's unconscious. I mean it comes from somewhere, and it may seem to be an accident, it may seem to be a happening because we don't know what the preceding steps were. Just as in intuition. We don't know how we reach it, but we do reach it by a telescoping of processes. There is observation, synthesis, analysis. But the final outcome is intuition. The final outcome is a happening which seems chance, but there is no such thing. It's just that we don't see the pattern. (68-A)

Q. You mentioned the American tendency to view things objectively rather than subjectively. Was this a particularly isolated part of the American character, or do you feel that it is widespread and continuous? Are we still this way?

A. N. No, we're not. We're changing a great deal, and I think the new generation is entirely different. It is very concerned with this lost individual self. I think America had an ideal concept of living communally, collectively, and it was an *ideal*. It was a *utopian ideal*—that we could live collectively without first being really born and maturing as individuals. Now Europe operated almost the reverse way: the individual was valuable, the collective was less developed. So each country had something to give to the other. But because I kept moving from one culture to the other I could see that the collective ideal wouldn't succeed unless the individual had something very wonderful to contribute to it, and that a mass of blind individuals could not produce a wonderfully universal collective life. The American ideal would have worked if we hadn't sacrificed the individual. Now the young today, I believe, are very concerned with this lost self, and I was asked when I was in Germany why our young people were reading Hesse so much. The Germans were quite amazed, because Hesse is a classic. He is considered passé. I think that the young are looking for all the things that were not developed in this ideal of the collective life—of joining before you even know what you are, or who you are, or what you are doing. (72-W)

Q. Can you become so subjective that you lose all contact with people and outer events?

A. N. That's the fake legend about subjectivity. That is really the sort of cliché which has frightened people in literature for the last twenty years—that subjectivity was a little trap that you walked into and you stayed inside and you could never come out again. And this is the thing I have been trying to say all evening: that it is only the starting point; it is only a way of looking at things and recognizing that all we have to look with is our own emotional experience and the sum of this experience. The richer we make this, the richer our vision will be. It's not a little trap that you can never come out of. It's the center from which you can touch on all the realms of science or history or whatever is happening in the world. It's a starting point; it is simply the way to illumine things. It's like carrying a little light, a flashing light. (68-A)

Q. You mentioned removing the obstacles so that you can get closer to others, reveal your secrets, and share with them. I was wondering when you do that whether you don't lose part of your own identity and become dependent?

A. N. No, because, you see, as you exchange, as you share, you are exchanging knowledge. I mean you don't lose yourself. You can lose yourself emotionally when you love someone, let's say. You can lose a part of yourself. We have all had that feeling— identifying with a loved one and losing some part of our personality. But that's a different thing; that's a fusion with a person we love, which woman tends to do very often. But once you have acquired your identity, you can share. You see when I was twenty and I was unsure about what I was, I didn't share, and I spoke to you about the years when I didn't talk. In other words, while I felt unsure I did not share. I didn't even talk with Miller very much or with Durrell or with anybody whom I felt was overwhelming to me. But I proceeded in the diary to build up this self—until I got to the point where I knew my identity, and therefore what I give to another cannot diminish me. Nothing is lost. What you give isn't lost. (73-I)

Q. You must be terribly dismayed by the trend in society toward the social. One of the newest "sciences," for example, is that of *social design*. It is a tenet of the flower children as well as of the hardened politicals; it is manifested in the commune as well as in the national communistic society.

A. N. What I see is that every time someone goes to the group for a solution, even in the commune, he presents an individual problem. I come back to the concept that we cannot live communally, we cannot live in groups, unless we bring to them an already evolved human being. This is happening also in the women's movement. Part of the women's movement is saying that all the problems are soluble through political action. Of course we know that isn't so. Some of the women bring their own private neuroses and give them to the group expecting the group to solve their problems. Of course, it can't. (72-Y)

Q. I am interested in so many things, and I have a terrible fear because my mother keeps telling me that I'm just going to be exploring the rest of my life and never getting anything done. But I find it really hard to set my ways and say, "Well, do I want to do this, or should I try to exploit that, or should I escape and completely do one thing?"

A. N. One word I would banish from the dictionary is "escape." Just banish that and you'll be fine. Because that word has been misused regarding anybody who wanted to move away from a certain spot and wanted to grow. He was an escapist. You know if you forget that word you will have a much easier time. Also you're in the prime, the beginning of your life; you should experiment with everything, try everything. . . . We are taught all these dichotomies, and I only learned later that they could work in harmony. We have created false dichotomies; we create false ambivalences, and very painful ones sometimes—the feeling that we have to choose. But I think at one point we finally realize, sometimes subconsciously, whether or not we are really fitted for what we try and if it's what we want to do.

You have a right to experiment with your life. You will make mistakes. And they are right too. No, I think there was too rigid a pattern. You came out of an education and are supposed to know your vocation. Your vocation is fixed, and maybe ten years later you find you are not a teacher anymore or you're not a painter anymore. It may happen. It has happened. I mean Gauguin decided at a certain point he wasn't a banker anymore; he was a painter. And so he walked away from banking. I think we have a right to change course. But society is the one that keeps demanding that we fit in and not disturb things. They would like you to fit in right away so that things work now. (73-K)

Q. You said there were personal reasons why you lived in Los Angeles. But if you could choose, where would you choose to live?

A. N. That's difficult at this point. I really don't know anymore. I don't really know because I feel rooted in America now, and I

would feel very uprooted if I went to live in Paris, although it's a
city I love. I love the way of life in Paris; I love the cafés; I love
the easy communication; I love being very near people. But if I
went there I would miss the very strong roots that I have acquired
here, very strong friendships.

You are, as a culture, in a state of formation and dynamism and
change, and in Europe that is not present. I participate in that, I
like change, I like not knowing. We're always in a state of flux,
we're always in a state of transmutation and change and experiment and questioning as a nation. And this I like. In Europe there
is an established culture; you communicate very well on the basis
of the books you've read and the paintings you have done and so
forth. It's all sort of *there,* and it's very enjoyable. There's no effort, there is no risk, and there is no gamble. But I like this constant evolution that you're going through here—revolution and
evolution.

Q. Have you ever been into the interior?

A. N. Like the Middle West, you mean? No, I suppose not; I've
seen the Middle West. But only the colleges, you see. I get a sort
of ferment from the colleges. I don't see the little towns that people sometimes tell me about. I haven't seen how poverty-stricken
or how difficult it would be to start from there. I haven't seen that.
No, I haven't seen that because I have been privileged to have contact with the *ferment* in Milwaukee, for example. I see them starting their women's studies, which is the atmosphere that I like.
Whereas in France you do feel that tradition is so heavy and so
fixed that any change which is happening in the young is much
more difficult; they have a much more difficult time.

Q. But you refer to evolution happening here like it's ours, not
yours. So I wonder where you feel you belong the most?

A. N. I said—I started to say—that I felt rooted and in tune with
this happening.

Q. Yes, but when you stated it you said *your* evolution.

A. N. Yes, but I feel in tune with it and I feel a part of it. And I
feel that I have, somehow or other, felt it. Because I've made a lot
of prophetic statements in the diary. Statements of criticism of

America, and of things that I wished for America, the things that are happening now. So that suddenly the timing, the conjunction, was right between what is happening to America now and what I like. Whereas I might not be in tune with what is happening, say, in France. (72-D)

Q. What were you against in the forties? I'm interested.

A. N. In the forties I was against everything.

Q. Could you name a few of those things?

A. N. It was a very alienated society. People did not communicate with each other on any meaningful level. There was no recognition at all of the subconscious life. It was the complete acceptance of the persona—that's the best way I could put it. There was an acceptance of the war; there was no effort at making new values. There was an acceptance of the pragmatic life, the pragmatic American ideal of the commercial life, and of the cultural values. Everybody was more or less united in that. The shock I had of going from one culture to another suddenly enabled me to see more sharply. There was a very beautiful article in the *Studies of the Humanities* at Santa Barbara by an American who had been exiled for ten years. He came back and of course saw an entirely different America. Now he *saw* the change, the new change, the new America very well—better than if he had stayed here, because he had the shock of returning. And he wrote a beautiful article about what had happened. In the forties there were rigidities, there were dogmas, there were standards. You had to be on the left, you had to be political. Everything was, let's say, standardized. And the students were inert and lifeless, just receiving this in a very unquestioning way. There were none of the rebellions and the evolutions and the questioning and the challenging that we have now. The forties were a very static period, a very difficult period.

Q. Have things really changed all that much? You seem to feel that the way things are going now people are becoming less alienated and the artist is becoming more respectable. But I really wonder. The 1970s seem to be a period when things are sort of reverting back.

A. N. No, I don't see it that way. I wonder where you got your impressions, and I wonder where I get my impression of the movement forward? We would have to compare the sources of our interpretations.

Q. I just wonder if things are changing all that much, changing at all.

A. N. Ask yourself if you are really noticing the change, or if it's you who hasn't changed, perhaps. You know, it's possible. We have to ask ourselves that too in connection with our environment, with what is happening. Whether we have closed ourselves to it, whether it is really happening but we haven't been in tune. Because sometimes we do not tune in.

Q. Perhaps what he's saying is that in the sixties there was a lot of idealism, and if we were to change to that idealism it would be an almost absolute change backward from what we know.

A. N. Well, I think that the idealism changes course. In the sixties we had an idealism about what was going to happen historically and it didn't happen. We weren't able to stop the war, and that gave us a period of despair, the feeling that nothing could be changed. I am talking about a change that is really very organic and very slow, and if we continue to believe that the change will come from within, from our change of consciousness, this consciousness finally pushes the wall down. And if we did lose some of our idealism and impetus about the state of the world, and about being able to put an end to the war, sometimes that idealism can be transferred to another thing. I think that happened with the young. They decided that we couldn't change that monolithic power structure through direct means, so then let's change ourselves. Which I think is a good change because in changing ourselves we are going to exert pressure. After all, you're coming up, you're stepping into the various jobs, and you will do them differently. So I believe that this return to saying very well then, we will work with ourselves since we can't do anything about the oil companies or whatever it is we're fighting, was a positive reaction. I believe the turning to ourselves was right. Because it created a new kind of human being. This is going to exert pressure finally, but

it takes time. We mustn't lose heart in the middle you know.
Q. Do you think then that the idealism now is different from what
it was then?
A. N. Yes, I think we have displaced our efforts into something
that *may* be perhaps more effective. Because what we thought was
that if we changed the system we could have an ideal community.
But what we found then, of course, is that in the system we always
get the corruptible elements and that it ends up always in some
form of tyranny against one group or the other. So if we displace
our energies by changing ourselves, this is bound to affect our
values, our cultural values, and what will happen outside. I see already some of you in jobs that I have seen occupied by slick and
false and phony personalities. I see you taking over some of those
jobs, working as interviewers, journalists, commentators. I can see
the wave coming from below and getting into these stiuations and
handling things differently.
Q. Yes, but would you feel crushed if another world war came up,
or something like that, which would falsify your theory?
A. N. In some ways I think my theory is probably born to be
crushed by the acceptance of evil. We will always have evil in the
world, but that's not a reason for dropping out. That's what I'm
trying to say. It's not a reason for giving up, because then what
would happen? We would have a completely dark world, a nightmare world. So I think we owe it to ourselves and others not to
give up because we failed to change something we wanted very
much, but to work with this feeling of a cellular change, a change
in consciousness.

Terrible things happen in the world of events, but we cannot
despair. To give up is to lose. Somebody has called *Diary* IV "the
refusal to despair." That is why I put so much stress on building
an inward life—so that you have resistance to withstand what happens outside. So that we don't collapse. What happens if we don't
have this very strong inward life is that external events just simply
cause you to break down, to collapse. Ever since I was a child, I
have had a feeling—because I was uprooted, because there *was*

war, there was *always* war—that I had to have something stable and strong. A core. ... I feel a responsibility for despair. I feel we have no right to despair. (72-G)

Q. Have you developed more respect for politics than in your second *Diary,* when you knew Gonzalo?

A. N. Yes, we need political action. But when I see the things that are being done to welfare or education or in medical assistance, I feel we need a counterpoint to that or else we lose faith. And this has been my concern because I have had so much to do with students and seen their loss of faith and their negativity. In other words, they know what they're against but they don't know how to build a different world. And this is what I want woman so much to do—start building a different kind of woman, a different world, without spending too much time on extremes. (71-B)

III
Women Reconstructing the World

I don't know what a "radical feminist" is, but I *am* a feminist.
... And what I discovered, when the diaries came out, were the
thousands of women in lonely little towns who had no one to share
their aspirations with; who had some creative disturbance and rest-
lessness and felt that they had potentialities but did not know how
to develop them and were very much lacking in self-confidence;
who were apt to invest in the people around them the faith that
they should have had for themselves.

Now, it is true that I believe liberation is never achieved by one
segment of people; it has to be simultaneous and it has to happen
to all of us. But I also think that men have learned from woman's
great quest for her identity, have learned that we have to peel off
the programming, the conditioning, the education, the taboos, and
the dogmas that have been inculcated in us. The restrictions were
stronger for woman because the pattern was very rigid and very
limited, and she was shut in within her personal world. A few women transcended that, and the women that I used to read about—
because I've always read women writers, and they were a great
inspiration to me—were the women who were able to *free themselves*, who did not *demand* their freedom, who were able to *create*

it. I will tell you later the story of a woman who achieved her wishes under amazing obstacles.

I became aware when the diaries came out that woman's problem was deeper, that her self-confidence somehow had been damaged, that she often looked to others for an image of herself. Men, as D. H. Lawrence said, were the ones who were making the pattern; men would decide one year if we had to be thin and another year if we had to be fat, or whatever. The pattern of our lives was really set by men. I think your response to the *Diary* is greatly due to the fact that we have had very few histories of the growth of women from the very beginning. In other words, I began with all the limitations and restrictions and taboos and dogmas which we all begin with, which were given to me by my culture—in this case straddling two cultures, the Latin and the American—which were given to me by religion: all the possible restrictions and limitations to growth. . . .

So women have had greater handicaps. This I am very fully aware of. And I have been radical in that sense, that I have even argued with the analyst on therapy for woman. I have argued with the analyst about his image of me. I maintained a stubborn continuity of personality, but it was done through the diary. I don't know whether it would have happened without the diary, because the diary was not only the confessional, the mirror, it was also the log of the journey. It made me fully aware of the difficulties of the journey. It made me fully aware when my life was stagnant. I was fully aware of the trap that women fall into, the conventional marriage and life in the suburbs. So the diary was a reflector and didn't allow me for one minute to be blinded or to be diffused or to be confused by the outer images that were imposed on me. My concession was to play the roles that were demanded of me but to maintain my integrity for myself *somewhere* very strongly.

When the *Diary* came out and I heard from many women, I heard about their timidities, their lack of confidence, their reliance upon others. If someone criticized their work, for example, they would almost fall apart. Then I remembered my own vulnerabilities and my own hesitancies and my own timidities, and I wanted you to know that they can be overcome. (73-G)

I want to stress this tremendous lack of confidence, this timidity and fear in woman, because I think that we have talked a great deal about the outer obstacles, the legal obstacles, the historical obstacles, the cultural obstacles, even the religious obstacles to her development and her growth. But we haven't focused enough on what happened to woman psychologically.

Otto Rank, in his book called *Truth and Reality*, stressed this very much when he spoke of two kinds of guilt that we have: a guilt for creating because we seem to be taking too much room or taking space from our fellows or asserting ourselves, and a guilt for not creating. By creating I don't mean only or specifically painting or composing music or writing books. I mean creating everything—creating a child, creating a garden, creating a house, creating a community, whatever it is. For me creativity is an all-encompassing word.

So we have guilt for creating and for not creating, and these women are caught really between the two: between the fear of asserting themselves, because then it would affect somehow the people near them, and the fear of not creating, of not realizing one's potential. I can give you an example of this. I was very obsessed with the idea of growth, and I used to think that if I grew too much I would overshadow my younger brothers or even some day overshadow my father, which was a terrifying thought. Now I don't know where I got the idea that I was growing into a giant redwood tree, or that I could possibly take the sunlight from other trees, but I really did. That was a tremendously erroneous concept, for I discovered that when a human being grows, this growth positively affects her environment, it affects the people around her and actually urges them to their own growth rather than the other way around. Our growth doesn't wither other people around us, it incites others to do the same. It inspires. I found that the more I expanded, the more I grew, the better it was for my environment. The effect of this would be always positive and would always be setting others on fire.

Women forget that, and they think that perhaps whatever

they achieve is at the expense of their personal world and will somehow destroy their personal world. They never thought that whatever they became was in turn poured back into the personal world and enriched it, that they were enriching their children, they were enriching their husband, they were enriching their neighbors. We stopped really believing that the enrichment of the individual is actually what enriches our collective life. We forgot that. And for woman it was worse because she was not expected to produce in the first place. She was not expected to create. Culture didn't demand it of her; it didn't demand of her to become the best doctor or the best lawyer or the best painter or the best writer; it didn't demand anything of her except the fulfillment of her personal duties. So this was not an incentive for woman to develop whatever gift she had.

But where did woman get this lack of confidence in whatever ability she has? Is it because she chooses models with exceptional gifts that she cannot imitate? When I was young and I was reading, I chose models that I could not possibly become. I wanted to be George Sand; I wanted to be a member of the French Academy; I wanted all kinds of impossible things, but as I grew mature I suddenly realized there were some things possible to me that had nothing to do with exceptional gifts.

Now the women's movement has been caught between the concept of self-development and growth and trying to find the obstacles that stand in the way of this growth and this self-development. We found some of the external factors; some of them were legal, some of them historical, some religious, some cultural, but we find it awfully hard to say that some of them come from within us, that as a result of all these elements, we had lost our self-confidence. We had lost our impetus toward creation. (73-D)

Woman's helplessness has given her a great deal of anxiety. We have had statistics about women breaking down more than men. That's a well-known statistic. My feeling was that they broke down because they had a surplus of anxieties because of helplessness. I mean the dependency on the man, the vicarious living through the man which I described in the novel *Ladders to Fire.* I described

Lillian and I said she *breathed* through Jay. She experienced everything through him; when he wasn't there she wasn't enjoying life.
In other words she received the whole dynamism of life from him.
This is a very bad thing for *the man* on whom the woman is dependent. Every kind of vicarious living is really victimizing the person
that you use for that purpose. And woman tended to do that.
(73-J)

Now we were not helped in our culture as women because first
of all we weren't taught rivalry, and man was taught the fear of
rivalry to such an extent that he considered the growth of woman
to be also a threat to himself, which is very tragic. And this really
comes out in the whole culture too. Rivalry takes prominence.

Not too long ago I was in Morocco, a totally different culture
where rivalry does not exist. I was doing an article for a magazine
and I had two guides who were always vying for getting the job to
take me through the town. When I took one I would say: "Aren't
the other one's feelings hurt?" And he would say: "Not at all, we
are all brothers."

This concept of mutual benefit is something we haven't considered enough in connection with women's development. Man
never thought woman's growth could be really an enhancing of his
own life, a liberation of his own burdens. Two people to carry the
load, the burdens of life, instead of one. We never thought of that,
we never thought how greatly unity and closeness could really
lighten this burden. (73-A)

Man is driven to competition and to win. Woman has been
driven the other way—not to compete and not to win because win-
ning would mean that she was stronger than her children or stronger than her brothers. And often she doesn't want to overshadow
or outdistance her husband—or she doesn't want to overshadow
her boss.

There is always that feeling which keeps her from growing. The
feeling that if she grows she is going to impede someone else's
growth and that her concern should be not to take too much space
and not to expand. . . . So woman carries many, many burdens. One
is this going backward instead of forward into self-expansion and

also erroneously considering this self-expansion to be aggressiveness. This word has always been used to discourage and disparage women who had a thrust toward growing. (73-A)

I often myself used to confuse what I called my active self with aggressiveness until a semanticist pointed out to me that there is a difference between activity and aggressiveness. Aggressiveness is moving against someone; activity is simply the dynamic creative will that I want to awaken in you. (73-D)

Another thing we must sort out is the way we have labelled things. We have said: "This is masculine, and man must behave this way, and this is feminine." Now we know very well that that is not true, that all of us are composed of masculine and feminine qualities, and I hope one day we shall say instead: there are some women who are courageous and there are some men who are tender; and there are some men who are intuitive and there are some women who are very scientific-minded. These ideas about roles are limiting to both men and women. That is why I believe woman has to work at liberation with men, because we can't do it by ourselves. We have to do it really all together. All races. All men. All women. It has to be everybody.

And it has to be simultaneous. Because when you feel free and the other person isn't, it's not an achievement. You're still bound, you're related, you're in some way still dependent. If one feels free and the other doesn't, the relationship doesn't work. So it's very important that we work *with* our differences—whether sexual or racial—whatever they might be. We have used everything with almost satanic genius, we used everything to make separatism. We've used religion to separate us, to divide us; we've used race to divide us; we have used everything that we pick up. Now we use the feminist movement to divide us from men. And that's what I don't want. (73-I)

Then there is another thing which plagues women, which comes also from the culture, it comes from religion, it comes from the family. That is, the thing that the culture encourages men to do, it discourages women from doing. It is made very clear to woman that her first and primary duty is to her personal life—whether it be to the husband, or children, or family, or parents. That is the primary thing. This is supposed to be her role in life. Now if a woman has really accepted that, then if she transgresses she has more guilt than the man. Our culture tells the man that he has to go beyond the personal because he has to achieve. He is excused for not being a particularly good father, or a particularly good son, or whatever it is that he doesn't fulfill in the personal life.

Yet woman *gains* something from this great emphasis on the personal life. She gains a very great humanism, which is a consideration of human beings as persons. Man, in his progress toward ideologies, toward science, toward philosophy, toward all the objective forms of thinking, separated himself from the personal. He rationalized in ideological terms in such a way that he became removed from any concept at all that his personal life was really at the root of his profession and his occupations and what he was interested in. Woman never lost sight of that personal life, and now something which started as a handicap, today I consider a *quality* which woman can then carry into her wider interests. But she has to retain this sense of the personal, because from that comes her sense of humanity. So she becomes a lawyer, she becomes a philosopher, she becomes a priest—it doesn't matter. What I hope she doesn't do is simply to annihilate all that she has learned through the centuries, which is the value of the individual. (73-A)

Certainly there are some negative things which were inculcated in us very early. They are cultural, they are racial, they are part of the family life. But despite that I see women beginning to take a pride in themselves and also to realize that they are capable of skills. Whenever we were told that we couldn't do something, we accepted it. I was told for years that I couldn't think clearly about politics. And I believed it. Why did I believe it? I suddenly discovered that I wasn't incapable; I could balance my checkbook and I could do all sorts of little things that I was told I could not do.

Printing, for example. Everyone laughed when I bought the press and they said: "Of course you're not very good at technology or mechanics." But I learned to print and I learned to love it, though it *was* very difficult. A woman printer was, you know, an unusual thing, and they would say that the tray would be too heavy and that typesetting was too complicated. These are notions that it's going to take some time to overcome. (72-E)

Now women have a problem today, beside the problem of guilt, which is that when a woman breaks through these taboos and transcends them, then she is said to be a special kind of woman. Now I have been studying women's lives the last few years—I have always read biography anyway. I have always been interested in the lives of other women. The women who transgressed and managed to overcome these taboos were not really exceptional women at all. They were stubborn. And I can testify to that because I too started with all the handicaps, incapabilities, and helplessness. I was not trying to earn my living, I was afraid of the world, I didn't talk when I was twenty. I taught myself (I know you won't believe that); I taught myself to talk by the actual act of writing. I learned to communicate with others, and it was the fact of the diaries coming out which made me able to communicate with you. (73-A)

So now I want to tell you just one story of a woman who achieved her liberation in spite of amazing obstacles. She is Frances Steloff, who owns the Gotham Book Mart in New York. I became aware of her history just recently on her eighty-sixth birthday.

She came from a farm where there were too many children; she couldn't go to school, and she couldn't get an education. So she came to New York, just like any other young woman, and got a job in Brentano's bookstore—the worst job of all, because it was near the turning door where everybody caught cold. She withstood that and sold magazines. Then, when she had saved one hundred dollars, she decided that she wanted a bookshop of her own. The owner of Brentano's, who by that time felt friendship for her, said; "But you're absolutely mad. You won't survive one summer in New York. With one hundred dollars what are you going to do?" She said: "I want my own bookshop." And back of that was her wish to be self-educated, to be near the books, to find the books that she had been deprived of and that she loved even without knowing the contents of them. With her hundred dollars she opened her bookshop near the theater section in a little cellar place where you had to go down three steps. And the publishers were impressed by her daring and gave her credit and gave her books. (73-G)

But what she did with this bookshop was to be so warm, so friendly, so inviting, such a listener, such a hospitable person that the bookshop grew and grew and grew. And not just as a bookshop; it grew as a center for people to meet. Writers met other writers, the critics met the writers and the painters. Everybody came to the bookshop. She let you browse. It was in great disorder always; you couldn't find the books, but it was a great adventure. Then she opened her backyard and scattered around those metal boxes that you see in the quais in Paris. She showed great imagination; she filled them with books, and then the parties used to take place in the backyard. And because she was an early believer in health foods, she served only tea and health crackers. Everybody came.

This bookshop became the heart of the literary life of New York. People would beg for parties. The Joyce Society had their meetings there every few months. People came from other countries. We heard about it in Paris. And when the war came we asked if we could send our books to her so that they would at least be out of Europe and sheltered from the destruction of war. She immediately wrote "yes"; she didn't know who we were, what the books were, just "yes."

This is the instinctive, intuitive, nurturing quality that we are worrying about now, that women would like to escape. But this woman created something with it, and at the same time she educated herself. Edmund Wilson came to her bookshop, all the critics came, and she learned from them. As they asked for certain books, she studied them. She educated herself to the extent that her adopted college of Skidmore (where I went to give a lecture the other day) gave her an honorary degree. She was able to give her college a rare library of Joyce items that nobody else had because she was always saying "yes" and putting things down in her cellar. There was a flair and an instinct about her, an intuition about human values; she said she judged a book by whether she liked the writer himself or not. She made her bookshop a true literary center, and this is what I call the creative woman. And today, at eighty-six, she's still very lively. Frances Steloff and I talked about the remarkable adventures of women we had known. She had a list of her own; I had my list, and on the way to Skidmore for three and a half hours we talked about the marvelous women we had known. (72-L)

She is still there, you can go and see her. She has white hair, she is very beautiful, and she eats sunflower seeds! That is the secret of her longevity. (73-K)

Then I discovered that perhaps the most adventurous woman in the realm of ideas, in the realm of the inner journey was a woman called Lou Andreas-Salomé. You may have been reading about her in connection with her correspondence with Freud— which slightly alters the burlesque quality of Kate Millett's book about Freud. Because he had an enormous respect for Lou Andreas-Salomé. Their correspondence shows a great sense of equality, shows him listening to her ideas, their exchange of opinions about his work, and his faith in her. It was in one of these letters that he says that woman is closer to the unconscious and remains closer to the unconscious than man, has fewer interferences, has a less over-developed sense of rationalization.

Lou Andreas-Salomé started as a very conventional little girl in Russia: very much impressed by her general father, very much captured by religion, very much under the rule of the strict families of the period. But she promptly, at sixteen, began to declare her independence. I consider her to be one of the independent women, the woman who is capable of creating her freedom rather than demanding it, of creating it under adverse circumstances, in other periods, with all the obstacles that you could possibly imagine.

Now the first thing she did was to renounce religion, which was a tremendous shock to her family. She said she wanted to study philosophy, that she had lost her faith. This was the beginning of her inner journey. For this she had first of all to leave her family. She went to Germany where, in the period of Nietzsche and Rilke and Freud, women were not allowed to study philosophy. She won her way into the philosophy course and was very brilliant. Her friendship with Nietzsche began. She was at the same time both a muse and a woman who created. She achieved both. Every time she had a relationship to a man, the relationship was tremendously fecund. Rilke mentions the change in his poetry during the six years that they lived together. So she studied philosophy and then came to the conclusion that it was not the answer either. Religion was not, philosophy was not, but psychology might be the key to human growth, to the problem of growing and expansion and understanding. So then she went to study with Freud.

Very little is known about her because the biography by H. F. Peters, who teaches at Reed College in Portland, has been out of print.* But you may find the book in the library and it is worth reading. Because this is a woman who absolutely created her independence at a time when woman was surrounded by taboos, when in Germany if you lived with a man you were expelled from the country. And she insisted on living not with one but with *two*! With Nietzsche and another, because they wanted to talk about philosophy all night. Nobody believed that. In other words, she created her independence. And she was absolutely guiltless. She was able to avoid the guilt about breaking relationships when they came to a natural end, which was not done by women in that period. So at fifty she became the first woman psychoanalyst and developed from there a great deal of writing, of journal writing, and articles and essays, and a book on Nietzsche. And yet we know so little about her, which is part of this ignoring of woman. People thought of her only in the function of having inspired Nietzsche, having inspired Freud, having inspired Rilke. They never thought of her in terms of her own work, which hasn't even been translated from the German. But what a remarkable woman she was, and one who had a great deal of influence on other women in the feminist movement which was beginning in Germany at that time.

What I find there that is inspiring to other women is the pos-

*My Sister, My Spouse, to be reprinted by Norton and Co., with a preface by Anäis Nin.

sibility of not having to wait for social changes or political changes. We have to work at them. That's understood, that's our duty. We have to work at changing the laws, we have to change and equalize the situation of woman. But we have to work above all on this psychological freedom of accepting and understanding what one is as a woman, so that the impetus for change and the influence of culture come from within, from a very deep source.

Other women I admire for their adventurousness found the only solution to their independence was to abandon the culture in which they were born, which was Victorian England. So four of these English women, born in the Victorian period, completely oppressed and stifled by the taboos and by the life of England at the time, dreamt of escaping. The only way they could dream, the only way of escaping for them was to try and reach other cultures, to escape from England itself.

They are described in a remarkable book called *The Wilder Shores of Love* by Lesley Blanch. The first life she studies in the book is that of the wife of Richard Burton, who dreamt for twenty years of being married to him and waited for him. At that time, the concept of achieving fulfillment or adventure was through the man—the typical Victorian attitude. She could only reach other cultures by her marriage to Richard Burton. But she finally married him and followed him to all these places that she had been reading about. She fulfilled her wish to travel and to see exotic countries and to step out of the Victorian culture. And did it very successfully. For twenty years she was the successful follower and assistant adventurer.

Then there was another woman called Lady Jane Digby, who also wanted to escape from the taboos and restrictions of English life. She married an Arab and led an Arab life to the extent of even participating in raids upon foreigners in the desert, completely identifying herself with another culture, which was really a way of escaping from the taboos of her particular culture. But it was an adventure, and in this case, successful in the sense that there was the escape from restriction into wider forms of life. Her life in Morocco was exceedingly adventurous and beautiful and exotic. She was deeply loved by the Sheik Abdul Medjuel el Mezrab. He gave up his seraglio for her, and she taught him really to live for one woman. So this is a beautiful adventure story of a daring woman who braved all the taboos of her time and place.

The third woman was Isabelle Eberhardt, a Russian-born girl who was an emigré to the south of France. She had no money at all, had a very difficult upbringing and childhood with her step-father. She loved her brother very much, almost too much, and then also wished to escape the whole restrictive shabby kind of existence that they led as immigrants in the south of France. She went to Algeria and dressed as a boy. The Arabs knew perfectly well she was not a boy but they respected her. She led the life of the Arabs, a nomadic life—which was in her blood anyway because she was a Russian from the nomadic part of Russia. She had a horse, went everywhere, covered an incredible amount of ground, lived in cafés, listened to the music, took hashish. Absolutely immersed herself and lost herself in another culture and became a part of it. She was able to commune with it, to be at ease with it. And for this same reason, because she understood the Arabs so well, she was a close friend of General Lyautey. When he needed to understand the situation in Algeria, he would send for her and had a high respect for her interpretation of the Arab character.

In addition to keeping a diary, Isabelle Eberhardt also wrote many travel articles, which unfortunately were not preserved at the time and then were found by a man who rewrote them, tried to make them more glamorous, and falsified them. So we know very little about her except what Lesley Blanch tells us about her true character and her vow to immerse herself in another culture and to escape thus into what she felt was the beauty of space and a larger existence. She died a very strange death, which was predicted by astrology: that she would die drowned in the desert. No one understood what that meant. But when she was only about twenty-four years old, there was a flash flood in the desert and she was drowned. Although her writings were tampered with for publication, the original diaries and papers are in the Bibliothèque

Nationale. Lesley Blanch found the original writings of this re-markable woman to be very pure, simple, and profound.

The fourth character was Aimée Dubucq De Rivery, a young woman who was the cousin of Josephine, who married Napoleon. When Aimée was going back to France from Martinique, she was abducted by the Turks and sold to a harem, the principal harem in Turkey. Now you would think that this is the ultimate imprison-ment for woman and that she could never escape from such a sit-uation! But she managed to bring about a revolution in Turkey. Such a woman, it seems to me, points the way to the fact that there is no trap, there is no imprisonment, there isn't any situation which one can't find a way out of. She created a very serious historical revolution which changed completely the whole trend of Turkish history. From a harem, and through her son whom she had ed-ucated and trained with the French ideas of republican life.

So I find these lives inspiring, and they've always led me on and on to what I call a stubborn sense of adventure against difficulties, to consider difficulties only as a challenge to your wits and to your strength. (73-J)

What I am trying to say is that we are not exceptional in our be-ginnings, we are only exceptional in our stubbornness, in this thrust towards growth which is almost a natural state. There are obsta-cles, but our intelligence and our awareness enable us to recognize and confront them. We know them. All of us have at some time or another become aware of them: the religious beliefs, the family beliefs, the oppression by the family, the very dogmatic form we have given to marriage. I believe in marriage but not the dogma that we've made out of it, the rigid dogma. You see we make every-thing rigid and it's all out of fear; we make these rigidities, and then we can't live in them and we suffocate in them. We make dif-ferent patterns of lives and to get security we give up our free-dom. (73-A)

I was trapped, which at one time or another all of us are, either in an arid period, a nonfertile period, or a depressive period. Or a passive period even; there are a great many times when we are passive in the face of destiny, forgetting that we really are able to be the captains of our destiny. We are taught a kind of passivity; the culture has taught us that a certain passivity is a feminine quality. So the day that I was told by Otto Rank that I was responsible for the failures, the defeats that had happened to me, and that it was in my power to conquer them, that day was a very exhilarating day. Because if you're told that you're responsible that means that you can do something about it. Whereas the people who say society is responsible, or some of the feminist women who say man is responsible, can only complain. You see if you put the blame on another, there is nothing *you* can do. I preferred to take the blame, because that also means that one can *act,* and it's such a relief from passivity, from being the victim. (72-H)

It is also very important that woman should let go of her blind anger. You see there are some angers that come from damage that has been festering, from anger that hasn't been expressed, or anger that is not understood. That is the destructive anger because it doesn't achieve anything and it doesn't clarify anything. We have to know that it is the repression of this anger which makes the explosion, which makes the destructive explosion, and not the anger itself, provided it has not been repressed, provided it has been expressed properly.

I have a lovely story about that. Judy Chicago is one of the leaders of the women's movement. She came one day to her husband with some grief or other, and she was very vehement but very chaotic and didn't express it well, so that her husband couldn't understand it. The next day when she had put some order in her ideas, she came up and said it again. And her husband said: "Is that all you want? But that's very simple!" It was a matter of expression, and anger of course doesn't express anything. It always overshoots its mark. So I think it's important at this moment that women should deal with the corrosive angers and determine whether they are angers that have accumulated from accepting a situation which really comes from one's own passivity and then has to blow up, or whether they are angers that are justified by inequalities in positions, salaries, or social conditions or laws—those angers that can be turned into energy and can become constructive. (73-J)

I never condoned the suppression of the anger. What I meant is I didn't want us to go through a stage of blind, violent anger which is not effective when we want to create. We have gone through very violent torture; I didn't want women also to go into a tantrum about their situation. That's what I meant about anger, but not that we had to repress it. I had angers like everybody else. I was angry because I wasn't published. I was angry about the passive situation in marriage and not being able to earn a living. I was angry about many things. But I felt I had to examine this anger and see whether it was a hopeless, foolish one. For example, fighting the publishers who wouldn't accept me. What good would it have done? The publishers are a monolithic empire. So instead of that I bought a press, and I put all the energy which would have been wasted in anger into action. What I didn't want to see women do was to get angry in a way that would only hurt *them* and that wouldn't create anything. I wanted them not to subdue anger, because it was a *just* anger, but to do something with it. It's really a transformation of anger into action. Because otherwise we transform this anger into blind violence, which is what a lot of the people today are doing—defacing things, breaking things, destroying things. The anger is there, but it's a useless kind of anger. (72-K)

That is why I'm so concerned with examining and with clarifying anger. So that it will be effective, so that it will work. Some people seem to say: "You got rid of it, why did you get rid of it?" I got rid of destructive anger because it wasn't very happy to live with. For example, when I was furious with the publishers who wouldn't do my work when I came from Europe, and I bought the press, this energy went into publishing the books and it was a release—getting rid of an anger which was toxic, and putting the energy into something else which delivered me of it. Which is what I call liberation—being freed from things that are not very good to live with. (72-E)

Now that is why I stress that there are two ways of going about liberation: one, of course, is the political way, changing the laws and fighting for equalities. There are so many ways of doing it. But the other I stress simply because it is the one I know: the psychological way, which is the removal of obstacles so that you can create your own freedom and you don't have to ask for it. You don't have to wait for it to be given to you. And the women I chose as my heroines were women who created their own freedom. They didn't demand it, they didn't ask for it. They created it. Something in themselves made them independent women, and this kind of independence I stress.

Because the other feeling that has been taught women really is the blaming of society or the blaming of men for the situation in which we find ourselves. Now I found through psychology that when I put the blame on others I felt I was practically saying: "I am a helpless, passive victim." And it's a depressing thought! So the day I saw beyond that, at a certain moment in psychology, I *saw*: "No, not at all. I am the master of my destiny." When I feel free and independent and behave in a certain way towards a relationship, that affects the relationship. I can have an effect on it; I can have an effect on the person I am working for, on my publisher. It is very easy to blame society or to blame the man, but it actually makes you feel even more helpless. Because that means that you are waiting for the man to liberate you or for the government to liberate you or for history. And that takes a long time. It takes centuries, and it's too slow for me. We have only one life.

At first I felt the development of my independence was helped by the absence of the father, the lack of training. But later on I missed that guidance, that philosophical guidance, and turned to a psychologist as a surrogate father—though whatever I learned from psychology I converted to my own use. I am quite amazed at women now who say the psychologist is doing us harm, that he is imposing his ideas upon us or that he is forcing us to accept this pattern. Because actually what happened to me with the psychologist was that he would say something and I would question it. I would challenge it.

So woman has a tremendous job to do at this moment in sorting out which part of her is cultural, religious, racial—what the programming has done to us—and what is left of that genuine woman. Which is what I had to do. I had to peel off all the roles that were imposed on me and slowly, slowly, tunnel my way out. And psychology is a help because it constantly confronts you with your genuine self.

Of course my genuine self was in the diary, and I used to have great nightmares everytime I saw a fire engine. I would say: "The diary is burning!" I couldn't understand why I kept thinking that if the diary burned my real self was burning. Because I, myself, had put it in there. I began to understand that, and I was able to open the diary only when I could accept that I was not exactly the woman that the role-playing had imposed on me. And slowly I began to shed these roles. I kept the ones I considered genuine, the ones that are really a part of me. This separation of our organic genuine self from the programmed self is a job we have to do now. And nobody can do it but yourself. You can get objective help from psychology—and I don't mean necessarily therapy—but just what we have learned from psychology about how we create false personas. I used to say in the diary that I was so aware when I was playing a role that I felt like the poet in the Gilbert and Sullivan comedy who tries to be something else and then gets paralyzed by a cramp! When you play a role, you feel that it is a role; it doesn't suit you, and your body is awkward. I had that feeling when I was playing the role of the perfect friend or the perfect wife, daughter, sister. I knew I was uncomfortable in my skin, in my body. Slowly the role-playing disappeared, and the genuine self was born.

You can see the story in the *Diary*. You can see how first of all I tried to be the ideal woman and that didn't work. Then I tried to be the mirror for others and the muse, the one that helped to get their books done. I didn't even practice my own rebellions, but I was always protecting the rebel, and we know that if you protect the rebel it really means that they are doing for you what you won't do for yourself. So, much later I understood why I was associating with Rank, who was a rebel against Freud, with Artaud who was a rebel against the surrealists, with Gonzalo who was a revolutionist. I used to feel absolutely responsible for them to the degree that I questioned myself: "Why do I feel entirely responsible for them?" I found the answer in Rank, who said that the shadow self, which we don't want to live out, we project onto others. We feel responsible because they are living a part of the self that we are denying; we feel we must protect them from the consequences, for we know that the rebel often pays for his rebellions. In other words, I protected them because I couldn't be as directly a rebel as I am now.

So you see how slowly we emerge. Not letting others play roles for us, not asking our freedom or demanding our freedom from others, but creating it ourselves. (73-I)

We look for alibis outside, and I don't want women to do that. I don't want women to look at the outside, which sometimes is very discouraging and very hard to change and a giant Goliath, but to begin with the idea that within a circle women create a cell, a humanistic cell, a creative cell which may actually have much more influence than what we try to do in a collective way. We try to feel less lonely by getting into groups of women. But that isn't going to heal us of past traumas. A group can't do that for us. The group can't restore our confidence which has been shattered by some experience, a group can't make up for personal and individual traumatic experiences and put us together again. These are things that we have to do by ourselves. (73-D)

We live in a culture where there is too much criticism, too much division, too much hostility, and too much undirected and unclear anger. This troubles me very much because I've seen it appear also in the women's movement. I found that when I went to the various colleges to open up the women's studies there was already this tendency to what I call negative criticism among the women themselves; they were forming other rules, regulations, and dogmas, trying to box in women. This is the last thing in the world I feel that we need. We need to be liberated, to think individually. Every woman's problems are different, and they cannot be solved entirely by one formula. . . . The liberation of woman has to take many forms: the problems of the Chicano woman, the problems of the Black woman are different; the problems of the artist woman are different. They cannot be solved by a totalitarian kind of formula. . . .

There are various ways of liberating women. My concern is with the women who have no confidence, no pride in themselves, no courage in their creativity. I have emphasized very much in my talks to Women's Studies the value of the personal and have also been misunderstood. I said that women, having had a slightly more restricted field, because they were thrown back into the personal, developed a high skill and a talent, a particularly beautiful relationship to the personal world which was the thing that man disparaged and called a small kingdom, a small world and a limited world. I was trying to make women realize that this personal world has an enormous value at this moment when we are in danger of dehumanization through technology, through science, through this expanding of the universe, through all the things that have made us think in terms of millions rather than in terms of the personal. And when I was talking to a group of women at Columbia University there was a woman on my right who said: "Of course I can see you haven't been to Washington, trying to persuade men to do this and that for women." Now I looked at this woman. If she entered this room, you and I would both feel that we didn't want to help her to do anything, because she was so terribly angry, terribly hostile, terribly combative. It was an attack. I said to her: "Perhaps you should see Beatrice, who runs this feminist group and is a psychotherapist, and I should go to Washington, and perhaps then we might get something done. . . ."

I found that kind of persecution turning up again, woman against woman, and I found it very difficult to take. I don't know why. I don't know why I find that much harder to take. It seems like fair combat with a man—a combat between differences, and I acknowledge the differences. With men, its ideological, it's a difference of nature and a difference of temperament; this is perfectly admissible. But somehow part of yourself turning against you seems very hard to take. This is what I'm pleading for: I would like women to be more tolerant towards each one's way of working towards liberation. Because there are so many ways and there are so many different kinds of problems and each woman has her role and has her usefulness. . . .

I think it's awfully important at this moment to have an inter-

pretation of liberation which is wide enough to include certain women who are timid, who are fearful, who are on the periphery, who
are untrained, who are approaching *my* work because it doesn't ter-
rify them. I think it's very important to realize that we need various perspectives, and that each kind of woman will deal with a respective level of development. Some women require tenderness,
the soft approach; some women need an indirect approach. They
are approaching their liberation very timidly and not on exacting
or very certain, clarified terms. (72-E)

Liberation means not to work through dogmas, but to work as
if every woman's case is different. I don't think we can make a
generalization. There are problems in minorities that can be
treated that way by general activities, by political activities. But
there are some which are very individual. So I do mind when one
side of the feminist movement is rigid towards the many ways in
which you can achieve this liberation. And of course the diary
proved two things: it proved how much you could do alone and
what you cannot do alone.

When I lived on a houseboat I had a servant I called the
"mouse" because she was so frightened and timid. She had a difficult pregnancy and was afraid to tell me, because in France to
be a servant is to be a member of a very unhappy clan. Even
though I had been kind to her she just wouldn't confess to me that
she was in trouble. So she tried to abort herself. Then when she
was in serious trouble, she finally confessed and I brought her a
doctor and paid for it. Now at that time, as an individual, I didn't
think that such things could be dealt with or could be changed.
And I learned from the women's movement that there are situations which can be corrected through political action, and that the
story of the little mouse was not an inevitable tragedy. She nearly
lost her life from fear and loneliness in her experience. But I wish
many militant feminists would learn to be tolerant towards the psychological, emotional, individual work that we all have to do.
(72-H)

I'm talking about liberation in *inner* terms. I'm not talking about
this freedom that you can get by going out and challenging the

abortion laws. I'm not talking about the things that you can do to protest wars. I'm talking about the necessity for inner change, the necessity for getting rid of the guilt, the necessity for being aware of what you are going to grow towards, the necessity of considering that sometimes the obstacle is not necessarily the man but an obstacle in ourselves created by the childhood, sometimes an obstacle created by the family, sometimes by our own lack of faith in ourselves. (73-A)

This is all to say that sometimes we don't have to struggle against monolithic conditions and feel frustrated and get angry, bitter, and defeated. We are fighting Gullivers; we are fighting giants. But if part of your strength goes into this slow, careful, organic evolution which I describe in the diaries, you learn how to emancipate yourself, how to unburden yourself. And this can be done without causing men to feel rivalry with you. We have to consider the relationship to others as vitally important. Our liberation has to be synchronized. We cannot achieve it alone. We can't have one group liberated and the other not. I think it has to be done simultaneously and synchronized between men and women and minorities and all of us together.

There has to be a completely new concept of what liberation means. I'm stressing the possibilities of psychological liberation because that's something we can do. And once you have that, then you have the strength to go and demonstrate or to fight a law or to go out into action in the world. You do need that conviction that things can change, but if you live expecting outer change only, then you might well feel that we're not getting anywhere. (72-L)

* * *

Q. There's a writer who said men will depend, the fate of the world will always depend, upon the wishes of women. What do you think about that?

A. N. My answer to that will be a collage that I received by Janko Varda, who was a Greek collagist. He had never met me, but he sent me this collage as a fan letter, a huge fan letter, and it was called "Women Reconstructing the World." Now I know that sounds very ambitious and very arrogant, but I think that this is the moment we have come to and that women can effect a positive change in the world if they will become very articulate about their wishes and transfer the quality of personal relationships into professional relationships. I have already watched women lawyers. I listened to this one woman plead in court, and I felt that she had bent the law a little bit in favor of the human situation—that she was being more human and less a lawyer. So I really do believe that. (73-H)

Q. Could you comment upon the trend of women going into professions? Do you think there will be a conflict between their personal and professional lives, and that they will sacrifice the one for the other?

A. N. I don't see the need of doing that. I haven't done that. I have a very heavy workload and I've never had to do that. Because fundamentally I think it doesn't have anything to do with the profession; it has to do with your capacity to concentrate and focus your attention on what you're doing. If you're doing professional work your attention should be on that, and then you should be able to shift and your attention should be wholly on the private life. In the end, the success of it depends on whether you are in touch at the moment and if you can make the shift.

Some women will have to make a striking or difficult shift when they are out in a hard professional world—as in the case of a friend of mine, Jill Krementz, who is a photographer. She was on duty the night of the Harlem riots, and so she went to Harlem and took the photographs. She came back the next day and had a terrible row with the boss who said that a woman had no business to go there, and that she should have called a man. Now this woman was a highly sensitive, perfectly feminine woman, but she had the courage and the guts and she went and did her job. . . . I think it's a matter of how much focus, how much attention we can put into each world. There is no conflict really. We need both. I don't think our professional life by itself is a very happy state, without our families and personal life to look forward to. (72-G)

Q. You emphasize creativity as a way of converting anger, and you channel your anger into writing. But what of the woman who can't create?

A. N. There is always creation to be done. I don't think of creation only as an artist doing painting or composing. I think of creation as creating a room, a dress, a child, a plant, a dish. I mean everything is creative as long as you are creating in life. To me everything is: relationship, creating all kinds of things, your own person that enriches the community. I think of creation in very general terms, and we can always channel anger into creation. For example, there is a little community in Sierra Madre where they didn't have a nursery. Instead of waving banners and getting very angry, a friend of mine there went around to all the shops and made each shop—the carpenter, the toy man, everyone in the village—contribute to building this nursery and running it. They weren't going to get it from the government and they weren't going to get it from Governor Reagan. So they did it alone. They got what they needed. And that's what I mean by creation. Just that. Doing the thing that is not being done for you. We have become a little too accustomed to demanding things and expecting them to be done for us. We know the government and we know everything they've *not* done. Then we're angry, when the energy for that anger could have achieved what we wanted. (72-K)

Q. When Gonzalo asked you, in the *Diary,* why you never allowed yourself to "explode," you replied: "It is not compatible with being a woman." Would you explain why you gave that answer?

A. N. I had always been preoccupied with the sublimation of anger, anger converted into energy or creation. I wanted to convert all our negative passions, things like jealousy and fear, into positive ones. The role of women as peace-maker was deep-rooted in me. Because there had to be balance to man's love of war and his natural belligerence. It is still a problem for me, the question of how to accomplish revolutions and evolutions without violence. Being a woman still means to me preserving and loving life more than power, with which men have demonstrated too tragic an obsession. All history is a struggle for power. (72-X)

Q. I agree that much of the anger women are expressing today is a destructive anger, but don't you think it is a natural stage we have to go through? We have to create this revolution, we have to crash through.

A. N. No. I see it as something that should be evolutionary rather than revolutionary, and I think there will be an evolution in relationship to man and he will realize that if we free ourselves we will free him. If we don't panic him by some kind of monstrous growth, then he will realize that we're freeing him too, from a lot of taboos and a lot of very suffocating things. That's why we have to work with intelligence and try to involve the man instead of revolting. Because we know that revolutions don't lead anywhere, wars don't lead anywhere. If we wage war on man, as Millett started to do and so many of the feminist women, I think we produce opposition. This is causing destruction, and we did that just at the time when man was coming closer because of psychology. The realization that he too sometimes has personas and irrationalities, the knowledge of dreams—all that was bringing us closer. We all have subconscious lives, man too; he is not always objective, he's not always abstract. So just as that was happening, we started trying to win by *war,* which I just don't believe in. (72-K)

Q. I've just read a book by Ingrid Bengis called *Combat in the Erogenous Zone,* and it seems it's just utterly impossible to establish any kind of meaningful relationship with man.

A. N. *Some* men! You can't make a generalization like that. I disapprove of this book very much because she exposed herself to very unselective experiences, and then was very angry at the men. She didn't select her men, she just went *hitch-hiking* with them. She made no selection at all, and then she blamed the men if accidents happened. I don't think one can generalize from that. . . .

My bad experiences never caused a break. They never caused alienation either from men, women, or children. And I think that what we are really suffering from is just a lack of capacity for relationship. It is not a problem exclusive to the relationship between men and women; it is something which is taking place in all relationships, and which I think this generation is trying very hard to overcome. Because relationships are never perfect. You have to assume that there is creativity involved, wherein we are going to try to make ourselves more understandable to the other person. Women are no longer willing to make that effort. They were usually very good at it. They were usually very good at maintaining relationships, which was sometimes difficult because the man didn't have the time or the willingness to analyze or to go into interpretation. I think that's a very dangerous track for the women's movement: to think that we can only really become totally grown women, emancipated women, and fulfilled women by breaking off relationships with men. (73-D)

Q. You have written that "the tragic aspect of love appears only when one tries to fit a boundless love into a limited one. All around me I find that one love is not enough, two are not enough. The women I know seek to add one love to another." Can this need "to add one love to another" be reconciled with legal marriage?

A. N. I believe in a few years we will dispense with the legal marriage. Marriage and divorce should not be in the power of the law or lawyers. Society will have to recognize all children as equal, legitimate or illegitimate. And marriage should be merely a free choice of the one at the center of one's life. The idea of multiple relationship has always been granted to man. It will have to be granted to woman.

Q. You have often said that "the only abnormality is the incapacity to love." Are exclusively homosexual men and women more limited emotionally and creatively than are heterosexuals?

A. N. No, psychology would not say that. What I have found in my own personal experience is that there is in homosexuality more immaturity and narcissism. As far as creativity goes, they are equal. Whether homosexual or heterosexual, if we do not develop properly and mature, we become distorted in life and in creations.

Q. Do you still believe that "to be violated is perhaps a need in woman, a secret erotic need," as you wrote in *Diary* II?

A. N. This may be part of the primitive programming of woman, which psychology has analyzed in various ways: one, as a test of the man's strength; the other as a way of eluding the burden of sexual guilt. If someone with a will stronger than hers "rapes" a woman, she is not responsible for the sexual act. These dreams may disappear when woman is freed of guilt for her sexual desires. (72-X)

Q. Would you differentiate between the love possible between men and women and the love possible between women?

A. N. I wouldn't differentiate. I think that relationship and love are very complex and that sometimes they work better in one combination than in another. Our greatest difficulty is simply finding the person who is suited, who really is suited to our temperament. I don't think it matters whether it is a man or a woman. But the alchemy, the balances, and the oscillations have to be there and also the effort to create the relationships. Because I don't think they are miraculous. I think they have to be created too. (72-M)

Q. Do you think that bisexuality will naturally come as a result of men and women freeing themselves into being human beings?

A. N. Yes. I think that that kind of freedom has always existed. We just didn't acknowledge it. We culturally confined it. Sexually we never were honest about it, and I think it is wonderful that we remove taboos on whatever directions our lives take. I think the only taboos should be on not loving. (73-C)

Q. Would you say something about monogamous relationships and just that whole question about what's happening today?

A. N. That's such a transitional thing. I don't think we know yet what we're doing in getting what we call our liberation from the artificial binding of two people together. I think we're trying to get rid of taboos, but we're in a transitional stage. I came from a culture which regarded marriage as a stable thing; it was meant for the children and the family, and therefore you don't upset that. But one could have lovers. French culture accepted that. Now, America never did. So then we had to choose between eliminating marriage and saying: "Well then, we will have a relationship". . . . And we're in that transitional stage of asking, what is freedom, freedom to love? There is romantic love, there are other kinds of love, all kinds of love. What are we going to do with these various ramifications of love and how are we going to keep a stable relationship? Sometimes people don't grow in unison; sometimes after ten years our development diverges; and then there are intermittent passions which I think are legitimate. In other words, we should be able to live out all our potential to love. So I don't know what's going to happen.

We've looked at marriage too dogmatically, I think. We've made divorce terribly humiliating and difficult. The law should never interfere with that; it should be very easy. And the law was made *under the guise of protecting the children!* Now the Latins never found that a problem; they protected illegitimate children as well as legitimate children. The law takes care of them in inheritance. So there was no excuse for the binding quality of marriage which we said was for the children.

I think we're in a very interesting, very difficult time. Also how are we going to handle freedom, letting the other person be free too? Because we have our human jealousy, we have our fears, we are possessive. I had friends who felt always a passion for someone else and who would say: "But if I yield to that then my relationship to my husband will never be the same." They were afraid of the continuity and stability of one relationship being damaged by another. It happened that the Latin cultures had a different plan. But I don't think we can take another cultural pattern and adapt it to ourselves and say that the marriage should be stable, and that we should be able to circumnavigate it.

But I *will* say, to give you a little hope, you *can* find a person who answers to all the multiple needs. I think you find it when these conflicting elements in yourself stop conflicting, and when you're willing to make certain balances in yourself. When you know which are the most essential parts of your life, and which are peripheral and ultimately not very important, then you really are willing to make minor sacrifices. And I don't mean major ones. And then there comes a time when we ourselves have an inner unity so that we are able to find the person we need. There is a possibility of that kind of relationship.

Lawrence put it in a beautiful way, I think, in his metaphor of star equilibrium. He said the possibilities for relationships are like a five-pointed star, with the ideal relationship being one in which two individuals balance each other at all points. But sometimes you relate only on this point or with one part of yourself to another person, sometimes on two, and only rarely do you find a match for all five. But it can happen. I know it's not a fantasy of women. And then it can become monogamous, in the sense that it is self-fulfilling. (72-D)

Q. Do you believe in free love?

A. N. I'm sorry. I can't answer that. It's so individual. I would phrase the answer negatively and say that to me the only crime is not loving. So whatever form of loving you've found, practice it. Whatever form it takes. Because I think the real thing is just to love. Free or not free, married or unmarried, are really things that are too individual. It's different for each individual. There are individuals who are more expansive, there are individuals who are capable of several loves. I don't think that can be answered; I don't think you can make an answer for everyone. (72-M)

Q. One of the incidents that's always stood out in my mind is in the first *Diary* when you go with Miller to the whorehouse, and see the two lesbians. I thought it was a fine example of your ability to record people without moralizing. But how did you feel about these women?

A. N. Particularly that the women responded to each other, that that was their way of separating themselves from the experience of prostitution. Didn't I make that clear? That touched me because naturally at a certain point every woman has considered that. At the time when I met June I could have thought that the love of woman was really the salvation from the difficulties of man, and I came very near to that. If June had wanted to, perhaps I would have been thrown in another direction. Anyone can be at any time. Because relationship to man seems so difficult. Instead of that, she was older than I and she didn't initiate me. Somehow my path went the other way.

Q. As a reaction to bad relationships with men, some women are saying that the only good relationships are with women, and the idea is put forth that such relationships are ideal, without any understanding of the problems that go along with female relationships.

A. N. That's why I said in one novel that I thought in the end it seemed to be narcissistic. It seemed to me that my love of June was really not *for* June; she was the woman *I* wanted to be. There was this attraction to a projected part of myself. It was really identification; I realized that we were not two people, but that she was really the woman I wanted to be. I felt that it was a narcissism. So I don't think it's a solution to the difficulties of relationship. The difficulties of relationship have nothing to do with the partner that we choose. I would have had the same difficulties with June if I had thought that that was a refuge from the brutalities of Henry which I only knew of in his writing so far. June came first, before I knew Henry well. I had a shrinking away from him and his world and June seemed much more subtle. She was living out her fantasy. If I had gone that way I would have had other kinds of difficulties, because she was taking drugs and she was very destructive.

Q. Right now, in general, I am much more comfortable with my women friends, much more willing to confide. Even with men who have an understanding of the movement, I don't feel that they always relate to me as a whole person. My sexuality always gets in the way, causing a barrier.

A. N. Well, I think this is a barrier we have to work at. I really worked awfully hard at it with Henry. I didn't accomplish anything. It didn't change his writing about woman. I didn't do it consciously, but I was always explaining June or defending June or trying to see women as human beings and what it might have been like with his first wife. But it didn't affect his writing, because already he was fairly set in that kind of attitude. When I grew mature enough to realize he was not the person to see woman as a whole, then I found other types of men.

Q. I felt that Miller and other men idealized you, related to you in a different way than they related to other women. Why were they willing to relate to you differently? They would treat you like a person, but they wouldn't do that with other women. Why were they willing to relate to you differently?

A. N. Well, I have asked myself that too. Was it only because I was writing? Was it because I was able to talk with them? Having been brought up in Europe I was taught to be able to dialogue with the man, to talk without getting angry or frightened. Was it that or was it what I said last night about Lou Andreas-Salomé: was it that I myself felt equal, that I acted like a person who, whether the sexual relationship exists or not, sets the level herself? That's what I meant by saying that according to our evaluation of ourselves men will accept us, as they accepted Lou Salomé in 1861, who came and went and left relationships when they were no longer alive and was utterly free and had no guilt and couldn't be made to feel guilty. I couldn't be made to feel subservient. So there was something in me too.

Q. Isn't it just another form of objectification to idealize you and put you on a pedestal?

A. N. But that was also the fashion of the time. A woman was either a prostitute or ideal in some way. But I think woman can change that. I changed that into comradeship, into writing and honesty. I escaped; let's say I was an exception. But it must have been my own attitude towards myself. I had a pride in myself as a woman.

June and Henry began the duel of the sexes, the duel of power. And you know June was a myth-maker, and the question of truth and the question of jealousy was on a instinctive level. What happened also was that being a writer I did inspire Henry to write and I did inspire Durrell to write and that's where the respect came from really. Because I did have that particular power, by such absorption in writing and such interest in it, to make them feel like writing. It may have been bringing them to respond on that level. (71-B)

Q. In *Diary* IV you said: "D. H. Lawrence wrote against merging. But it is this merging that I love and seek." How is the desire to "merge" related to woman's search for her own psychology?

A. N. It's a tendency women have had all along, not to merge but to submerge their personalities in those of their men. This can be dangerous, depending on the choice of partner. On the other hand, some women choose a weak person, someone who will not interfere with their growth. That's a negative way of seeking freedom.

Q. In your concept of love, is merging, then, at times indispensable?

A. N. Yes. But one would have to define the word very carefully. It would contain all kinds of things: empathy, sympathy; intuitive understanding of the other's feelings. Also there is the complex and interesting role of rhythm. Merging cannot be constant. Lawrence speaks of this. There are times when the man has to be alone and the woman has to be alone. They have to possess their own souls. (72-X)

Q. You mentioned your demons, and I'm curious as to the one of jealousy. Was that ever a problem in your relationships?

A. N. Yes. But even that, when I met what I thought then—as a young woman who had a young woman's crush on a mature and full-grown woman—when I thought June was the most beautiful woman I had ever seen, I converted whatever jealousy there was into love. I loved her, and I managed to fight that jealousy. But I used to think about it. Everybody has jealousies. I'm never going to deny that. We all have. Also I was reading Dostoevsky and I thought: "Dostoevsky is always talking about jealousy and how jealousy becomes love; so this thing that you're jealous of is really the thing that you admire." What really happened was that I thought June was the acme of all women. So then you love, and that was much more pleasurable than jealousy.

Q. The thing I fear is being left out—that's my feeling of jealousy. I feel deprived.

A. N. That there's not enough to go around. Yes, there is a sense of loss. Beyond jealousy there is a fear of loss. That's what makes a jealousy.

Q. And the problem is then instead of being cast out to somehow get included.

A. N. It's hard to do, and I wasn't conscious of that, but I remember that I was troubled by it. I had a choice of feeling that

June would deprive me of the relationship to Miller or June was going to be included and I was going to love her. It wasn't a conscious thing, it's unconscious. I have an unconscious drive to turn jealousy into love, to transform my demons. . . .

Colette has a beautiful story, especially beautiful in this respect. It's about two women: one is the wife and the other is the indispensable secretary to a very famous playwright who is terribly egocentric and terribly spoiled by women. The secretary is always there with the wife, sister-like to her, indispensable. Then the wife suddenly discovers that her husband is having an affair with this woman. But she needs her. She says: "Who am I going to sit here with in the evening waiting for him to come back?" So they sit together and knit together. She really created a relationship to this woman which was more human than her relationship to the impossible, primadonna husband, and her feeling toward the woman is marvelous. So the jealousy disappeared because she really had a great human need of this woman, a caring and tenderness. It was marvelous, especially when she decided: "What will I do? Send her away? And then I'll sit here and wait for him alone. We used to both sit and wait together." I know it's sort of old-fashioned in one sense, the acceptance of the man, the enslaving by the husband; but still the relationship between the two women is beautifully and delicately expressed. (72-D)

Q. That we are women going to universities, that we have read your books, that we are in the audience right now is a certain reflection on our own growth and self-confidence. But there are millions of women in American society who need to know about this much more than we do, and they're just not being reached at all. What can we do about it?

A. N. Well, I think that the growth is being transmitted. It was transmitted to me by other women in the past. It is being transmitted to you. And you're going to transmit it; we influence many without even knowing it. What you know today and what I know and what we share is something that you are going to pass on to other levels of women who don't have access to it, perhaps who haven't been to the university. I find that naturally whatever I learn I want to share, I want to give it. I'm an educator.

We have to begin somewhere, we have to begin against the falsification we've called elitism—saying that some women have been favored by certain backgrounds and education. We need those women to show the way. The women who showed me the way were women who knew more than I did at that time. So we need that, we need guides. We mustn't turn our backs and say: I have no right to be an educated woman or to have reached a certain point (which I reached very late), but rather try to communicate. For instance, my effort to answer all the letters I get. I am trying to reach women in little towns who are very lonely, who are completely isolated and cut off, who are really greatly in need. I do the best I can. But I think we, each one of us, have much more influence in a radius. The more you work upon yourself, the more of an influence you're going to bring to a group of women, ultimately to many people.

We're influenced beyond direct influence. When living in France, for example, I never joined the surrealist movement. I wasn't a part of it. But we were breathing it, the way you're breathing psychology today. It was in the air. It was in all the books, it was in all the galleries, it was all around us, it was talked about, we heard it. So whether we wanted to or not, we received something from it. And I think that whether these women know it or not they are going to receive from you, from the educated women, what we're privileged to talk about together.

It's coming out. It's coming out in books and it is being transmitted. It is distressing to see what the *media* transmit, of course. That's our greatest enemy. But women *do* read, often ravenously. We are trying really to sort out now and establish these patterns for ourselves. But somebody has to begin, somebody has to make a pattern—somebody who has had the time, let's say. For instance, my interest in psychology is my contribution. It's the way I can contribute to the liberation of women. . . . What we have to do is contribute according to our skill and within our medium. In our own way, do all we can. I'm writing in magazines.

We can influence and we can change. That's almost the only

change left to us: how we can change ourselves and, therefore, others. It will grow, you see; it's like cells. It begins with one cell and then it multiplies. You have no idea what an influence you might have, what radius, wherever or whatever you work at. I see now women lawyers functioning differently, women historians. I see now libraries springing up that are collecting books about women and by women. In Berkeley there is one that asks for gifts of books by women because they don't have funding for it. So we're trying to build a history, trying to give woman a consciousness of herself and her abilities. But you see how a woman like Frances Steloff becomes an important symbol; because she really started without any privilege and created her own life. Now what gave her that hunger and that drive is something else. Where did she get that? (73-I)

Q. When I hear people talk about women's liberation it makes me want to assert the other side of it, that men suffer just as much from women's lack of development as do women. Could you speak a little about *men* and man's liberation?

A. N. Oh, don't be misled. In the woman's movement there are several movements. There are different types of women, there are different types of problems, and there are different ways of solving them. Some women are at the moment *so* concerned, so *fearful* really, and that makes them both aggressive and hostile. Don't worry about that because the majority of women, I think, are fully aware that we will never be liberated except together; that it is in relation to others—men, children, professors, fathers, mothers—that women will only and best achieve their liberation. There *are* some women, of course, so fearful now and so uncertain that they think that by excluding men from their talks they will reach some knowledge of themselves. It's only a temporary awkward stage of the women's movement.

Man also has hated the roles that are imposed on him, and when we say that a man can't cry and be a man that's an absurd statement. Men have been just as conditioned and programmed and put into tight roles as women. I always felt, as a woman, the necessity to dialogue, to explain ourselves. I remember Rank used to let me write on the side of his lecture in red ink what I thought about his lecture. It was so important to do it like that, to do it together, and to convince and to be articulate towards each other. And I think in the end the men who are sensitive and intelligent realize that they will be liberated by a woman who doesn't project some passive need and expect man to create a world. We've burdened men through our own passivity.

Now the part of the women's movement that I believe in is the women who are quite willing to take the responsibility for the *whole* thing: that it takes two to create a relationship, that it takes two to accept what an analyst says, that we don't have to accept everything that is said to us, that women haven't done enough of their own private thinking. It's a difficult moment for men, because the women say that they have to talk together and they have to *be* together and they have to get their strength. I think it's just an awkward stage and that many women have gone beyond that. . . . I think we're going to get into a much more comfortable state where each one will *be*—the real meaning of liberation.

I was talking to a woman's group in Los Angeles and one woman said: "You consider yourself a liberated woman." I said: "Why? Do you doubt it?" And she said: "Well, you're not a lesbian." I said: "Well, liberation means that I have to be whatever I am, doesn't it? Whatever I am, whatever you are? It doesn't mean that I'm going to become something else that does not happen to be me." (73-K)

Q. I must say the lesbian issue is becoming very distressing to me. I believe people have the right to be whatever they wish, but now it seems like it's turning the other way.

A. N. Now it's become a law, another law. In other words, just as we are getting free and beginning to think as women individually and trying to remove all the taboos on homosexuality, on lesbianism, on every form of love, why should we suddenly say that you have to go against your nature and be something that you are not. It's as much of a restriction as we used to have in the male world. You see it is a weakness when you have failed in something, in a relationship to a child, to a man, to a woman, to just walk out of it and say that now you'll have a relationship with another kind of person. I mean it is a weakness not to face this failure. And it will pursue us in every kind of relationship we have.

Q. Well, as I understand it, many of the lesbians refuse to accept that their lesbianism was caused by failure in their relationship with men. That they absolutely deny. They say it is not that they failed with men but rather that they simply have a very strong feeling for women.

A. N. That's perfectly acceptable. But they cannot impose that on all women and say that we can only express our loyalty to women that way. I have a love for women which is very strong; but lesbianism is not necessarily a natural thing to me.

Q. Well, the issue is whether or not woman-love means necessarily the enactment of sexual love. That's the issue. Whether or not you can or cannot love women without acting it out sexually.

A. N. You can. You certainly can. Absolutely and very deeply, very, very deeply. (72-E)

Q. It seems to me that some women are so untypical that it might be possible for them to stand in the same relationship to another woman as a man would.

A. N. Oh yes, and I think between men too, when one is extremely feminine and the other extremely active. No, I think you'll find very much more subtle mixtures than just a man or a woman. But I think in general that the birth of that kind of relationship has usually been the young woman admiring the older woman she wants to be, or a young man admiring the older man. There is a certain hero worship rather than a sense of the other. In the Greek days there was a great deal of the master creating the young man.

Q. But wouldn't this be a recognition of what you lacked, an attraction to the other?

A. N. Yes, but it is still part of you. It is not detached from you. If I love some person who is what I would like to be, it is still *me*—not someone who is totally different from me or balanced toward me and different, the *other*. Much later, I think, I was much clearer about the other. June was really not the other; June was another facet, the unconscious woman in *me* that I couldn't reach or express. It could have been a man too. It happened to be a woman. (67-A)

Q. Do you think the subjection of women to men follows from the kind of society in which we live?

A. N. Yes, it's inherited. It is passed from one to another. My mother's ideal was certainly passed on to me as a child. I told you I made an ideal of my Spanish grandmother because the whole family would say that she was so wonderful; she was such a marvelous woman. I used to hear that as a child and I used to think: "This is what I must become." Her name was Angela—very symbolic! So those things weigh on us, those things play a role, and of course the only way you find this out is in therapy—how strong are these ideals set up in childhood. Any time that I wasn't like my grandmother I thought I was a monster. So I had to get rid of that, and I had to make new ideals. Not my mother's ideal and certainly not my father's ideal of woman, which, from the *Diary,* you know was not workable. And then religion which interfered with my reading so that at sixteen I stopped being a Catholic. Right then and there I fought the dogma. Each step along the way I realized had to be a private evolution before you could really become effective. At least I felt that. (71-B)

Q. How do you feel about the women's liberation movement in terms of the whole question of the individual versus the group?

A. N. Of course there was no question of the group at the time when I was going through my various evolutions. But we substituted for that a very close one-to-one friendship with women so that we would talk. Without being a group, we did talk, two women at a time, about our problems, our difficulties, our lives—and very honestly. A different kind of talk from the talk we had with the man. The group work today achieves very different things—you see, they bring social solutions. I didn't know these solutions, for example, to the problem of abortion. I knew that women suffered from that and lost their lives and risked their lives and that the whole thing was a very tragic thing for a woman. But I didn't know the solution, because individually, you don't often arrive at these things.

Those are the things you have to do as a group, and when you study law and when you study history you learn that those are social problems. The only problems I could resolve were psychological ones, the kind you could solve by yourself through conscious evolution or by helping each other. Both are valuable. But what I still feel strongly is that when the individual has worked on his own evolution, he has something to bring to the group and that a great deal of the work we should really do outside of the group so that we don't bring to the group our problems only, but some solutions—those that you have been able to arrive at alone. (72-Z)

Q. But don't you think that the group can help the individual to achieve the same kind of evolution and development which you reached alone?

A. N. There is one danger in it, which I always felt about the group. That is: does it strengthen your individual creative will, or are you dependent on the group for your development? The fact that I had to do it alone, I do not regret. It was lonely and it was more difficult, and I certainly would have loved to have been with other women who were writing so that we could have encouraged each other. But I found that encouragement in Paris because the writers were much more fraternal and there was no competition. I did find a fraternity of writers. Miller and Durrell and I encouraged each other and strengthened each other. We do need the others, but what I want to say also is that the group can weaken us. Because it makes us think like the group, and so we don't learn to think alone. We don't learn to bear our sorrows, and we don't learn to overcome them on our own. So that when we do find ourselves alone as Sylvia Plath did, then we can't rescue ourselves. (73-D)

Q. Do you think that if women were raised exactly the same way as men are, with the same expectations, that they would be the same as men, or do you think there might still be a difference between men and women?

A. N. I hope there is going to be a difference. I think there is a difference. I think the very restrictions which were put on woman which made her emphasize the personal world caused something very good to be born. Whereas men dealt in terms of nations, in terms of statistics, abstract ideology, woman, because her world was restricted to the personal, was more human. Now that she is beginning to step beyond her confines, I hope she can bring to the world the sense of the personal value of human beings, some empathy and some sympathy.

Q. Would you say then that while you would like woman to be able to enter man's world on an equal basis, you would prefer that the values which emanate from the female personality be more operational, assume more importance in the world at large?

A. N. Yes, I would agree with that. And I hope woman carries these values into the major themes and major preoccupations of our time. I have been watching women critics, women lawyers, and I see a difference (except among those who have imitated man and have gotten where they are just by imitation). But, I mean the women who really have kept their womanhood. For example, women lawyers take more consideration of the human situation while women critics are less apt to assert their own personal convictions about how a book should be written. They are more apt to listen to the case that is made by the writer. Long centuries of listening, long centuries of receiving, of receptivity, which was so highly developed and was in some ways a limitation, became a gift also. (72-Y)

Q. You are a very beautiful woman, and there can be no doubt of your femininity or desire to be interesting and beautiful. But some women today feel that beauty is a threat to an intelligent woman, and that an intellectual woman ought not to bother about her appearance. Were you ever aware of this conflict; was it ever a problem to you?

A. N. No, I always accepted that that was part of being a woman, and I don't think that it is a threat. I never felt, for example, that it interfered with my intellectual relationships with men. If I wanted it to be on that plane and that was my particular interest in that special person, I found that it could be as well fulfilled as it would be with a woman. There isn't any reason why the sexual interplay should be a threatening one to woman. The other part—about looking their best and all that which women have gone against—it's an understandable rebellion against the slickness and over-standardization of beauty, against the fashion industry's attempt to make women feel that if they don't reach that perfection they are nowhere at all. But I feel that that's a negative reaction. I think every woman has to bring her own natural beauty to a point, which doesn't mean we have to look like the models in *Vogue* or *Harper's Bazaar*. I think that the emphasis upon anti-aesthetics is a false solution, and that through it we'll falsify a relationship to men. (72-F)

Q. I wonder if you could talk more about relating to men? I have really good relationships with women but lousy relationships with men. And I'm trying to move with it, you know, move toward men, but I'm really having a lot of trouble.

A. N. Well, don't rush it. Don't rush it. Do your construction job first, and then you'll be much more able to cope with the translation that has to take place with the man or with connecting the links or creating the relationships. You know I have friends who used to laugh at me when I said we have to create a relationship. They thought relationship is a miracle, it just happens, it comes, we find it, and there it is. But it's not true. I never found that to be true. One friend was amazed at things that happened in a relationship over the years. And I said: "Yes, we created that. This friendship was created with talking, with struggle, with crises." So wait until you feel right within yourself, and then you'll feel right towards the men, and you'll even be more concerned with the fact that they're not feeling any better.

The turning to other women for confidence, that's a temporary thing. It's probably a necessity right now. For instance, I had to build my confidence which was thoroughly destroyed by my father. He left me nothing at all because he was hypercritical. He was a perfectionist, and he was a Spanish father on top of that. And that's quite a combination! So when that was destroyed I had to be reconstructed. Now it happened that I was helped by men to do that. I was lucky enough to have my confidence supported by marriage, by man! So I didn't have that particular problem, but I did have a problem. (73-K)

Q. You said sensitive men have always been able to relate to women. But what about the others? Can they ever become sympathetic and understand women?

A. N. If we help them. Because, of course, we are the ones who make the men. At least we raise the boys. And still do, I hope.

Q. Will this involve the change from the concept of different sexes to one of androgyny?

A. N. Not necessarily. It implies seeing the other's point of view, being able to talk their language. As I said once in the *Diary,* we need to translate woman to man and man to woman. Of course we are all androgynous in one sense. We all have what we call masculine qualities and feminine qualities. But we have them in different proportions. So that doesn't really matter. But in teaching the sons, in teaching the men, I think that a great deal will depend upon how we make them feel. Some militant women have frightened men, and I don't think that's very effective. (72-K)

Q. Did the development of the women's movement surprise you, or did you see it as the inevitable development of human evolution?

A. N. No, I read a book a long time ago called *Cosmic Consciousness.* I forget the author, but he was a man with a big white beard and he had predicted this in a very mythical and occult kind of way, which we sort of laughed at. But I remembered it—the revolution of the Blacks and the revolution of woman. And you know this *has* been going on in history. I mean there have been moments when women have won extraordinary positions in history already, and I was always very eager to see that happen. What surprised me was one aspect of it, the angry aspect which I didn't want to identify with. The other I was completely in favor of. (71-B)

Q. Have you seen flaws in the feminist movement?

A. N. What I saw at the beginning was confusion. I saw a great many hostile and angry women who didn't know what they were angry about and who were not effective in their anger but would just sputter and have volcanic eruptions. I see much less of that. I see more unification and I see more effective action in the movement. I don't know exactly what you mean by flaws. The weakness was a blind one—anger. The weakness was not knowing how to unify in order to accomplish the things that we wanted. Woman is trying now to expand, and after all there is a great deal of emphasis on preoccupation with her expansion. But ultimately I think these things are going to fuse. We know very well that there are men who have all the qualities I was talking about, who are humanistic.

But at this time we are at a very crucial moment. We are seeing the development of woman, which is lagging behind the development of man, and therefore *he* will have to forgive us if the emphasis is on *her*—woman.

Q. What I thought is that the movement has to be coincidental or there won't be any movement at all.

A. N. They have to be coincidental. The proof is that *you* are here. However, there is some work to be done by women which is going to be temporarily very intense, very obsessional, and very one-track. Because we have some time to make up for. We have a lot of things to make up for; we have to catch up. We don't even know our women writers; we don't even know our women artists We are only discovering women now. So we have a lot of work to do, and I hope that men will be patient while we're doing it. (73-A)

Q. The other question then is, is it not true that not only women have to focus on women but men have to focus on women?

A. N. Men have to focus on women, and that's why I don't want to alienate them. And I don't want the women, the dogmatic feminist women, to alienate me. Because I can be useful. This is really a plea. I don't want to be alienated by a magazine that says if you're not a lesbian you're not a feminist, or that you're not a feminist if you don't use their particular language, or that you're not a feminist if you don't adopt all of Millett's book. This is what I mean. I don't want a dogma to be imposed. Since I have fought all the dogmas in the world—from the Catholic to the psychological to the psychoanalytical—in order to establish my own feminine vision, I certainly am not going to accept either being told how to become liberated or how to liberate other women. (72-E)

IV

The Unveiling
of Woman

This is a tremendous moment for women which we are witnessing, because, in spite of their not realizing it, our women have been as veiled as in the Orient. They have veiled their thoughts through a long traditional sense of secrecy about their feelings; they have not been articulate. They have written as men, they have painted as men, and we did not really know what they felt. But now *we* have come to the moment of unveiling of women which is just as critical as the unveiling of Oriental women. We are unveiling our thoughts, we are unveiling our feelings, and for that we need extremely expressive, articulate women who will at least know themselves, know what they are trying to tell others, know who they are. (73-A)

This moment, when women are really trying to unveil and unmask themselves and show their true nature, is a time when they need to refine their expression and to reach the ultimate understanding of language so that we can talk together. But I don't mean the kind of talk that we usually practice, which Ionesco described in *The Bench*. In that play two people sat on the bench and talked for hours about the weather, and taxes, and about nothing at all. ... I mean the other kind of talk which relates to the deepest part of the self. (73-F)

I would like to see women become very articulate about their feelings so that they can talk—try and make men see the point of view that we would like them to be aware of. And I think that awareness has to do with language. For a long time we have denigrated reading and what we call literature. But literature teaches us to talk together, and I would like to see women creating their own language. Not fighting like men, but trying really to find a language for their feelings, a language for these things which come from the unconscious, which are instinctive. (72-Z)

The need of language at this moment, for woman to write well, to express herself, is almost as important as the actual evolution of her growth. The *Diary* shows this, that the more I wrote, the clearer my thinking was, that the more I expressed myself, the more I was able then to express to the men or the artists around me what I felt or where I stood. It's a great involvement with language, and the language in the first *Diary* is not as developed as it is in the second, or in the third. And it was finally by writing that I taught myself to talk with others. So I can't stress enough for woman at this moment the need for articulateness, the need to care about language; because again the thing that can create misunderstandings and alienation and estrangement is the inability to speak, the inability to write. We need you to write, we need you to speak, we need this revelation of woman who is not only trying to be revealed to herself but needs to be revealed to others. (72-B)

I owe to writing everything. I owe to it the fact that I can sit here and talk with you. Because when I was twenty I was mute. I know you don't believe that, but I didn't talk at all. And an aunt came one time and said to my mother: "I'm awfully sorry, but you have a subnormal child." When I was thirty I listened always to other people, and I never said a word. I was really mute. So I taught myself to talk, and I owe to writing the fact that we can talk together now. To me there is no question about it, there is no doubt of its meaning to our life. (73-H)

Now I can communicate with women who are very far away—in Japan, Poland, Italy, Canada—all over the world, on the basis of the purely feminine experience, the struggle that is a part of our experience, the added struggle we have, which men don't have in becoming an independent person. (73-D)

That's why I connect articulation with growth, and I say that the women now who are trying to find their identity, who are seeking to expand, who are seeking to find other dimensions in their lives, *need* the expression. Because expression is tied with our awareness. We cannot be aware of something in a non-language state. Our awareness somehow is connected with language. So it's very important at this point that women who have operated on a combination of instinct, emotion, intellect, and observation, a synthesis which we call intuition, somehow must learn to articulate, to become focused.

Women have known a great deal of what we call soft focus. I mean a diffused awareness. Because they are sensory, they feel things with their whole bodies, and all these senses are unified more than in men who can proceed into an abstract ideology. So even though women are now doing abstract mathematics and abstract science—I don't mean that they're incapable of doing it—usually all the parts of themselves are involved, and this requires a much more complex language and expression. (73-H)

The feminine point of view has been much more difficult to express than the masculine. If I may say so, the feminine point of view doesn't go through the rationalization that the man's intellect puts his feelings through. Woman thinks emotionally; her vision is based on intuition. For example, she will have a feeling about something, and she may not even be able to articulate it. I found it extremely difficult at first to describe how I felt. But if you go into psychoanalysis the question always is: "How did you *feel* about that?" not "What did you *think*?" And since woman very often has not taken the second step, which is to explain her intuition—by which step she reached it, the one-two-three of it—she is not able to be as articulate.

Now I have tried to do this (whether I have succeeded or not), and because I was writing a diary that I thought nobody would read, I was able to put down what I felt about people or what I felt about what I saw without the second process. The second process came through analysis, which was a method also of communicating with man in terms of a rationalization of one's emotions so that they seem to make sense to the male intellect. So there is a difference, I think, which is very profound but which is beginning to disappear. Because I think when the younger generation goes through any analytical experience it discovers that the dreams of men and women are the same, the unconscious is universal, and that *there* the things stem from feeling and instinct and have not gone through the rationalization process, and therefore this is a *feminine* point of view. (72-W)

There is a wonderful woman commentator named Maryanne Mennes who asked if she couldn't be given the role of commentator on politics on television. And she was told: "Women are not logical." She answered: "But are events and history at the present moment logical?"

I wonder if you know that D. H. Lawrence obtained a great deal of his knowledge of woman by reading the diary of his first love. He was very curious about women's feelings. He was not indifferent; he just found it difficult to understand them. But we do owe him a tremendous debt for his effort to find a language, which for me was the beginning of a pioneer work in a struggle to find the language which was not the language of ideas—which is very easy to do, the language of our minds, of concepts—but the language for feelings, instincts, emotions, and intuitions; that's the hardest language to gain. (72-B)

There is also an extra problem that women have about writing that men don't have and that is guilt. Somehow woman has associated the activity of creating, the creative will, with a masculine concept and has had the fear that this activity was an aggressive act. Because culture didn't demand achievement of a woman. It demanded it of the man. So the man had no guilt for locking himself up and writing a novel and not paying any attention to his family for three months. But women had been almost inbred with the sense that their personal life was their first major duty, and that their writing had to do with self-expression. She confused that with subjectivity and narcissism, whereas we never spoke of a male writer as a narcissist. (73-B)

These are very real problems, and Virginia Woolf's "room of one's own" is sometimes impossible to have. Judy Chicago, a woman artist who leads the woman's movement in Los Angeles, said she went around visiting all the women painters and found that none of them had a studio of her own. The husband was a painter and had a studio separate from the house where he could work and be away from the children. But the woman was painting in the kitchen, with the kids, or in a bedroom. She still remained part of the house. A friend of mine is a writer. She and her husband took a house in Albuquerque and her husband built a studio separate from the house because he is a writer. He writes about American Indians. But she has to write her book in the middle of the house with the children, all the interruptions, the visitors. So this is something that the woman has had to cope with. (72-D)

I would like now, however, to tell the story of one life which is oppositely pertinent. This concerns a couple who are both artists: she is a painter and her husband is a sculptor. Suddenly the wife began to talk to women's groups and to feel that she was too rigidly molded into the pattern of being the mother, of being home at a certain time to make dinner. All her duties were surrounding her, and they were strangling her. Finally she felt that she had to break away. She broke away with the help of a consciousness-raising group, rented a studio, and stayed alone for six weeks. Then she suddenly realized, when she came back to talk things over, that the pattern that she thought the husband and son had instilled was *in her*. *They* didn't expect her to be home and make dinner; they could do it themselves. All of that so-called tight duty, tight pattern, which really didn't let her paint freely and go on painting if she felt like it, was self-imposed. The husband was perfectly willing to help her with the duties and to let her have a studio separate from the house, so she wouldn't know what was going on in the house. They were perfectly willing to cook their own dinner. So she began to find out that most of the things that strangled her were really of her own making. This happened very recently, and so I think if we study some of the restrictions that we feel, we will find that it's not the other person who imposes them. I think, of course, we have to educate each other. I think we do have to explain to each other what we're going through and *know* what we're going through. So I find myself begging women to be very articulate at this moment, because if they can tell what they are going through they will get cooperation in the end. (73-N)

But it took me a long time to realize that instead of worrying about conflicts—putting everything always in opposition, either I write diaries or novels or, either I'm a wife or a public figure, or either this or that—I find now I just do everything. I take everything in, and, strangely enough, as soon as the conflicts cease, you find that you have energy to do all the things you thought you had to choose between and eliminate. So now I find time to write, I find time to correspond, I find time for my friends, I find time for my private life. Because I'm not in conflict; I'm not using my energy in pitting one possibility against the other. If I'm writing I'm not disturbed when somebody calls me for help or some crucial need. It's the pulling actually, it's the conflicts that drain us. It's surprising how much you can take on instead of eliminating. (72-G)

Now the other conflict is to create as women, because we do have different experiences and a different point of view. We have been educated by men and formed by men. Man invented the soul, he invented psychology, he teaches us the arts. So woman had a more difficult time really writing as a woman. The reason that I escaped that difficulty was that I never had a formal education so that I went my own way and had to find my own forms and had to do my own exploring. So in one way it was harder and in another way it was good for me, because I had to find my own language as a woman, distinct from Miller or Durrell or other men around me. (73-H)

George Sand really materialized for me the concept, the real concern of the woman who starts to create and thinks that when she creates she is assuming a masculine role. George Sand, you remember, used to wear pants, and she used to smoke cigars and carry a little dagger in her waist. And when I first wrote my book on D. H. Lawrence, I thought I could only write at that period by wearing slacks and taking a man's name, a pseudonym like George Sand, or George Eliot. But I quickly got rid of that because I was working with Dr. Rank. He showed me the falsity of this concept woman had, her belief that she was really stealing the thunder of creation from man, that it was something she had no right to and that the only way she could assume strength was to be an imitation of him. This really caused devastation among women novelists of a certain period and many of our women writers. . . . What we are trying really to settle now is to accept that we don't know to what degree each one of us possesses a certain amount of what we call masculine qualities, creativity or will or courage.

What we have to recognize, what we are trying to avoid, is being forced to play a false role. If a woman has creativity as George Sand had or Rebecca West or these women I was talking about, then she should be able to let it out without guilt or without thinking in any terms of a transformation of sex or loss of femininity. I feel that I was able to do that, not at the beginning, but towards the latter part of my life. I had to learn to distinguish between the false selves that my culture had enforced on me as a woman, my religion and my culture, and the true part of my femininity which I wanted to preserve. (73-J)

You have all read the biography of Zelda Fitzgerald, I imagine. That is for women an important book to read. There is a very dramatic moment in the book that almost shows the cause, the motivation, the inception of her mental illness. She had written a diary and a very famous critic at that time wanted to publish it. But her husband said: "Not at all. I need this diary for my own novels and I intend to use it." This episode is referred to in two biographies of Zelda. I notice it perhaps more than I would others because I felt that this was the inhibiting factor in her writing career. She felt that her husband was doing this too well; she really felt subjugated by his talent; she admired him; she gave up her own work. At that moment she really gave up a way of existence or a creativity which might have saved her. So she tried other things for which she was not talented—painting, dancing—all those were substitutes which didn't work. I think the tragedy of Zelda is very interesting to study; I really think that writing might have averted her tragedy, that it would have provided her an equal life as an artist. (72-B)

I always read women writers and I was very shocked by Judy Chicago, one of the leaders of the feminists, who said: "I began to read women writers two years ago." I said: "Why only two years ago? I've always read them, I've always noticed, I've always respected their concern and their focus on the personal."

This personal focus was actually treated in a very derogatory way by men critics—as a very small kingdom, as a minor world, as a world that didn't have stature because it wasn't concerned with larger movements of history. In other words, they made an extraordinary division between the larger world and the quality of the personal world, which woman, because of the prescribed journey and restrictions that surrounded her life, perfected—this personal world and this small kingdom. But if you read the critics, women were disparaged for being concerned with it.

When the great French writer Colette was nominated for membership in the French Academy, the objections to her were certainly not against her beautiful style of writing but against the fact that the subjects that she treated were not large enough. She treated love between man and woman, she treated her life on the stage, the relationships between women and women! And all this was not considered really a great concern, but only minor. Now this is an amazing idea if you examine it. Because the source of our human life, the source of our personal happiness all the time depends on this personal world. From it we take our inspiration and our strength for work, and even the artists take from it their strength to achieve. In other words, it is the center of our life usually. The woman had made it the center but it was not minor!

The discovery I made from my own work was that while being accused of all these many things in my twenties and in my thirties, of being subjective, of being concerned with the personal world, I suddenly realized that when you went deeply enough into the personal you touched the sources of our human life and our humanity. Now my great hope is that at this marvelous moment for women, they should remember that one of the gifts they have is that they remained so very close to the personal life, and that the qualities that were discovered in the personal life, the value of human life, the value of tenderness, the attentiveness to others' moods, the need for compassion and pity and understanding, the things that women practice every day in their daily lives, in their small kingdoms, are enormously important. (72-G)

When I wrote the book on Lawrence it was really an act of love, and it was very consistent with my way of looking at things. Because I don't believe there is objective criticism. Man created falsely objective criticism to separate himself from things, to separate himself from what he was looking at, but that doesn't give you the truth any more than becoming involved in it. Also it deprives you of experience. It depends on what you want, whether you want to be an academic critic sitting up there and writing a cold analytical study or whether you want to experience the work. When I wrote the book on Lawrence I said the duty of the critic is to understand and then illumine for others, but first of all to be in love with it, to identify with it. I did not write about Lawrence objectively. My critical faculty was simply what you might call a need to analyze so as to clarify. (73-K)

A remarkable woman, Sharon Spencer, who is only in her thirties, has written a book called *Space, Time and Structure in the Modern Novel*. Instead of judging the modern novel from the criteria or standards of a certain set of values already established, she did just the opposite. She accepted the premise of the novelist and the novelty of his form and studied all sorts of people who had opened up the conventional form of the novel, such as Cortazar— you have probably read his *Hopscotch*. She studies what she calls the open-ended structure. The opposite of the structure we are used to. Her book is extremely academic, extremely intellectual, intelligent, and at the same time there is flexibility, acceptance of the concept that lies imbedded within the work instead of imposing an already existing concept of criticism. . . .

A woman, among the critics, whom I should also mention, is Bettina Knapp, who wrote a book on Artaud. If you would like to know more about Artaud than you found in the diaries, she studied both his life and his work and their relation to each other very completely and thoroughly. She knows French, she went to all the sources that were available, even Artaud's relatives and his mistress in France, and gave a complete relationship of his work to his life and his life to his acting. As you know, Artaud was involved as an actor in films; he acted in Dreyer's *Joan of Arc,* and was a very amazing performer. He tried to establish a theatre of cruelty which is the theatre that we finally came to use today—the theatre in the round where the action takes place so near that we almost feel that we are on stage, and we feel that what is happening there is happening to us.

There is another woman critic called Anna Balakian who has written on surrealism and symbolism and has also written a remarkable book on André Breton. Interestingly enough, she also wove together the life and the work in equal proportion. The critics found the only thing they could say was that they thought Breton had not achieved a very important revolution, but I think that we all know now that surrealism, whether we like it or not, has influenced us. (72-B)

I also think that woman has served as a muse—sometimes this beautiful word covered being the assistant artist—and that now she has the responsibility of being the artist herself. And up to a point I think *men* will be very much liberated when the women stop trying to live through them vicariously. When I was young and timid about being a writer (and I didn't think I was one at twenty or twenty-one or twenty-two), I was living vicariously through the writers that I knew, and I was hoping that they were going to do this writing that I didn't want to do. I let them be rebels for me, and I let them write for me. Then I suddenly came to the realization that it was not *right* to expect them to do the writing that I had to do. So I think men will be free of that burden of having someone living through them and expecting them to fulfill what is woman's job. And it was my job to speak for women.

One night I remember being with Durrell and his wife. She was very silent; they were quarreling a little and she turned to me as much as to say: "You speak for me now, you talk." She felt I could say what she was feeling. So we have been shirking that job of being the artist, of being the writer, of being the philosopher, of being the psychologist. Because culture didn't demand that of us. It demanded it of the man; the man was expected to perform these things and perform them well. But woman was merely expected to fulfill her personal roles. I don't think we have to discard those roles. I never wanted to discard anything, and I decided to do them all. I took them all in. Continued to be a woman, continued to be the muse, continued to be the assistant artist, but at the same time doing my own work. (73-H)

Speaking of the obscure role of woman, it is very interesting that only a few years ago they honored the letters of Madame Lafayette. Only by these letters did we find out that Madame Lafayette played as strong a role as Lafayette himself in the relationship between France and America. Friends of mine who are historians didn't know this at all, that while he was here fighting she was the one who was raising arms and equipment and receiving the American messengers and continuing to persuade the French to help the American Revolution. So she played a leading role, and Lafayette admitted it and said she was his other self, that while he was active here she was active in France, putting pressure on the French government to send help. (72-B)

A woman who understands what a man is doing if he is an artist will be far more valuable than what we call the muse, which is really the assistant artist or assistant politician. The role of the muse in myth was always that of the inspiring one. There is a very remarkable one in the history of letters called Lou Andreas-Salomé. She was a muse in the sense that every man that she came in contact with somehow was tremendously inspired, tremendously awakened—from Nietzsche to Rilke to Freud—and recognized this debt. And I don't think that she could have been that if she hadn't been herself a philosopher, a poet, a writer, and a psychologist. It was because, as Freud says in one of his letters to her·

"You always understand what I'm trying to say beyond what I have said." So it was her own development which made her such a good friend and such an extraordinary influence on others. (72-J)

Now the few books we have that we think are revelatory of woman's life have always suffered from a certain eclipse, either in public recognition, or by the critics, or by the women themselves. I think that woman was inarticulate about her feelings because they belong to a realm that we have not expressed very much in literature. . . . Also there was a certain fear in woman of what she had to express. There was a certain fear of what she was going to reveal, and one reason for the fear was the judgment of society upon her work.

I'd like you to see a difference of judgment upon two French women who call themselves the female Henry Millers of France. Francoise D'Eaubonne, whom you don't know because she hasn't been translated, wrote a book that she sent to Henry Miller, telling him that in France she was called the female Henry Miller. This book, however, was completely condemned and then disappeared. The same public who gave Henry Miller his great appreciation could not take this kind of openness from a woman. We had the same difficulty with the judgments passed on Violette LeDuc. I don't know how many of you have read *La Bâtarde*. This is an extraordinary confessional work, a naked, honest, even ugly self-revelation. She has absolutely no vanity and no desire to beautify her conduct or herself. Criticism of the book had absolutely nothing to do with the fact that she's a very skillful writer; it was all on a moral basis. Her behavior, the nature of her relationships—this is what the reviews were concerned with. These inequalities are still true. . . .

Many, many years ago a woman named Anna Kavan, whose last book called *Ice* was finally published by Doubleday, wrote two remarkable books: one was *Asylum Pieces* and the other was *The House of Sleep*. *The House of Sleep* was made up entirely of dreams, just as I made up *House of Incest*, and it revealed her world, as very few people have done, through her dreams. *Asylum*

Pieces was a series of short stories, written with the most extraordinary clarity but going into the irrational mind with a tremendous understanding. In each case the person felt herself separating from the common source around her, and she was trying to explain what she felt. She was struggling to articulate these so-called irrational states which we have become more familiar with in our modern times when the stress of events has put such great strain on our psychic health.

I would also like to speak about *Nightwood* by Djuna Barnes. *Nightwood* came too soon. It was written in 1925. All of us read it at the time and T. S. Eliot said, in presenting it, that he didn't mean only poets could read *Nightwood*, but that it did require a certain initiation to the poetic language, a certain refinement of the sensibilities. So *Nightwood* was read only by a few. Djuna Barnes is today eighty years old, and Kent University has finally put together an anthology of criticism and essays and studies of her one extraordinary book. Why it was so overlooked I'm not too sure; it's a masterpiece of style, it's a very lyrical book. It's a story of the relationship of two women and a fabulous character, a doctor, and I want to read you a part of it. She is so marvelous because she was one who knew that we could not describe the nocturnal world without the poetic metaphor; we could not penetrate the unconscious or the emotional or irrational life without this subtle language that has two meanings and works on two levels. So in *Nightwood* there is a chapter called "Watchman, What of the Night!" [Reads the chapter from *Nightwood*.]

I want especially to introduce you to your greatest dreamer of all. She is a woman who has done for American literature what Joyce did for Irish literature. She is Marguerite Young, who wrote *Miss MacIntosh, My Darling*. The book is almost entirely oceanic, almost entirely a nocturnal book. What she has done is to take the stock characters of Middle Western life, the ones who are most familiar, the most corny characters that you can possibly imagine, and by plunging into their unconscious lives has shown that there is no life without tremendous interest if one goes deep enough. So we have the country doctor, the suffragette, the old maid, the nurse, the hangman, all the people that you might imagine as having perhaps only one dimension. But suddenly, through her use of inner monologue and her way of going into this oceanic unconscious, the country doctor becomes an extraordinary character. Every one of them has an extraordinary dimension of life. She does it without the play of words of Joyce; she does it by a kind of efflorescence, a tremendous proliferation of images.

If any writer here ever feels that she or he is for a moment stranded in a desert and cannot write, I think that just reading a little bit of Marguerite Young would set off whole waves and vibrations of images of such richness that it would be contagious. It is difficult reading and you probably won't read from page 1 to page 1000 as I did; you have to take small parts of it and read it aloud. Because it has the lulling rhythm of the very long phrase which unfurls like a wave, rises and curls but always returns to earth. I think that she is our Joyce, and that her portrait of the young girl who pursues throughout the entire book the question of what is reality and what is illusion is very pertinent for woman. She pursues the image of the mother and the nurse and cannot find in this nurse any substantial, warm reality. She uses the symbolism of discovering that she wore a wig, as if this were a supreme disguise. She can't find the warmth that she needs in her. The whole quest is based on the search for human contact through a long, long journey of dreaming, reverie, directed dream, and a tremendous development of the image.

There is a book called *The Sweet Death of Candor* by Hannah Lee which also came too soon and treated very remarkably the difference of sexual appetite between a husband and wife. The husband made the wife feel that she was abnormal, and she labored under this delusion for many years; then discovered that she wasn't, and that there was a disparity between them, a disharmony in their own marriage. She wrote that very bravely and beautifully about ten years ago, and the book was also treated as rather outrageous.

There is great inspiration for women in the journals of George Sand or in her biography by Maurois. *There* was an independent woman whom no one could tame, whom no one could oppress, and whom no one could really hold down in any way. She began very early to express her freedom through writing; her behavior was free, unconventional. She had great courage, great creative activity (stronger than some of the men around her). Her vitality was enormous. But in spite of that she maintained and expressed all through her life very strong maternal feelings toward other writers, toward her children, toward other artists. There was always this sense of the human relationship; she was never happier than when the house was full of people whom she could protect or help, people who were weaker than herself.

In concentrating on relationships, Maude Hutchins is very similar to Colette whose theme was so often her mother and her childhood, or relationships between men and women. There was always this intense focusing on one particular relationship which she studied and unravelled with great delicacy. Maude Hutchins did the same thing in the *Diary of Love* where she is extremely erotic in a very beautiful way. There is also *Victorine* and *Love Is a Pie*, where she treats all this with a very great sense of comedy. Maude Hutchins has written a number of books and they are all very good.

Marianne Hauser is another very little-known writer who has done amazing short stories and novels with a great sense of craft. She is now a teacher at Queen's College, and all her books are worth reading, particularly *Ishmael*, where she took the legend of Casper Hauser and for the first time told the story from a woman's point of view, entirely different from the way the legend was presented by Wasserman. (72-B)

One of the things that surprised me most when I talked to Women's Studies groups about women's writing was that women did not realize their potential. I talked about how women writers had developed an extraordinary faculty for perceiving human relationship within a very small circle, and that this quality could be transferred to larger issues, could be preserved and adapted to larger issues. Somebody once said when women are good at this it is called interpersonal relationship and when men do it it is called diplomacy.

I say we need to and can transform this feminine talent into diplomacy, always with the hope of putting an end to war. But when I talked about that, the women were not too interested; they took almost a masculine point of view—that this personal world was very small. As they used to say about the diaries. They used to say: Of what interest is the story of one woman? I say the story of one woman is no different than the story of a million women. I mean, one woman speaks, that's all. One talks or paints for the others who can't. (72-E)

The crucial issue, which some of the women's liberationists don't recognize, is for women to discover and appreciate the true nature of *femininity* and to strengthen that. They don't have to become men and they don't have to create the world in the same way. I think it will end up really with women finding their femininity, and that, in the Jungian sense, we will realize that we all have feminine and masculine traits and that we have to be allowed to live them out as they express themselves. Usually the artist is the one who accepts this feminine, intuitive side and stays close to the unconscious. That is why for me it was easy to relate to the artist. But later on, when women come to understand themselves better, men also will not be troubled when they find the woman who is very strongly creative, but they will let her go ahead in her own way without regarding her as a threat or a fearful tyrant.

When I once said I would rather be married to an artist than be one, I was really being a coward. I was really dropping out. I was saying that I would help the artist but I was not going to try to *be* one. There was nothing wonderful or sacrificial about that. The muse is a very suspect character, because I simply was refusing to take the responsibility of being an artist myself. So I had decided I would be the helper, the assistant; it was really much easier. So when women complain about being forced into that role, I have *my doubts.* Because I played that role too. After a while I realized Miller wasn't going to write the book I wanted to write, and that Durrell wasn't going to write the book I wanted to write. It was up to me. And it took me quite awhile to take that on my shoulders and say: "Very well then, I will assist and be the muse but I will also do my work." (73-K)

I always said I would like there to be a lot of good writers around; I would feel much better in a universe where there were a lot of good writers and a lot of articulate people. I like the creativity of other people. I felt that the more universal it was, the richer. I never thought of it in terms of competition. The word competition came out the other day. We never once in all our friendships—Durrell and Miller and I— thought in terms of competition. We thought simply of enriching each other or giving the other the sustenance he needed, but we also felt that we were giving to each other. There was no idea of competition. And today I would like to see marvelous women writers, more of them. I will encourage them, I will nurture them. To me that gives us strength. I don't understand competition because I think it's a weakening element. I feel stronger if there is another woman writing and saying things that I can believe in. I feel much stronger when you talk about things in a way that is perceptible to me and acceptable and eloquent. It enriches my world; I feel as if I'm receiving something. (72-E)

I'm sorry that we have to go through this phase of working as women and saying "women writers," because this brings us back again to those distinctions. I wish we didn't have any distinctions. But we're still working with them, and until we have found our way into anthologies of writing and into the museums and exhibitions and until we're treated as among the best artists, that distinction has to be made. I'm sorry it has to be done that way, but I think it's only a phase. (72-Z)

* * *

Q. Edmund Wilson said that one of the great difficulties in his life was that he was attracted to intelligent women and that they were always impossibly neurotic. Do you think it's true that a woman who feels and creates is generally more neurotic?

A. N. No, I don't think that. At that time my differing from his opinion, my divergence from his ideas of writing were very frustrating to me and they would cause neurotic reactions in a sense. Today I would simply say: "Look, your idea of writing is different from mine, and I am sure of mine." But back then I wasn't as sure of myself. I still needed the father or the big critic who would say: "You're fine, you're going along fine, you're a good writer." And because I needed that then, whoever didn't do that became a very threatening force, and that's a neurotic reaction. He was trying to make me *doubt myself*, when I had spent my whole life trying to reach a certain type of writing. Now if I had been absolutely secure then, as I feel today about my work, I could have said it very simply. I wouldn't even have had a quarrel with him. I could have simply said: "You live in the eighteenth century and I'm trying to innovate something in twentieth-century writing; I'm writing as a woman." I wouldn't have been neurotic about it. We're only neurotic if we feel that something is harming us. (72-F)

Q. The symbol of creative inspiration for the man has always been the muse, or the angels, or the feminine. What is it that women must get in touch with in order to be inspired?

A. N. The same thing, I think, in reverse. I don't know why we have never had a word for the man who inspires the woman. We never had a Mr. Muse. But I have received a great deal of inspiration and stimulation and education from man, and I recognize that both men and women can inspire such centers of creativity in each other. I don't know why we made the muse feminine. But I do know that creative women have said that certain men have inspired them the same way. And I have always said that I never would have created if I hadn't had a very deep and rich personal life.

Q. Can women inspire women and can men inspire men?

A. N. Absolutely. Why not? Of course. Inspiration is—I don't like to use the word abstract—but it's a pure quality which has nothing to do with the sex. Women can inspire women, and certainly very often in my early stage a woman was the symbol of what I wanted to be myself. So I would have these great attachments to the woman that I really wanted to be. Like June. I felt June was free and I was not. I was very much tied by my cultural conventional life, and I envied the freedom that she had attained by fantasy-making.

I didn't realize how dangerous her freedom was. So women can do that for each other. We never know what is going to stimulate the center of creativity. (73-J)

Q. Would you speak more about what you see as the feminine qualities and the masculine qualities and how they relate to each other?

A. N. I think at this point we're awfully mixed up about that. We have wanted to label everything, and in labelling masculine and feminine we have said a man has no right to weep and a woman should be weak and passive and not active and not aggressive. We have made these artificial distinctions. But I think we're now in the process of realizing what Baudelaire said: that in every one of us there is a man, a woman, and a child. The successful relationship will depend on the rhythm of these components. George Sand was a very strong woman, a very strong writer, and she had difficulty in mating, finding someone who would fit in with the particular way she was made up. . . . There are courageous women, and there are men who are very tender and weep. There are also men who make very good mothers!

I think we are in the process of getting rid of this pattern imposed on women: that all women must be a certain way, that all women must bear children or get married to be fulfilled—which is what people like my mother would say—that this was the only means of fulfillment for woman. I think we're getting rid of all that. We're in the process of transition, and so we have to be very clear-minded and lucid at this moment. We are separating the genuine from the not genuine and it's a task which each one of us is going to have to do separately. Women in groups can help each other feel less lonely and they can discuss many things but they can't do everything. Especially if one is traumatized or has very deep-seated hangups, as you call them. (73-I)

Q. Have you ever used a pseudonym?

A. N. No, I never have. Oh, I think once in a very small article for a Canadian magazine when I was very young and didn't dare put my name to anything. But I never have used a pseudonym. I know my name sounds like one. (73-D)

Q. You are a preeminent woman and I find your point of view to be entirely female and exciting. But do you think we have that in America, a good female point of view?

A. N. Yes we have. In writers that we hardly know. But the women writers that you have favored, for whatever reasons, are women who have imitated men. I consider Mary McCarthy, Susan Sontag, and Simone De Beauvoir to have masculine minds. But we have had women like Djuna Barnes. . . . Maude Hutchins. . . . Marguerite Young. . . . Now these are the women we don't read. Very interesting, but it's our choice. Because we have feminine women writers. (72-W)

Q. Do you think that the male as such has been one of the chief sources of pain to the creative female?

A. N. Yes. But because *we* set him up. *We* accepted him as the philosopher, *we* accepted him as a historian, *we* accepted him as a psychologist, *we* accepted his influence on our education. *We* gave him this kind of power. And when you go through the process of psychoanalysis, the process of self-discovery, you realize that you should *not* give anybody the power to decide what is right and wrong in your creativity. I mean the critic should not be outside; it should be within yourself. And when you reach maturity, which I finally have after a great many years, I find now that I'm the judge of my own work. I need opinions and reactions, it's true; but they're not fatal. They wouldn't keep me from working. (72-F)

Q. Two writers whom you are very frequently associated with are D. H. Lawrence and Henry Miller. Do you feel that there is a discrepancy between your encouragement of women to take an independent view and your relationship especially to these two male writers?

A. N. I don't see any contradiction in that. I think every experience comes at a time when that experience is what you are ready for. At the time, in Paris, there were no women artists or women writers that I could have associated with. I would have associated equally with them because I have always had very close friendships with women. But they were on another level, the wives of the artists. Djuna Barnes, the one woman writer I did want to know, and who had a great influence on my writing, didn't answer my letters. So it was not an accidental choice. It was the fact that the men were doing the writing, the painting, and whatever was happening around me, so that they were interesting to me. I never found at that time a female Artaud or a female Miller or a female Durrell. I would have been equally close to them. I used to read women all the time. But today, when women are coming forward, I have women friends who are as valuable as painters as the men that I know, are as strong as writers and as exceptional, and so now my friendship has been balanced between men and women and I don't discriminate. (73-B)

Q. D. H. Lawrence is accused by a lot of feminist writers of being chauvinistic and dogmatic about women. I was wondering if you felt that way.

A. N. No, I don't feel that way. I don't think we can just get rid of a writer because he had one limitation. I think we have to take from Lawrence the great contribution he made in trying to find the language for sensations and emotions and instincts. He tried to understand woman. He was part of his time. He did have a limitation, but it was also part of his period. I don't think we can sweep him off and say he was no good because he failed in this particular thing. That's what I don't like. This is what I call dogmatism. Lawrence gave me a great deal as a woman. He was the one who said that women would have to make their own patterns, that they were being created by man. You can find negatives or partisanship in almost anything if you want to and some of the feminists have tuned in simply on that very limited range. You can take any writer out of context and condemn him for this reason or for that reason, for some prejudice or some limitation. But you have to take Lawrence as a whole and see his contribution. He put me on the track that there was a language for emotions and instincts and sensation. (72-G)

Q. Would you talk a bit about Henry Miller and your perceptions of him in terms of women's liberation?

A. N. Well, this is a very delicate subject, because Millett gave you a very distorted image. She's a very angry woman. You can always quote out of context. You can always fail to understand at what period a writer was writing. Lawrence's ideas about women were very old-fashioned, but they belonged to his period, and being a miner's son, his experience was limited. He had a very naive and limited understanding of women. Miller was a Brooklyn boy. He had a very limited experience. He was very distrustful of woman. Nevertheless, what Millett did was to take his humorous, comic stance seriously, without realizing that this was picaresque writing. All he was trying to do really was to revolt against Puritanism and be a picaresque writer, such as we had in France in Rabelais. Everybody accepted Rabelais as a comic artist. And nobody understands Miller as a man whose treatment of woman is quite different from the stance which he took—which was the stance of that period, the Hemingway stance, the stance of Mailer today. So you have to make the distinction between a stance, a phony stance in the case of Henry Miller who meant it as a humorous, comic treatment and his treatment of certain women, including myself. I certainly wouldn't have had a relationship with a chauvinistic man!

Millett's is a very one-sided image. Why did she lavish so much time and scholarship and care on blaming men for what they did not do? I never expected Henry Miller to make a delicate, subtle, nuanced portrait of a woman. Why didn't she write about women? Why didn't she spend all that energy writing about women who *had* written portraits of women and who *did* speak for themselves and who wrote biographies and diaries? This is what I feel about Millett. And I want it very clear because there's a distortion there. The same is true for Freud. Freud lived at the beginning of psychoanalysis. Of course he had limitations! Every one of us has limitations. The thing for women to do is to become aware of the limitations, just as I did when I was being analyzed by Allendy. I asked him once: "What is my true self like?", and he made an absurd description and I laughed. He visualized me as his own fantasy of a Creole woman sitting in a rocking chair fanning herself, in a long white dress. This was his fantasy, but we have to know enough about ourselves to say no, that's not me. And in the case of

Miller, I think Millett lost all sense of humor and understanding of the comic anti-Puritanism that he represented. (73-G)

Q. I get the impression, from the absence of women in the *Diary,* that you were more influenced in your development by men than women.

A. N. There were women writers like George Sand, Djuna Barnes, and George Eliot. These were the women artists. But the women who were around me were the wives of artists, and they had long ago given up and were just playing a shadow role. Nevertheless I have life-long and very strong friendships with women. That's all in the *Diary.* Now artistically, as far as thinking and education, you mustn't forget that I was deprived of a father and of a teacher too because I left school very early and never went back. So I had to make up for that by getting my education from different artists, from the psychologists. We didn't have women psychologists at that time in France. We didn't have women philosophers. We're just beginning now to have them, and women historians.

So we didn't really have guiding women. The women I knew were not able to do that. They were not psychologists, they were not philosophers, they were not painters. I was educated by the artists, and the artists happened to be at that time more men than women. The women were the friends; the women acted the role of the sister, the consoling one, the understanding one, the one that stood by, the one who was loyal, the one I could share things with. But they didn't *guide* me. In life I couldn't do without them and I loved them; in art I chose the leadership of the men artists who at the time happened to be stronger than the women I met.

I wanted to meet Djuna Barnes, for example, who had a tremendous influence on my work, but she wouldn't meet me, she wouldn't answer my letters. So don't forget that the women themselves kept separate. Not as they do now. For instance Djuna Barnes could have answered my letter, as I am answering my mail today. And that is why I'm doing it. Because I thought it was unkind of her not to answer a beautiful letter about her work, about *Nightwood.* But she didn't. She still does that, you know, she's absolutely inaccessible.

At that time too, you must remember, women were *beginning* to make their way as artists. In Volume V of the *Diary*, for example, I have portraits of Cornelia Runyon, the sculptress, of Frances Field, the painter, and of Peggy Glanville-Hicks, one of the women composers who is now being recognized. All their concern at that time was how to get recognized. Peggy was very unhappy and very frustrated and very bitter. So she couldn't help another woman artist. She could only do the work that she did, and I could only listen to her work. But such a woman couldn't play leader. (73-A)

Q. Do you feel that if woman had invented the soul it would have been a different soul? Do you think we would have looked at it from a different point of view?

A. N. I think that's yet to be discovered, how woman will formulate all these elements—religion, metaphysics, science. Already I had a great encounter in Stanford when I was invited by the scientists, the men who are making the integrated circuits. I think you know what that means: that's a miniaturization of computers into something the size of a wristwatch. I saw the whole process first in the laboratory; and then what they really wanted to do was to quiz me about the creative process—what steps?—how did it happen?—so that they could compare this with the computer's thinking. I have gone through that second step because I wished to communicate with man. I did rationalize and analyze these processes. Not in the diary because the diary was written automatically. There was *never one* erasure in the diary. It was completely a habit, a spontaneous habit, almost automatic writing. But my other writing, in such a book as *The Novel of the Future,* is analytical. We don't know how woman is going to formulate all those truths yet, but I think it will bring man and woman together. Mainly the study of the unconscious is the thing that really brings us together, because in the unconscious man behaves far more as the woman always has, when she has not taken the second step of intellectualizing. (72-W)

Q. As a woman artist with a type of sensibility that is often dismissed as "trivial" by critics, have you encountered special difficulties?

A. N. Yes, but once women become critics, women writers will be in a stronger position. Woman has been reviewed and criticized by man, essentially. Many male critics were very wonderful and others were highly prejudiced. They thought woman's sensibility was superficial and limited. But I know several women critics who have tackled their work with such vigor and clarity that now, I feel, something is going to happen to women's writing.

Q. If women critics possess the sensibility to understand women writers, what, then, accounts for the fact that when your novellas came out in the 1940s so many women critics ruthlessly attacked them?

A. N. I believe that the women who attacked me during the forties were imitating men. Women critics who imitated men were particularly keen on separating themselves from what men defined as "feminine" writing, and to show they were not a part of this, they attacked it. (72-A)

Q. Can you say if there is a particular critic whom you feel best understands your work?

A. N. The first critic of my work was a man, Oliver Evans, and the book was titled *Anaïs Nin*. But he did not understand my writing; he took it too literally and was not transcendental or symbolic enough. The best critic is a young woman, Evelyn Hinz, who has done a very objective—cool, but not cold—study of the entire work. The title of her book is *The Mirror and the Garden: Realism and Reality in the Writings of Anaïs Nin* and the title and focus derive from *Ladders to Fire,* where the problem of illusion and reality with respect to the psyche of the woman is dramatically symbolized. She has a great understanding of D. H. Lawrence, and her initial interest was Lawrence's work. But in reading my book on Lawrence, with its concern with his efforts to understand woman, she began to take an interest in my work and wrote her book. (72-Z)

Q. Is part of your uniqueness as a writer due to the fact that you venture into realms which relate specifically to woman's situation and experience?

A. N. My own subjective attitude towards reality was all I really knew, what I could see and feel. I read a great deal, but I didn't imitate men writers. I wanted to tell what I saw. So it came out as a woman's vision of the universe, a highly personal vision. I wanted to translate man to woman and woman to man. I didn't want to lose contact with the language of man, but I knew that there was a distinction of levels. (73-M)

Q. How did you earn your living when you were writing in Paris? Did you have a job?

A. N. No, at that time I was dependent.

Q. Were you married?

A. N. Yes. But I was writing just as much when I was not a dependent before marriage when I was posing for artists in the evening and modeling for Jaeckel's Fur Store to take care of my mother and two brothers. I was writing just as much. When I was sixteen I was earning my living, and I used to give up my lunch hour to write. So it's not right to say that I wrote a great deal because I didn't have an economic problem. We shouldn't tell ourselves that. We can do it under *any* conditions. (73-K)

Q. You continually emphasize the difference between woman's creativity and man's creativity. You don't, in other words, entertain the idea of androgyny, which many women are discussing. You seem to emphasize the reverse.

A. N. If so, it's mainly because we are *rushing* now into a sense of liberation. We're emphasizing a total denial of womanhood and think that this will free us, because the image we previously had of woman we found oppressive and limiting and restricting. But it's up to us to change that image, and we don't have to give up our femininity, we don't have to throw out the whole female concept.

I think, going back to Jung—the yin and the yang, the positive and negative—everything is interrelated. So there is no reason why we shouldn't retain that aspect of woman that we are related to by nature, which is greater closeness to nature and greater closeness to instinct and intuition. We did not develop our rationalization as man did; we didn't go into science and into philosophy and all that rationalization of what we feel and the final abstraction of it. We were saved from that, and I want women to realize that that was a wonderful thing, in a way. We were prevented from being the head of the oil company or the head of the bank and so saved from corruption and abstraction and dehumanization.

Woman, having been limited, developed—as animals do, insects do, when they are deprived of one sense—they developed another sense. We developed a very high sense of humanism and of the depth of the personal, as I said in the *Diary*. I didn't know how strong it was until the *Diary* came out and I realized that in telling a personal story we also tell a story that is collective. There is no difference. Man is always saying: do an objective piece of writing, be objective, become objective. But they finally became not objective but dehumanized. They really went off to the moon, and some of them stayed there! So I would like us not to throw out all we have developed through the centuries. . . . It's a shame to throw it out and talk about unisex and all that. That's not what we want. What we want is to be accepted for whatever we are and the recognition that some women have more masculine components than others, some are more childish, some are more feminine. What we want to do is accept whatever components are genuine. (72-K)

Q. Another aspect of the humanism of woman is that, traditionally being more involved with children than man, she thinks of the future. Because if women were to consider that there was no place for their children in the future, then their despair would be so terrible that there would be mass suicide.

A. N. That's a very interesting point. That's a great concern of women. But also—and this is the same thing that you're saying—remember when we read Ellsberg, his comments on all the *Pentagon Papers:* that not once have the Vietnamese been mentioned as *human beings.* Now I know that for women, to see a body killed—it doesn't matter what body—hurts a woman. I don't think woman can think of it in terms of numbers—anonymously. There's a closer sense of the body, of the preciousness of life—put it that way. (72-Z)

Q. This suffering, be it in terms of human relationship or be it just in the ability to feel more than some other people, does it make life more difficult for a woman and particularly a creative woman?

A. N. It has made life more difficult for the creative woman. In other words if a woman often lacked self-confidence, which I think she did, and was dependent on others for praise or for approval, it made her very vulnerable. And when I speak of neurosis I really mean nothing more than what we used to call romanticism: that is, wanting the impossible and then being unhappy if it was found to be impossible. I wanted not only to do my work but to be approved, to be helped, to be admired, to be inspired by the man, and that was not always forthcoming. Although I must say that for the most part men have helped me in my work.

Q. Would you still need male approval, do you think?

A. N. No. I think part of our maturity, what I call outgrowing the neurosis, is really that we ought to be able to do our work and believe in ourselves without such approval. But I don't think any of us do. There is always someone whose judgment we need. (72-F)

Q. We would like to discuss the question of what is missing in art today, and then relate it to women. Are there particular characteristics of women which could make art more meaningful for all mankind?

A. N. What I have found in general (and I really don't consider myself an art critic) is that the depiction of despair, of the gutter and the trash of our lives and the complete negativity really, of life —the opposite of life, the cult of the ugly—the underworld—this sort of satanic underworld is man-made.

It is not very familiar to woman. Her love of life is more persistent, perhaps, or more obstinate, more tied to her senses, to human relationships. She does not want to give way to despair. Man has taken this despair from history, from ideology, from politics. He doesn't value his personal life as much. To me the personal life has always been nourishment which made life worth living. I have never been able to stand history at all because it always seemed to be stories of war, greed, and intrigue. It's just a horrifying thing to read history. I like to read personal biographies in which an individual finds life worthwhile and finally succeeds. Whereas, in history you will read the story of general catastrophe, which is what we are seeing now. I think woman is very untouched by that. She doesn't contemplate destruction and death as modern art has done. I see so much of that in modern painting. (72-Z)

Q. You were talking too about the function of woman and how a woman acts in terms of an agent, almost a catalyst, for the rest of the community, and I think you described it as "woman is nature, woman is the mirror, poetry and art," and you said that the mirror is also an expression of fear, the fear of truth. "The mirror allows us to contemplate nature while out of danger." That struck me as a tremendously graphic way of describing the function of woman.

A. N. There are several things involved there: the mirror sometimes I use as a form of art, where we reflect nature without being in danger, where it's transmuted into a form that is no longer lethal, as experience can be, and then there is also the mirror that the woman always was for the male artist and the mirror that I am in the diary when I portray others.

Q. Does it mean also that in some sense the woman's suffering enables the rest of humanity to see deeper and to see some of the kind of mystical values underneath things while at the same time not endangering themselves in any way, not becoming neurotic themselves as it were?

A. N. There is a difference between genuine suffering and neurotic suffering. I think some of the things that woman suffered were absolutely real, conditions which made her life as an artist very difficult. There were many many more obstacles than there were for the male artist. That's the genuine suffering. The neurotic suffering comes when this creativity and this growth is frustrated either by social conditions, family conditions, educational conditions, whatever the atmosphere is. Then it becomes neurosis, it becomes negative. But I think the neurosis theme in our time is almost a collective one. I think there has been a collective frustration for all creativity and all expansion of the individual.

Q. And the danger of course is that instead of directing or channelling that suffering into some kind of creativity you can go over the edge into a kind of neurosis and withdrawal.

A. N. Yes, but then that's happened to men artists too. We've had the poets go mad; we've had Rimbaud walk out of his poetic existence; we've had the madness of Artaud. And we have recently had the poet who wrote *The Bell Jar*, Sylvia Plath—those suicides who were not able to fulfill themselves and decided in favor of death. But then women usually choose a quieter way of withdrawing from activity which is simply to live in the home and give up the piano, or give up the painting, or give up the writing.

Q. But you think it's symptomatic of the same thing?

A. N. Yes, it's the same as Rimbaud walking out. Except that it's not so dramatic. The average woman just withdraws into her personal life and takes care of her children, of her personal life and gives up the other challenge.

Q. And it represents the same kind of loss, in the last result?

A. N. I think it does. I think it represents a great loss in terms of culture, in terms of history. Because woman did have a major contribution to make. I found a most beautiful quotation the other day from Maryanne Mennes saying that the whole process of culture had been too much in favor of the masculine principle and that the day that those two worked in unison we would really have something very wonderful.

Q. But it certainly hasn't happened yet.

A. N. No it hasn't. But it's happening. The balance went too far into the masculine concept of the world and now women are trying to straighten it out by going too far in the other direction, by isolating themselves and separating from the man and having their own sort of fanatical prejudices too, which I really don't go along with. But that's a transitional stage. Maybe when both sides feel strong enough they will work in unison, when the woman doesn't feel so endangered. If I hadn't felt so endangered by Wilson we could have had a very interesting friendship, a friendship of opposites.

Q. But the interesting thing, one of the most interesting things to me about your writing, is that you never seemed to be *too* threatened. There is always a kind of strength in you, and one can see it and one knows that no matter what comes along you're never going to go under. I mean I think you expressed it by saying, "I care. I care very much, but I will never die from caring." Whereas the other writers that are part of this program—Joan Didion and Dore Previn—may well die from caring too much. One gets the feeling from both of them that the edge that's keeping them back from dying is very thin indeed. What do you think are the qualities in you which made this less of a danger?

A. N. I think there was always the primary concept of what it meant to be an artist. For example when I refused destructive experiences such as drugs, I would always say: "Because I am a writer—I must stay lucid because I'm a writer." I was determined to transmute the sorrows. Whatever bitter experience or whatever difficult experience or frustrating experience, it all came out in work and that was my salvation. And even today, if I have to fight a very deep depression, I sit at my desk at 7:30, and I begin to work and the depression goes away. So my salvation somehow was always in the work. (72-F)

Q. Could you say something more about Sylvia Plath?

A. N. About Sylvia Plath the most illuminating thing is not what I could tell you but in an article I have read in *MS*. magazine which I would like you to read. It's a very fair study contrasting the beauty of her poetry with the complete inadequacy of herself as a human being and as a character. Which would then explain her immediate surrender. (73-D)

Q. Could you comment on your feelings toward Virginia Woolf as a writer?

A. N. I have great admiration and respect for Virginia Woolf but I don't have the love that I should have. Because there was one aspect of her life which was missing for me, the passionate aspect, the sensuous aspect. So I don't have this great affinity for her that I have for D. H. Lawrence. (72-I)

Q. Would you say that Virginia Woolf gets into a nocturnal area?

A. N. Yes, very much so. She was a real visionary, the visionary poet using the novel, but the novel as a visionary poetic state.

Q. But she got in trouble didn't she?

A. N. Yes she did. It's true. But it's also true that women allow themselves to do that. We do think of the poets who flipped and lost their balance but we forget the ones who didn't. I mean it's true Virginia Woolf lost her balance, and we don't quite know why, whether it was organic or whether it was neurotic. We don't know enough about her. We don't know if it was a physical unbalance or depression or whether it was a psychic depression. We really were never told anything about her state. Her husband edited her diary and wanted to preserve that aspect of her, which we didn't preserve in the case of Artaud. Artaud explained himself when he made his descent into hell. But with Virginia Woolf that was left out of the diary—when she would lose her balance and then recover and then come up again and then finally couldn't bear it. So we don't really know the nature of it. Her diary now, her manuscript, has been given to the New York Public Library on 42nd Street instead of to a college, which is strange. And I don't know whether it will ever be published in its entirety because the first one we had, *A Writer's Diary*, was severely edited. (72-D)

Q. You would say, then, that one of the aspects of art today is that it's fragmented and that woman's ability to use her total intuitive perception is the quality she should bring to art?

A. N. Yes. The split only came when she found it impossible to play all the roles. I mean women have found it difficult to be mother, muse, wife, professional, artist. If she can handle all these things, she will have a wonderful synthesis. So our job is greater, but we really have more to achieve. And I think we also have been given some qualities, some extra-sensory qualities, to achieve them with. (72-Z)

Q. Who would you say are the best writers to read, the nourishing ones?

A. N. Nourishing writers? I think that's different for everyone. I think we read very subjectively. We read what we need. There is almost an obscure force that guides us to a particular book at a particular time; then we get in trouble when we try to rationalize that and say this writer is good and this writer is bad. I've never been able to say that. You see I can't say Simone de Beauvoir is bad, but I can say she doesn't nourish me. That's a totally different statement. And I think that differs very much. I have made a list

of women writers and their books which have nourished me. But
it is not a literary selection. It is a purely subjective selection and
yours might be totally different.

I'm very often asked how I feel about Simone de Beauvoir, how
I feel about *The Golden Notebook,* and I always have a very difficult time answering. I don't consider them nourishing books because they keep telling me how things are, but never show me how
I can change them. Now when Simone de Beauvoir writes a book
about aging she is bowing down to chronological age and saying
that at a certain time we become old. But we become old sometimes at twenty. Age is another thing which we have to transcend
and have a different attitude towards. It's not chronological. So I
feel the same way about the description of things as they are without an opening as to where we can go from there or how we can
transcend that, which I find in what I call the nourishing writers.
That is why, when I'm not in love with writers, I always say that
I may respect their ideas but they don't give me the feeling that
pushes me on towards life. (73-K)

I was discouraged by the outer details of Doris Lessing, and
maybe I gave up too soon. I may have made the same mistake that
Gide made about Proust when he said if a man takes fifteen pages
to describe a wakening he couldn't read it. Lessing took four pages
to describe a teacup that had a stain on it, and I just gave up. I
shouldn't have given up, but I mean there was too much detail, for
me, too much upholstery. (72-D)

Q. One of the things female sculptors, painters, film-makers,
frequently talk about is that we have no role model. If you go into
the Whitney or to the Guggenheim, you don't see any female art
on the walls. Would you agree that this is somewhat less of a problem for the female writer, and secondly, would you talk about female artists who have influenced your work?

A. N. Of course, being a writer, it is mainly women writers who
have influenced my work. But I could also think of women painters that I've admired very much and women musicians, women
composers and a person like Martha Graham. Her creations of
dances influenced my writing. . . . I think what happened with wo-

men painters is that the critics didn't treat them with the same attention. Think of women like Georgia O'Keefe. I'm sure it took her much longer to be recognized than other painters. And we also lack the female critics who would notice women artists and write about them. I mentioned Judy Chicago, an artist and a feminist, saying that she had only begun to read women writers two years ago. And I said: "But why? I always read them, I was nourished by them, I needed them." They represented a very different view of the world. At a time when all the male novelists were writing about alienation, I could cite five or six women who were writing books about relationships.

Q. You mentioned that Martha Graham influenced you. Could you spell that out a bit more?

A. N. I used to watch the way she composed the scenes of her dances and the symbolic way in which she handled scenes which, if they had been handled, say, in the Greek play, would have been stated directly and much less tragically. She used symbolism. I had her in mind when I wrote the last section of *Ladders to Fire,* about the party, the movement, and the motions of the party. I described the party, which I call the least-attended party in literature, in which everyone, because he had obsessions and preoccupations, was absent and did not really attend it; perhaps some through lack of self-confidence, some because they were expecting something that didn't happen. Each one was really carried away from the party. It was only their bodies that moved on the stage. And it was from her I learned this idea of movement, of the pattern that the lives of people make.

Q. Another woman you mention in the *Diary* is Maya Deren. Could you tell us something more about her work and how you felt about her as a female artist?

A. N. Maya Deren was a very courageous woman, a very talented woman, who really started the underground film and did a spectacular thing. She was married to a very fine camera man, Sasha Hammid, who did the "Mexican Village." But she had a very difficult time. She had to use her friends, who were not very good actors, and we had to have fake backgrounds and go to Central Park, go to the beach. She had to use whatever was available. But she had a great deal of imagination, a real talent.

The only good thing that ever happened to her was that she received a Guggenheim to make a film on Haiti. She spent two years there and became very, very deeply learned in voodoo practices. But when she came back she found that she needed more money in order to edit the film, as the laboratory cost was very high. I know she did not receive a second grant, and I don't to this day know if the film was ever finished. In frustration she was obliged to write a book about voodoo and Haiti, which is a very wonderful book. (72-Z)

Q. Are there things that you would never have believed possible that you see now?

A. N. I never thought women, for instance, would have their own publishing houses, would have their own newspapers. I never thought that we would have college courses on women's writing. In the past these things were very unjustly handled and women were often *not* really given the proper place because the critics were men and the teachers were men. So I think all this new activity by women is going to make a very interesting, better balanced culture. Of course there will be excesses, you know; there always are in a revolution. (72-F)

Q. What writers of today are translating man to woman and woman to man?

A. N. Well, that's a difficult question. I think of many writers. I lay stress on women writers because women writers were writing profound studies of relationships when men writers of the same period were writing about alienation. And when Paul Bowles writes a book which ends in a murder, and he says that it was only by murder that the man could find contact with another man, this is the kind of thing that the male novelist carried to excesses— writers like Mailer, for example. In this same period, women were writing studies of relationship.

Now, the translation of what woman feels for man is something that women are doing now. They are writing. They are saying what they feel. And I would like them to become highly articulate. I still maintain that it was because I was writing novels that I became better and better at saying what I felt in the diary. So we do need the craft; we do need to care for language. We do need to explain ourselves to others. We do need to become articulate so that man will understand what we feel. (73-G)

Q. In other words the responsibility lies with us to articulate our own reality because we have really been accomplices in the mystification of the female.

A. N. Absolutely, absolutely. This I really believe. This is why, when I have gone around, I have said: "Please write well, please articulate, please sort out what you feel." Especially since my realm is writing. That's my craft; it's something I can convey and I can teach and I can communicate. I emphasize that because I would like women really to believe that we do need that, that we do need this articulateness.

Q. That's why the woman artist right now is the most important?

A. N. She has to speak, she has to speak for other women. (72-E)

V
Proceed from the Dream

What a mystery it is that we still continue to dream! We get more and more scientific, more and more rational, more and more abstract, but we still continue to dream in symbolic language! So I always say: "Well then, we might just as well learn it, because it's not about to disappear." No matter how modern our concepts grow—even my desire to use some of the scientific terms as metaphors, as I did when I used the theory of the integrated circuits. ... Even so, if you have a *dream* you go right on using symbolic language, the language from *another period*.... Why do you think we were given that dreaming, nocturnal life? It's a strange thing, when you stop to think about it. What is it meant to do? Is it meant to be a warning of another life that is in us and that we have to get to know? (72-D)

This is what psychology has been trying to tell us, and I think we're now aware of that. That's why we have so many studies on dreams, more than ever before. We used to think of dreams as things that belonged to the Persian era or the Japanese Court. But very recently we've had many studies of dreams come out because now we are fully aware that dreams are the revelation of a life that goes on, that is part of us, and that the quicker we can make the synthesis the sooner we can walk into life with a total kind of strength, achieve totality. (72-M)

The primitives understood this. The primitives understood their dreams; they understood their prophetic function. They didn't need to have interpretations. And they had other modes of perception than we do. They believed in the spirit, they believed in symbolism. There wasn't any interference in receptivity. But we have lost that. So we have to relearn how to interpret our dreams, how to interpret the life of the spirit, and how to find our way to the inner life, the interior journey, which we have lost and are deprived of by our emphasis upon rationalism, upon logic. We were told that dreams were the irrational part of ourselves and had to be repressed and suppressed. (72-I)

There are some marvelous books by Laurens Van der Post, a man who was the son of a Dutch family who went to live in Africa. He was raised with the Africans, and he considers himself a "white African." He is a Jungian psychologist besides and also a poet. And he keeps talking about the African soul as a part of us that we repudiated, and that whenever we repudiate the minority, or when we repudiate any quality whatsoever in another person, it's a part of ourselves that we do not want to allow to live. So we are the losers, we are the ones who are sacrificing what he calls our night-soul, which is symbolic of Africa because of their belief in myth. He goes very deeply into the significance of African life and the beauty of their particular belief, its nobility. (72-J)

And there is a beautiful part in one of his books where he says the Africans never suffered from loneliness as we have; they never suffered from the feeling of the meaninglessness of their life, as we occasionally have. For they have the fraternity of communal life, the perfect understanding between them, sharing with one's neighbor, the nobility of sharing. They have codes of honor that we have really forgotten. And this annihilated all sense of loneliness. Then, as far as the meaning of their existence, they always had a sense of significance because they felt that there was a power, a force taking care of them. So they have no fear, they have no anxieties, and they never have a sense of meaninglessness. . . .

Van der Post carried it beyond politics and says what we have really tried to do is to kill our night-soul, our deeper self. We tried to kill our primitive spirit; we tried to forget our origin; we tried to forget where we were born. And so he brings politics and psychology together in this way: "The African belongs to the night. He is a child of darkness, he has a certain wisdom, he knows the secret of the dark. He goes to the night as if to a friend and to the darkness as if it were his home. As if the Black Pearl of the night were the dome of his hut. How the ghosts of the European mind are warmed with the memories of the African's response to the night. . . . It is an irony so characteristic of our basic unreality to blame the problem on him, to shoulder him with our fears and our sins and to call it a black, a native, an African problem. It is a striking and effective and plausible irony, but it is not true. The problem is ours. . . . We have trampled on our own dark natures, and we have added to our unrealities and made ourselves less than human. So that that dark side of ourselves, our shadowy twin, has to murder or be murdered. If we could but make friends with our inner selves, come to terms with our own darkness, then there would be no trouble from without." (72-N)

Now there is no going back in a literal or historical sense. D. H. Lawrence said that very very clearly. Lawrence was seeking all his life what he called a pure, pagan, primitive life. He was seeking that in Italy, in Spain, in Mexico; he went to New Mexico to seek it. He really wanted to become a part again of the primitive community, a pre-civilized community without any of the features of the modern world. But of course he found that you can't. This is a paradise that's lost to us. You can't go back, and he realized that in Mexico. The wish was there, the desire to penetrate the Indian life, to become as they were, one with nature. I think we all have wishes of that kind, but I don't think they are fulfillable. Still we can achieve the same oneness, in Western terms. And *this* is why I lay so much stress on psychology. Because I think when we live in harmony with our psychic selves we do find wholeness. We find the old religious sense, we find the communal—we find everything that we want *in the unconscious.* (72-G)

We don't owe it to the poet, because we've never listened to the poet. We *could* have gotten it from the poet. But we never listened to him, we never listened to the artist. An artist like Varda could have taught us how to live. At fifteen if I had met Varda I would have learned to live from him, Varda's philosophy. But we didn't do that. So then the next best thing was to have a philosophy which was psychology, which would help us then to live in a very difficult culture. We always keep forgetting too that we live in a very deadening culture, a very corrupt one. (72-I)

So another reason we couldn't go back was that this culture said any introspection—which is the way to go, your inner journey—is taboo. That's why we had to go through the experiment with drugs. We had to go through artificial means. Or we had to use the pseudo-scientific terminology of psychology. Because we were trained to think in terms of science, since science says you can explore the unconscious very safely, we believed Freud more readily than we believed the poet or mystic. So our culture did not prepare us, did not give the poet his status. The one with the vision is the artist: the man who has a vision into his subconscious and who is trying to convey that to us. But we don't even like the word "artist." We say it's elitism! Yet the artist is simply the man who has concentrated on his inner world and tried to project it, through painting or music or whatever it was, in order to give it to you. Our culture repudiated this inner world and disparaged the artist and devalued him. So this generation had to find its way back again to the inner journey. If you're fortunate enough to approach it as an artist you have no difficulties, no obstacles. But many of us have had obstacles and the obstacles can be overcome, because psychology at its best (not in its negative aspect) does teach us to take the journey into dreams.

What makes me sad in a way is that when people discuss psychology they only discuss it in terms of its beginning, which is Freudian. They never seem to have watched its continuing development. The last psychologist I have read is R. D. Laing, who is really a poet of psychology. He is a remarkable writer who has extended the boundaries, has really broken all the narrow confines of psychology. So I'm sorry to see that when people discuss it, they're still thinking in terms of its *origin*, which is way back, rather than in terms of its development. I have read many modern psychologists who are no longer dogmatic, who don't even say they are Freudians or Rankians or Jungians but who are really using their own insights. So that when we think of it we should think of it in terms of its potentials and possibilities and how it's expanding. Women, for example, are bringing new questions and new elements into psychology; they want to write their own and want to explore and want to show us how little we really know about them. So we have to think of things in terms of continuous change, as evolutions. I think we have to think of things as evolving, not static. Psychology is not Freud. (72-G)

Someone once said that in our entire evolution, every time someone, either the artist or the scientist, disturbed the already existing knowledge, or went into a new realm, he was always regarded as an enemy. Nobody wants to follow into an uncharted land. (72-Y)

And yet the interesting paradox is that we ought to be much more fearful of what we don't know. We should really be fearful of an unconscious that inhabits us, that guides us, that influences our life and of which we don't know the face and don't know the message. Actually I have much less fear since I confronted fears. What's frightening to me is people whose unconscious leads them, destroys them, and yet they will never stop and look at it. That's the minotaur in the labyrinth, which many people never come face to face with. There was a very remarkable percussion composer, Edgar Varèse, who always mocked psychology, mocked psychoanalysis, mocked psychiatry. He was satirical about it, wouldn't have any of it. And yet his whole life pattern was self-destructive. He was an innovator and a tremendous musician. But he blocked himself. His biography is out now, and you can see the pattern. You can see this demon that was driving him, the origin of it. He seemed to be a very fearless, strong, tremendous tempered man with great force; he even looked like a Corsican bandit. But he had no power over the forces that were pushing him. That is what frightens me. I find that more frightening than confronting one's demons. (72-D)

So this is what I mean when I say I made psychology a guide beyond its ordinary meaning; I made a philosophy of it. I learned from psychology respect for the dream, familiarity with the use of it, to know what was happening to me in my life. Secondly, what I learned from psychology was a way of overcoming obsessions. When a trauma crystallizes in you and forms a certain pattern you can become a slave of this pattern through your whole life. I would have been a slave of the father image all of my life. But what I learned from psychology was that these traumas could be unravelled, and you could proceed to the next cycle. I don't mean that you can be happy forever after and free of the father image, but that you can continue to live other cycles, which is life. You enter other cycles and encounter other patterns and other problems.

Some writers, for example, have been obsessed with only one theme. When I met Richard Wright, in the Village in New York, he said to himself and to us: "I must leave America if I'm going to become a writer who is not obsessed with only one theme. I must go away so that I can expand and not be always concerned with the way I was treated today by somebody in the street." He thought that this was a restricting experience which was obsessing him and thus preventing him from becoming a great writer. So he left America and settled in France.

If I had gone on all my life relating only to my father or trying to find substitutes for the father, as I did with Dr. Rank and the analysts in my twenties, I would have been a very limited writer. I had to free myself of that trauma and the other one, which was the uprooting, the break-up of the family, which has happened to a lot of us. So I had to overcome these one by one. And there psychology helped me as a philosophy. The philosophy of mobility, of having to get rid of traumas which would mold us into something from which we cannot escape. (72-G)

The whole art of psychology or the science of psychology, if you want to call it that, is based upon a reversal of the objectivity process. Not that we cannot *become* objective, but that we can only become objective *after* we have confronted our non-objective attitudes, our non-rational attitudes. To reach an honest objectivity means that we have to know what points of our nature are given to particular prejudice, what part of us is defensive, what part of us distorts what we hear. And it requires a tremendous self-honesty to begin to clear away these distortions and to clarify our vision. So that we can reach objectivity only after we have found what areas of our psyche are not objective. Also the basic recognition of psychology is that deep down, the greatest part of our life is unknown to the conscious mind, and that the more we bring it into consciousness then the more honest and the more objective we can become. We don't see others clearly, and what obscures our vision are the prejudices that the so-called objective person refuses to recognize. An objective person would say that he is not responsible for war, but a person who knows psychology knows that each one of us is responsible because each one of us has always an area of hostility, which is then projected into vaster collective hostilities.

So it takes a terrific honesty to recognize, first of all, that we are not born objective. There are objectivities of wisdom, a higher state which we can achieve but only after we know the composition of the camera and the recorder that we are—what our blind spots are and in what areas we are vulnerable. For instance in neurosis, the first thing that hurt me so much when I realized my neurotic trends was that they prevented me from having total confidence in other human beings. My father's desertion had left a damaged spot and if anybody invaded that damaged area—the critic or anybody representing the father or any authority—they would always get from me an irrational response. I had to clear that area and then become an objective thinker toward the father, the critic, or other figures of authority. But you can't achieve that by rationalization. (73-J)

But we were talking last night about trying to go beyond psychology, which is what Rank wanted when he emphasized that we all have so much creative will and that the concept of neurosis makes us dwell too much on the negative parts or the obstacle to our growth. We have to get beyond psychology in that sense and realize that we all have the potential creative will and that not all of it is neurosis. (73-K)

In the early days of psychoanalysis, whenever a patient showed willfulness, Freud would say that this was resistance. But Rank went further and said that this was really a hopeful evidence of the creative will, and that we have to let that come through. Since Freud there has been a great deal of development and a great deal of expansion in the whole area of psychology, and what Rank had a special interest in was the strength of the creative will, which is what animates all these different people whom I have been talking about. He had a great influence on my life. When I met him, in my thirties, he felt that creativity was a life-saving force in me, and he wanted to work on that rather than trying to solve all the human problems that I was surrounded with. (73-J)

So I want to stress the importance of the *wish.* The real magical element is the *wish,* and if we don't know the wish then we stumble about and we accept entrapment because we don't really know what we are going towards. Then we have no strength, we have no inspirational visions. I took dreams as the guide. Sometimes the dream was prophetic, it was a warning, it may have been a symptom of anxiety. But very often it was a *dynamic* dream, the real creative dream that propels you forward and illuminates the wish. And having once a vision of the wish, then we can move towards it.

The example of the wish which propelled me is the one which began when I was visiting some friends in Maupassant's house in Brittany, and saw a boat which had been thrown into the yard by a storm and left there. I said I wanted to sleep in it, but my friends said: "No you can't because we use it for a tool house." But the wish was born, there at that moment! And then that night I dreamt that I did get into the boat and travelled for twenty years, that I made this immense, formidable, incredible journey. Having had the wish and the dream, I returned to Paris, and there I—who never read newspapers—read an advertisement saying: "Houseboat For Rent"! Everything was guiding me. So because I had the dream, because I had the wish, I went to see the houseboat. It belonged to Michel Simon, the actor, and he wanted to rent it because he couldn't live in it himself. It was in the middle of Paris, symbolically between the left and the right banks. So the wish guided me, the dream guided me, and I fulfilled something which may have seemed, if I had spoken about it, an impossible wish. And the wish, which actually cost me only ten dollars a month, became an inspiration not only for the life I led for two years there before the war, but I also wrote a short story about the houseboat.

Living on the houseboat, of course, gave me a great many more dreams about voyages because I felt the river moving all the time under me, and it had an effect on the flowing rhythm of my life. Because I felt that I was in a moving, changing, fluid form of life, that the boat could leave at any time, and I had dreams about that. We moved only from bridge to bridge, but nevertheless the imagination was nourished. And so I wrote a novel, and then the novel created Varda's living on his boat, and it also created a young man who went to Paris to live on a boat and sell books. The books got mildewed, so he moved next to the river and his place became a very famous bookshop that everyone loves to go to. So one dream fosters and nourishes the other.

When I was sixteen, and I hadn't been trained to earn a living, the only thing I found that I could do was to join a models' club and be a model for artists. Now I was by far the least beautiful of the models in the club. I can say that quite frankly, and yet I was getting all the work. We used to sit around and wonder why, and I myself found the reason. The painters told me that when I came they felt like working, because instead of being bored and looking bored and sitting and watching my wristwatch and counting how long I had to sit in that chair, I was terribly interested that the painting should get done, that the painting should be very beautiful. I was participating in the painting. I didn't know it, but I was really helping the painter. And furthermore I learned all that I know about color from posing because I watched the mixing of the paints. I watched how it was done, and I acquired a permanent and very deep interest in colors. So what is magic is nothing more than psychic participation and carrying out the dream—this involvement in others' dreams or in others' works, this capacity to enter another world and participate in it. All the worlds are open to us provided we are willing to enter with some magic quality which is helping the work to be done.

Very often you have thought too that I have made friends with famous people. But I made friends with people long before they were famous, and not all of them became famous! What I did have was a great love for and a great obsession with the potential in young writers, in young poets, in a nonformed writer, in what I sometimes call a not-yet-born writer. I was always looking for some potential because another's creativity nourishes your own. It is something that moves back and forth. What you put into it, you receive back from others. So I was just as intent upon discovering or receiving as upon transmitting whatever I had learned, receiving but also being very much of a transmitter myself. Can you see what I mean, the interaction of all these psychic energies?

Even Freud, old man Freud the scientist, was about to publish a paper on soul transference. But he panicked because he felt that the scientists would then no longer take him seriously. So he hesitated and a disciple of his went ahead and did the study, which angered Freud very much. But he would have published a long study on the power of thought transference, and what I am talking about is really, in modern terms, this soul transference. If you transfer the wish for the painter to paint, he will paint. And if you believe, as we did, in each others' writing—I believed in Miller's, Miller believed in mine, I believed in Durrell's and he believed in mine—that had the most amazing effect on us, when we had nobody else interested in what we were doing.

So there is the whole mystery of growth, of expansion, of deliverance from the traps which life sets us, because life loves the drama of entrapping us and seeing whether we can get out. It's a game, a game of psychic courage, a beautiful psychic game, a game of magic. Every difficult situation into which you are sometimes thrown has some kind of opening somewhere, even if it is only by way of the dream—the way I transformed childhood, transformed adolescence, and then later on transformed friendships. I wrote about all of them, my friends and myself, as much in terms of our potential as our actual selves. I tried to imagine the future, just as Ira Progoff, in teaching the Intensive Journal, makes you imagine your future, which is really to create your future, to put your mind forward into what you might wish to go toward, even though the wish seems impossible. (73-K)

Now the romantics, of course, were absolutists. If they couldn't find what they wanted they would die of tuberculosis. I once read the whole history of the romantics. All of them. And all of them were really in a way saying: "I can't have what I want so I will die." A neurotic does the same thing, except he doesn't take such obvious ways out. So the Chinese said that the beginning of wisdom was the beginning of realization of the *denial* of the ideal. I was very impressed with that because in our twenties we do that, we set up ideals.

On the other hand, I think we do need to carry the blueprint, the image of something we want. I don't mean the impossible, the absolute thing, the romantic thing, the neurotic thing, the narcissistic thing like trying to find the twin who says "yes" to everything. I mean once you are ready to accept the reality of human beings, then I think you do need to have a blueprint. I say the dream serves to guide us towards what we want. We do have to have a wish—I don't mean that kind of impossible hope—but we do have to have some image of what we want to go towards, because that guides us.

For instance, I would read biographies as a girl, and I would say: "Now that's life, that's the life I want," or "That's the country I want to see." And then I would reach for it, and when the thing was open to me, I would seize it. Because I had read so much about Japan, when I was invited there for the publication of my novel, I went. I think that's not the same as that impossible hope that we dash our heads against. It is really the creation of a life within artistic controls, with its form and its pattern. I give the example of dreaming about the houseboat, then seeing it, then getting it, then living in it, and then writing about it. The dream was the guiding light.

So we have to have some image. Like Shirley Clark, who was a film-maker. She was extremely poor, in New York. She said she had always dreamt of going to India to photograph children. Of course at that time, in the Village, penniless as she was, it seemed an absolute impossibility. But she had this obssesion, so when UNESCO gave her a job to photograph children in France she said "yes," because that was a little nearer to India. She did the children in France, and then they gave her the job to go to India. She had a desperate wish, and it was really fulfilled. Many of mine were too. You know when I read biographies I found certain models, forms of life, that I wanted to achieve, and they made me go towards it. So that if we don't have an image, or if we aren't following a dream, then we also don't know what we are walking towards, and we don't help to make it happen. (72-D)

You heard such wonderful things this morning about the dream used to orient ourselves in our psychological worlds. But I feel now like talking to you about another aspect of the dream and how it can be used specifically for purposes of creativity. Aside from orienting ourselves in our spiritual world, which is a very valuable aspect of the dream, there is another one which we benefit from, once we have overcome the resistance to it and really pay attention to dreams. Now I paid attention to dreams both ways: to help myself in life but also to create. And then I went beyond that.

I kept a record of my dreams for a year, for a whole year, and then wrote a book called *House of Incest*, based on the idea that the first love was always within the family and was always, in an emotional sense, incestuous. But what I found was that if you just keep your dreams, and you're not relating them to your life or to an orientation, then you fall in love with them for themselves. You let yourself be seduced by the images, and you discover another language. Not the cerebral language, not the rationalistic language, but a language of images. So I kept these dreams, and since I was not relating them to my life, they seemed unrelated as the images are in a poem or a prose poem. I had learned very early from therapy not to be too concerned about the visible pattern, not to look immediately for the connection, but to allow these images to come floating up, to enjoy them, to look at them as you would look at a painting, to permit them to exist. Usually, unless we find some utilitarian use for dreams, unless they are guiding us through a difficult moment of our life, we tend really not to listen to them or to put them away.

So I just kept them, and it seemed that I had a very chaotic set of dreams. But then very slowly I began to relate them only in terms of feelings, and all of them clustered around the feelings of my life at the time. So then therapy helped me to find out what the pattern was that I felt I was caught in, which was the family and the early love. That was the explanation of the pattern. But it also helped me to find the pattern in the sense of art, in the sense of writing prose poems. I began to describe the dreams themselves, and then to dream about the dream, to dream around it. A beautiful image would come, and it's different from looking for a meaning to apply to your life. It's really as if you're writing the first line of a poem, and then you look for the second line and the pattern emerges only at the end.

So if you believe that the subconscious has wonderful patterns, if you allow it to form its designs, if you just trust to that design, in the end all these clusters form a pattern, sometimes a very unexpected one. I began to trust that to the extent that I would be working on a novel and would be interrupted by an image that would come to my mind. It would seem to be absolutely irrelevant to the story, and I couldn't understand why it had come. But I would obey it.

It happened when I was writing *Ladders to Fire,* for example, and it made a great impression on me at that time because I was very annoyed. I felt I should really go on with this novel and that it wasn't right for me to be remembering something irrelevant. But the image was very very vivid: it was associated with a concert that I had attended in Paris. I had looked away to the garden, and I had seen a three-way mirror in the garden, which is rather unusual. I had meditated on that while I was listening to the music. At the time the image didn't particularly affect me very much, but it must have made a very strong impression for me to retain it for ten years. And why did it come up at that particular moment? But I allowed it to come to my mind, this memory, and I wrote it down. I wrote about the music; I wrote about the three-way mirror, which was an unusual thing to find in the garden, and then of course I immediately became aware that the association was garden-nature, mirrors-artifice; neurosis, the reflection of reality rather than reality that you could touch. And I went on and on, and before I knew it had finished the novel. I was writing, I was giving in the metaphor, in that image, the key to the novel, which is the struggle of these women against their nature, the unreality of their lives, the reflection of nature in the mirror rather than nature itself. So it's the trusting to the image which I think makes the poet write the first line of his poem and then continue. And every novel I wrote from then on always began with a dream, and sometimes I didn't know where it was going to lead me.

Sometimes the dream links up with imagery from something that you have read or heard about. For example, I heard about the pharoahs having had solar barques to travel in after death. They had two boats always buried with them: one to travel during the day towards the sun and one to travel at night towards the moon. And of course we know very well that that's symbolic of the conscious mind and the unconscious mind. So such an image, though it's taken from history, if it stays with me, if it really penetrates me in some way, then I know that it links up with some myth that I am trying to make clear. So that image was not received from a dream; it was taken from the outside, from something I had read. Yet because it had vibrations and because it affected me and because it stayed with me, I knew that it had some specific meaning. So I began the novel of a woman's journey through Mexico, and then found that it was exactly the right image I wanted to hold the novel together. For when you write an impressionistic, free association novel, the pattern is very difficult to find, because you don't start by telling the story. Rather you're trying to find what is inside of the character and to follow the exploration of it. What led me was the feeling that Lillian's journey was dual. It was a day journey into the great beauty of Mexico, but it was also the nocturnal journey into the understanding of herself. And then I saw that the solar barque was the perfect image to consolidate, to fuse the meaning of the novel.

So the dream can be the beginning of a poem, it can be the beginning of a novel, it can be the beginning of a plot, of a search. I have one novel that begins with a recurrent dream which I had myself and which I explored in the novel until I uncovered what it meant. The recurrent dream was of pushing a boat through a waterless city, and all through the dream I was making a tremendous effort to push this boat and pull it across the city. It wouldn't float in the city. I had the dream for many years, and I never quite knew what it meant except that I wasn't living according to the dictates of the unconscious. I wasn't free, I hadn't found my water level, I hadn't found my real journey. Now it happened that I found it in Mexico, and so I described my first contact with the sea and the sense of harmony with the culture, and then suddenly I was afloat. That image became the key image of the novel too. And as I had the dream and wrote the novel, I never had the dream again. It had served its purpose for me, but it had also brought together the kind of novel which is very difficult to write, which is like a poem. It's a novel that doesn't have a plot; you don't plan ahead what is going to happen because what is going to happen is the inner voyage and you can't predict where it's going to take you. It's based upon an infinite trust in the meaning of the dream.

It was through this emphasis on dream imagery that I also discovered that there is another kind of language, the inspirational, which is the one that penetrates our unconscious directly and doesn't need to be analyzed or interpreted in a cerebral way. It penetrates us in the way music does, through the senses. This was the language I was talking about and why, for awhile, when I emphasized language, there were misunderstandings. The students have said: "We have too many words, we have too much language, we have too much talk." But I would say: "No, language is a precious, wonderful thing; it depends how we use it." If it's imagistic, if it's inspirational, if it comes straight from the unconscious, then it's something that absolutely sets others free and sets us all afloat. But it has to be the language of dream imagery, because that's pure, that really comes from the unconscious, that's the way the unconscious expresses itself.

One day a student asked me why we dreamt in symbols, why we didn't dream very directly, why as writers we don't say exactly what we mean. I said: "Because dreams are a language we have to learn. It's still an indirect language because we can't bear the naked truth, so it comes in the form of a symbol or a metaphor." When you want to write a novel which concerns that level, if you want to write a novel about what takes place in a person's mind, then you do have to have recourse to the image, to rhythm, to things that affect the body and which are received through the senses. So when a girl this morning spoke of composing music with themes from Jung, I thought that was a fascinating idea. . . .

Now I think the artist always had that contact with the symbolic level and always knew that this was the source of what he painted, of music and of all the arts. But for awhile that source was shut off in our own culture. Our culture put a taboo on dreaming, said that it was a waste of time, it was an escape, didn't have much meaning. One time, I have heard, when the Orientals were discussing schedules with the American Army, they said: "Do you mean to say that you don't have in your schedule a time for dreaming!" But our culture had placed a great taboo on that, a taboo on introspection, on seeking to find the meaning of it all, which is why we lost a terrible lot of writers. And that's also why, I think, we have the much more dangerous explosion of drugs. That was the mechanical way to unseal the tremendous taboo that had been put on dreaming, imagery, and sensation. That was a very tragic way of trying to reach the inner world. And the difference between taking drugs and what I am talking about is that with dreaming and meditation your creative will is involved; there is active participation; you're creating something with the image, while the chemical way makes you passive. I call it being a tourist in the world of images. It is a passive way of receiving the dream, not linking it to life or linking it to art work or to a poem. There is no living connection.

It is just like lying down and taking opium and having fantasies but with no connection between the fantasies and the fulfillment of them, which is the next step, the creation of your life. (72-I)

So before I end, I want to read you one part of another book which has meant a great deal to me, a book called *Dream Power* by Ann Farraday. She sees the dream not only as a symptom of some troubled mind or some neurotic state or some anxiety state but as a dynamic message of what is happening in the future, of what can happen. She uses the dream as a dynamic force, just as in the diary I also used the dream to express anxiety but later on used it as an indication of the kind of life I wanted, the dream used as a kind of blueprint. So as Ann Faraday says: "There is a widespread belief among the young people that during the past decade mankind has entered a new epoch. They characterize it by using the astrological notion of the Age of Aquarius, whose main feature is traditionally supposed to be the search for spiritual wholeness. . . . I have no views on astrology," she says, "but I hope they are right about the new age. Because unless people do begin to learn more about the inner springs of their behavior and to seek more authentic selfhood, it seems unlikely that the human race has much hope for any tolerable future at all." (73-F)

* * *

Q. You use the word psychic quite a bit, and since it's a well-used word I wonder what specifically does it mean for you?

A. N. By psychic I mean the inner significance. I have always used the word psyche to refer to the unconscious, to our spiritual life, to our emotional life. In Greek, psyche was the soul, the butterfly which sheds its cocoon and flies away. So to me, psyche is a term which synthesizes this idea of the soul and the unconscious. The psyche is the soul, which, as Jung and other psychologists have pointed out, exists collectively and individually, and is revealed in dreams. That is why we have to learn symbolism—to understand what happens within us. The psyche is a dual sort of current in our lives; it's from there that the richness comes, the whole tie with the universal world, and the whole potential for creation. (72-G)

Q. Several times you mentioned meditation and I wonder if that takes any special kind of form for you.

A. N. No, it's not what *you* call meditation. It's what I used to call, in the diary, my opium period. That is, when the experience is over, and the day is over, then I would mull over or relive or meditate on what had happened, because I wanted to understand it. It's a different kind of meditation. It's not saying: "Now I am meditating." It's meditation that takes place in the diary, if I write it at night; *after* an event, not *during*. Then there is that meditation over events which I used to feel I needed when I didn't want more experience than I could absorb. (72-D)

Q. I am interested in what you think about the value of Eastern thought and discipline for Western culture.

A. N. I haven't talked about that because I don't believe in it. I don't believe that we can adopt a religion or discipline or philosophy that is foreign to our own culture. I think we have to work out our own salvation, find our spiritual world in Western terms. I have spoken to many dear friends who have been in the East, who have been in meditation in Japan, who have been in Buddhist monasteries. What happens is that they find they cannot hold on to it. Because it has not been created by *you,* in terms of where you're going to live. If one were staying in Japan and remained the rest of one's life in a Buddhist monastery, I could see contemplating moving toward that way of life. But that's not what we're doing. We're trying to transplant it. A friend was saying to me that while he was there, he had the utmost serenity. I felt that too in Japan. You stay there, and you know everything is absolutley serene and beautiful. But you can't carry this over and really live it here.

Q. Could you then elaborate on your idea of what Western civilization has to offer in the way of spirituality—what do we have to counter this Eastern thought?

A. N. Well, it is difficult to answer that because it is so different for each person. I think you can achieve what we call your serenity, or your religious self, or your spiritual self, or mystical self or anything that you want to call it—the life of the spirit—with the means given to us. And it would be without dogma. Because I think that what we have freed ourselves from now is the dogma of religion. We are not so dogmatic anymore, we are not even dogmatic about psychology. We don't have these demarcations. So I think we are in the process of achieving a wholeness, an unlocking of the spirit, a freeing of the psyche, the whole thing, in our own terms, under the conditions that we live with here. We're not losing the marvelous help which we have had from the other side, the way the Japanese achieve serenity, their ascetic philosophy. All that is helping us to achieve our own. But you can't transplant their way, because we would have to change our whole culture, the whole Western culture.

Q. But isn't it just like your having come from one culture and become part of another?

A. N. That's a different thing. I was uprooted, and I put down my roots here. I had to make a new life also, and *adapt* to a new culture. But that's not quite the same as *adopting* a completely different culture.

Q. But there are teachers from Japan who live here. Don't you think there's the possibility of a cross-cultural thing happening?

A. N. Yes, without adopting it. It's duration quality is different from the dogmatic quality. I make a distinction here. Certainly we can be inspired by a culture that has always been more spiritual than ours. But it's still not something we can adopt. You'll find that it's not permanent, because it is something you have to earn. In the East they gained that organically and by centuries of discipline. It is a racial thing, and the very deep memory of thousands of years lies behind it. Taking an interest in it is one thing. I'm terribly interested in the Orient. But we're speaking now of adoption.

Q. Well, once you take an interest in it, you can't follow it through without the idea of adopting it.

A. N. But then you should move to the East. Because as a Westerner you cannot live the life of serenity and asceticism of the Japanese, and they cannot move into our culture. (72-I)

Q. I am curious if you have ever come in contact with the Tarot or used its symbolism.

A. N. No. I have a very stubborn streak about adopting other religions, occults, rituals. I always wanted to make my own. I wanted to have my own mythology. Somebody questioned me the other day about my use of the minotaur. I made up my own story about the labyrinth. I suppose that the creative person really wants to make his universe, in keeping with his own faith. For instance I never read astrology or the art of Zen, though I have friends who tried to teach me. Somehow it had to be created by me, just as children want to make their own poems. (72-G)

Q. Are you interested in the Carlos Casteneda method of exploring the unconscious, of inducing psychic states?

A. N. No, it's not my method to use drugs. That's not my way of exploring. In the diary I'm working on now I describe my one and only experiment with L.S.D. And the interesting thing, in this case, was that I went into it as an experiment. I was invited because I was a writer, and there was a scientist, there was a composer, and different kinds of people. But what I found after examination of this long dream, which I had and which lasted about eight hours, was that all the imagery that I had under L.S.D. was in my work already. Which proves that if you are working from subconscious images, from dreams, from a complete freedom of access to the unconscious, then you don't need drugs. And of course I had an argument with Huxley because he said: "You're lucky; you can just walk in and out of your unconscious, but some of us are not so lucky and we need L.S.D." But you see it's interesting as an experiment, to find that all the richness of imagery was similar. I could track it down. So my conclusion was that we had closed the door on the artist, at least America certainly did. We had closed the door on a way of perception which the artist could have provided.

Q. Was your experience with L.S.D. frightening?

A. N. Frightening? No, I didn't have a "bad trip," as they call it. I had only one bad moment of thinking I wasn't breathing very well, which could have been physical. It could have been a physical symptom.

Q. How much did you take?

A. N. I don't know. But I don't really believe in it, and I think that the imagery which we get through it makes us more and more passive. As I said in *The Novel of the Future*, I don't want to be a tourist in the world of images. I want to create something with them. If I see an image of a houseboat, I want to live in a houseboat, and get a houseboat. Do it! But the drug undermines completely your whole creative activity; it makes you passive. So that's why I don't believe in it. You do see imagery, but it's like watching a film; it doesn't change your life, it doesn't make you create a life. You lose your ability to create. (73-H)

Q. I have discovered that guys take drugs a lot more, both marijuana and drinking, than the women I know do. And one of my friends explained it to me in terms of yin and yang: women are yin and men are yang, and drugs are yin. So when a woman takes drugs it tends sometimes to intensify something that she already uses to the point where it's unbearable and causes great fears.

A. N. I've never seen that distinction between man and woman. I think that if you carry an unformulated nightmare the drug will bring it out. Whatever is in the unconscious comes out. (72-G)

Q. What place would you assign to the dream in your works, and what significance to the constancy of flow and communication between the conscious and the unconscious?

A. N. Unfortunately, we tend to separate everything. We separate the body and soul. We separate the dream from our daily life. What I found in psychology was the interrelationship between them, and I wanted to keep those passageways open, to be able to move from one dimension to the other, not to divide them even, so that they were really one. The next step was carrying it into the novel, always starting the novel with a dream, having that dream be the theme of the novel to be developed, understood and fulfilled if possible at the end in order to be able to move on to the next experience.

Q. In the diaries you stress one of Jung's phrases, "proceed from the dream outward."

A. N. That was a very important phrase and at the core of where I wanted to situate my work. But at the time, it wasn't Jung I was interested in so much as Otto Rank. He was extremely involved with the artist, and directly responsible for my concern with what I call the creative will, the transformation of life, the transcending, the metamorphosis of everything. It is only recently that I have been able to enjoy Jung. First I had to solve the problem of the creative will, which was Rank's great theme.

Q. In your writings you express a profound belief in the human capacity to grow beyond neurosis. What is the source of your optimism?

A. N. I never thought about the source. I always felt that impulse in myself, the way plants have an impulse to grow. We all have that impulse but then it gets damaged occasionally. It's in children, isn't it? They use their strengths, their skills, and explore everything, all possibilities. I believe that we can take notice of the damage which most of us sustain somewhere along the line, and we can overcome the damage. We all have interferences, discouragements, and traumatic experiences. I have met young writers who have stopped at the first rejection notice. So it's a question of how much we are willing to struggle in order to overcome the impediments. (73-M)

Q. My problem is trying to remember my dreams and always waking up before they are finished.

A. N. We discovered at the period when we were really writing them down and wanted to have lots of them, that eating something very indigestible would make us sleep badly and remember all our dreams! So we used to eat lots of cheese at night and wine, and sleep very badly but then remember all our dreams. It's really true. If we don't sleep well, we seem to stay more on that upper level of dreaming than if we sleep very deeply. I think they have made studies of that. (72-D)

Q. My problem is that my dreams are so very matter-of-fact. I realize that these too have a meaning, but what I'm missing is the kind of far-out, bizarre type of dream image, and I'm wondering how you could develop that kind of thing.

A. N. That depends on what you nourish yourself on. It depends on what books you read, what films you see, what paintings you see. My dreams have been influenced, say, by my love of Lippold's *Sun*. Seeing things like that will nourish your dreams with poetic images, and if you want poetic dreams, you'll have them. But I can understand your problem. Sometimes I'm angry because what I write, the dreams that I invent, are better than the ones I have at night. But it's a starting point. For as you have said and as I have said, they all have a symbolic meaning. The simplest act has another meaning. There is no matter-of-fact act. (72-I)

Q. Have you found that your deam life has gone in stages?

A. N. Yes, active and inactive sometimes. There are passive periods. When too much is coming in from the outside, the inner life becomes quieter. And then when I'm working, the writing is a waking dream. I consider most of the writing that I do, poetic prose, a sort of waking dream which you direct, which you expand. But as I said, there were periods when the dreams were very active and influenced me a great deal, there was a great deal of interaction, and other periods when there would be less. Periods of action would usually put an end to the reverie part, but when I go back to my work, then the reverie takes over. I think writing is a lot a waking dream, that kind of writing I do which is free association. (72-D)

Q. Did you keep a dream notebook at the time when you were living at Louveciennes?

A. N. Yes, I used to write a lot of dreams and recorded talks with friends about difficulties and problems. But the dreams, I found, were not interesting unless they were related to something. I found dreams in themselves are not interesting. I learned that from reading Michel Leiris. He just publishes his dreams. I find them very tiresome to read. I don't know why. I edited out a lot of dreams that I hadn't deciphered, that I didn't think were interesting, for just that reason. (72-Y)

Q. Can you say something about being afraid to pursue a wish, afraid that you won't be able to carry it through?

A. N. This fear we all have. The fear that we will not attain our wish, or that we don't have the capacity to attain it. The wishes I gave you were not too difficult; having a houseboat, for example,

138   *A Woman Speaks*

is not too difficult. But other wishes, such as becoming a writer who could transmit feelings to others and realizing it couldn't be done by writing with a rational mind, it couldn't be done by planning a novel ahead of time, that it was not a matter of logic but a matter of digging into the unconscious life where all the richness lies—now that was difficult. That was a wish that was difficult. I said I would like to write the way music affects you. That was a difficult wish, and it took me a lifetime to reach it. Now, as you say, one does have fears. You have fears, you have doubts. I certainly had doubts during the twenty years when America decided to be totally silent about my work. That gave me doubts, and I was dependent on friends to sustain me in my work when there wasn't any sign of a response. So there the wish had to be stronger. But it isn't so much a matter of courage, and it isn't a matter of becoming a hero. It really is not a heroic thing. I say it's a matter of stubbornness. I was very stubborn. (73-K)

Q. Your writing seems very dream-like to me at times. Is that your vision of reality?

A. N. No, it is that part of our life *is* dreams, and I have welded those two so that they are unified. There is the night dreaming and then there is the daylight reverie, and writing itself is a form of what I call waking dreams. So it seems dream-like, but it's not a dream. It's actually the way we live. We live partly consciously and partly unconsciously. Our fantasies and night dreams do influence us, and our life during the day influences our night dreams. So it is really a marriage of them. (73-B)

Q. You speak about the advantages of tuning into the unconscious and of the difficulties which we're experiencing because our cultural heritage ignored the unconscious. But I think that's somewhat misleading in that it ignores what seems to me the most basic reason why people in the past did not tune into their unconscious and that is that instinctual drives cause a great deal of anxiety both in normal and abnormal people and that the ego puts up defenses to prevent the destructive drives of the unconscious.

A. N. No, I understand that. But you see you are discounting the fact that we have learned much more about this than we knew in ancient times. We don't think any more in terms of possession and witchcraft. We know that we can explore it and by exploring it become aware of whatever evil or destructive element it has. We can—not dominate, because that's not what we want—but we can orient it. So you see it has ceased to be a dark and fearsome place, a Dante's Inferno. It really is a place now that the scientists and ourselves can explore with awareness and can understand. You're leaving out all the progress that we have made in our dealings with this unconscious force. And you are discounting its positive force. (68-A)

Q. How do you equate the diary you write with the process of psychoanalysis? Does one interfere with the other?

A. N. Interfere with the other? No, my faith in psychoanalysis was very solidly grounded and has remained permanent. I made it a philosophy. I made it the basic touchstone of my whole work. And in the *Diary* you can see that at certain great critical moments I turned to professional help because the confusion was very great, the difficulty of playing all the roles that man expected of me, and then the roles that I wanted to play for myself, what I wanted to be. In all these conflicts I was very much helped by psychoanalysis.

Q. But you turn toward psychoanalysis then only at critical points?

A. N. Yes. I don't think we turn to it unless we are at a critical point. For example, one cycle was the relationship to the father, and that had to be solved or else I would have spent my whole life looking for a substitute father. And then another cycle was the relationship to the mother, which got me into a different kind of trouble because I wanted to mother the whole world. And then other cycles came. The last cycle involved the question of whether to publish the diary or not. It was a very critical issue. I had to examine what we all feel, the fear of judgment, of being misunderstood, and of not being loved. So at every critical cycle analysis enabled me not to stay caught in the same cycle, which sometimes a writer does—he takes one theme and writes about one theme all his life.

Q. But analysis is such a long process, and I was wondering how you managed to get it all in.

A. N. It wasn't such a long process because I discarded the

Freudian analyst very quickly, and then Rank's analysis was what
he called dynamic analysis. He wanted the period very much short-
ened, in fact to two or three months. That was his belief; whether
he succeeded or not, I'm not sure. He did succeed in strengthening
the artist in me, in picking out the strongest part of my creative
will, and in emphasizing that to help me solve whatever secondary
problems came up.

Q. It's not so much the matter of time but the matter of money
that bothers me. If psychoanalysis is a necessity, it is also a luxury.

A. N. Yes, that's a very legitimate point. But two things are no
longer true in America. We have many clinics now, free clinics, for
psychoanalysis and psychiatry, and the luxury analyst is disappearing. The people who can't afford analysis now work in groups.
Three analysts I know operating in Los Angeles, in San Francisco,
and in New York have patients who pay, and they also have patients who can't pay. So I think that is one of the prejudices that
is no longer true. At least not in America.

Q. Don't you think frequently psychoanalysts do more harm than
good, and that many of them are more commercially-minded and
curious than public-spirited?

A. N. Yes, that's possible. But when you talk about analysis you
have to realize that just as there are bad doctors who make mistakes and kill people, so there are bad analysts. We recognize that.
But you can't always take a thing just from its negative side and
develop, as Kate Millett did, a prejudice against Freud, who after
all was only at the beginning of psychoanalysis. And also you must
realize that a great deal of psychoanalysis has seeped in *free* into
our culture; that we're living with a great deal more awareness
than we did twenty years ago; that we have received from it—not
directly, not as paying patients—but we have received the wisdom
of psychoanalysis through books, through literature, through writers, through many other channels, just as we received the influence
of surrealism in Paris even when we didn't join the movement. It
was in the air, we were breathing it, we were looking at it in every
gallery painting, we were absorbing it without even wanting to. So
you have absorbed a great deal of psychoanalysis without even

knowing it. And you just can't negate something which is part of our modern awareness. You can't just sweep it off and say it's of no use socially because it has been a luxury.

Q. But what about the general public? How available is all this to them?

A. N. We don't have to worry so much about the general public; those who want it really always find it. And the ones who don't want it are the people who criticized McGovern's running mate, you remember, for having a breakdown, and then finding out that he had consulted a psychiatrist, considered that a handicap. Those are the ignorant people who are holding back the use of psychoanalysis in education. I found lots of writing problems were not problems of writing, they were problems of emotional blocks and taboos. So we have benefitted even if we don't recognize it. (73-H)

Q. You give a great deal of credit to therapy, but how do you think today that therapy can help woman find herself and grow when it usually has forced woman to adapt to conditions.

A. N. That's a very old-fashioned concept of psychoanalysis. I have no doubt that there are psychoanalysts existing today who talk about adaptation to things as they are. But you have to read the modern ones; you have to read the women psychologists; you have to keep up with psychoanalysis and realize what it has become to understand it. It is still the only instrument we have to get rid of conditioning and dogmas and programming. We have no other way to do it.

Q. You can talk to other women!

A. N. No, because they don't have the objectivity and the wisdom that a professional has. You wouldn't go with a physical illness to a friend for help. Now, when we develop a neurosis due to traumas, complexes, lack of confidence, to all the things that beset us, when it becomes a neurosis, then you need professional help. You cannot help each other.

Q. What I think your writing did was to clarify and help other women realize that they weren't alone in what they were feeling. That was probably the therapeutic process that they hadn't gone through if they never talked with another woman.

A. N. That's true. That's true, but *why* didn't they talk to other women? I've always had deep and long-lasting friendships with other women. Why didn't all women have that? That was part of the neurosis or lack of trust which I was talking about.

Somehow, because I had a very devoted mother, I had confidence and trust in women. I didn't mistrust women. I've benefitted from the friendships. We did hold each other's hands, and we helped each other through crises. I don't deny that women can help each other. I didn't say that. But I say that when we are really confused and really in a tangle, it's like a physical illness. Then we really need a very wise and a very objective person to overcome the trauma. Talking with my other friends never made me overcome my shyness of speaking in public.

You see, I had to go deeper than that. I had to go very deep into childhood to find the origin of such fears. We still need professional help, and I *do* ask women not to be stopped by the old Freudian concepts. We long, long ago have gone beyond that, transcended that. There are innovations in psychology. There are women entering into the field who are writing remarkable things. I get almost a book a week from women psychologists who are helping women. There is no way of shedding the persona except the psychological way. (73-G)

Q. This has to do with the problem of women's finding their own psychology, a necessity that you stress in *Diary* IV. Can women seek their own psychology through psychoanalysis when ninety per cent of analysts are men and most are predictably committed to stereotyped views of woman's nature and her limited possibilities?

A. N. I have encountered the kind of analyst who limits the woman's world and doesn't take her art seriously. But I've also been treated by a very creative analyst, Dr. Otto Rank, who was terribly interested in the artist and would recognize creativity in a woman just as well as in a man. A superior kind of analyst is concerned with growth, and whether his patient is a man or a woman, he wouldn't limit or confine or constrict or do anything to inhibit any kind of growth: emotional or psychological. It's a question of finding this quality in an analyst. And the patient can feel that right away, I think, whether the doctor is the sort to encourage the fullest expansion. (72-X)

Q. Could you speak about the difference between your experience and the experience that Dr. Freud had in discovering the inner world of his patients? That is, I wonder what is the difference between your experience of developing insight and the psychoanalytic method.

A. N. I couldn't possibly compare them because one was a psychoanalytical technique and that was not the technique I had in the diary. I did practice psychoanalysis under the control of Dr. Rank for five months, but I was not a trained psychoanalyst. My way of approaching the portrait of persons was seeking to go into depth; I did want to know the unconscious self. I wanted to go deep; I didn't want to know people on a one-dimensional basis. But it's quite different from the psychoanalytical way that Freud handled people. In the first place the people that went to him were in trouble, and not all my friends were in trouble. (73-E)

Q. What's the difference between your discovery of your probing for your inner self and Jung's discovery of his probing for his inner self.

A. N. There is no difference except that I was able to keep a record longer and in more detail. Also it was a woman's story, that's one difference. Women have written diaries, but they very rarely began at such an early age and continued consistently until the fulfillment of this orientation. But there's no difference. As I told you, what I learned about the method of going in and finding out about yourself was from psychology. (73-F)

Q. When women write to you, in your responses I suppose you write your own feelings and answers to them. But do you ever encourage them either to see a psychoanalyst or to seek out womens' consciousness-raising?

A. N. It depends what the letter is about. There are some women who are already gifted, good writers who simply lack confidence, and then all they want is a judgment on their work or help or encouragement or comment. There are other women who are really in *deep* emotional trouble and who even ask me about therapy.

There are different requests. There are sometimes women who have written to me who feel that I made them transcend their depressions—that it would not last forever, that there would be a tomorrow. I've had people threatening suicide, and I've had to answer that and help them.

Q. I was trying really to make the point that women's consciousness-raising groups might serve the same purpose, provide the same help of a real personal nature to women, as a psychoanalyst would do, and minus the seventy-five bucks.

A. N. Well, that's ridiculous about the seventy-five bucks. Because there are many free clinics now, in the first place, and also there are many many analysts now who share their practice between those who pay and don't pay. So that's really not true anymore.

Q. Liberal, radical, *feminine* psychologists?

A. N. Yes, you can get that in clinics, and also there are many women psychologists. And then there is a change in psychology itself. We are not living in Freud's days by any means. That's why it's so ridiculous to spend all our energy trying to ignore Freud. Because we are not living in the Freudian era. We've gone way beyond that.

Q. We're not in Laing's era either. He doesn't have the power that a lot of other people do.

A. N. Yes, but all of us have read Laing. We have been influenced by Laing, we have heard him talk. So he's been an influence. You have to catch up with the present psychology. He's a very liberating force. He doesn't make a distinction between man and woman. And I know plenty of very good psychologists and psychoanalysts who are helping women. I think that attitude is part of this shifting of personal responsibility, of blaming the psychologist or the husband or the society for the position in which we find ourselves. Now the first psychologist I had, the first psychoanalyst I had, was a very limited combination of Freud and Marx—if you can imagine anything more dogmatic and more unsuited to me. Well, I left him! I mean I learned something, and then I found his limitation and left. (73-I)

Q. What do you think of the Intensive Journal Ira Progoff has been developing?

A. N. Very interesting. In fact he is the only man I have met this year who inspired me because he knows how to develop diary writing. For me, getting into it was such a natural thing that I can't quite explain how I happened to do it sometimes. But he is imparting the way to enter into it, and I find him very wonderful. I have been reading all his books.

And then of course I like his idea of imagining your future. The only thing I don't like—probably one gets rid of it later—is the dissociation between, say, your dreams or your past and your present. Because in my diary it all flowed together. It was like one big river dragging everything with it, both flashbacks and prophetic dreams. The way these are separated in the Intensive Journal would bother me at this point—the dreams, then what happened today, and how you imagine your future, or who you want to dialogue with. But I think he is very inspirational, a wonderful, inspirational man, and certainly beyond psychology. (73-K)

Q. Do you ever think that the artist who is torn with anxieties and confusion and whose energy is bottled up because of these, and then is finally released in a work of art, that that work of art itself is like a good session with an analyst?

A. N. No, we have had too many histories of tragic lives of artists, and the work of art was not necessarily the thing that saved the others. It may give us art, but it doesn't rescue the artist from his torment. We are talking now in terms of human life, and that was often sacrificed. Like Artaud. He went over the border. So that isn't really the answer. I think that was a romantic idea really, that suffering produced art, and that therapy wasn't good for the artist. There are sufferings that are good. But there is a suffering that is a waste and a corroding of the human being. (72-I)

Q. What specifically do you think are the qualities of a good therapist for people to go to?

A. N. I'll tell you. But first of all I think all of us could help each other if we decided to take what is good for us and leave the rest, not to become immediately negative and say: "I'll throw this away because it doesn't fit me or it doesn't suit me." I have somehow a gift for extracting out the knowledge that I received from men, the education I received from the psychologist, whatever I needed. I extracted what I could convert to my own use as a woman and as a writer. I never decided, for instance, to give up psychoanalysis because Allendy, the first analyst I ever met, was limited, was an old-fashioned Freudian in his time. It didn't bother me. I learned something from him, and then I passed on. I think all of us could do that—provided we know what our orientation is. It's like a bee choosing just what it needs. And then Rank showed also a certain error—because as he himself said at one point, we didn't know very much about women because women hadn't been articulate in psychology and most of the patients were men. He also made a statement, which turned out to be wrong, that all women who were analyzed and got rid of neurosis would go back into life and not create. Of course he was wrong. But it didn't bother me.

The amount of human error to me is not a reason for negating the whole thing, the whole science. I took what was good, what was fecundating, what was inspiring, and then went on to further research. I think that this open attitude, instead of condemning, makes us remain explorative. So that if it's a new science, we continue to explore it, the new things coming up, new knowledge, new facts, new experiments. And then you continue until you catch up with the present, and then you begin to create a future psychology. (72-G)

Q. When you speak about the importance of the psychologist as the interpreter, do you mean interpreter literally, that is the psychologist as analyst? I understand the importance of therapy in a specific sense and of psychology in a broad sense, but I hate to think that psychoanalysis is a necessity, that people can't get out on their own.

A. N. There are three aspects. There is therapy when you really need it, when you are paralyzed; there is psychology which you absorb every day through books and through education and which is in the air; and then there is the third one, which is the philosophy of psychology, and which is very profound and goes much deeper even than philosophy. This woman that I admire, Lou Andreas-Salomé, studied philosophy and found that philosophy was not really enough to understand human beings. So she turned to psychology.

So we do need that, and there is nothing humiliating, there isn't anything wrong with our needing that. We go to physical doctors when we are in trouble, and there used to be religious ways of curing one's self. Now we have psychology. There are all sorts of ways of curing problems. But this is *our* way of curing ourselves, the *Western* way. (72-I)

VI
The Personal Life
Deeply Lived

I know that you think that you discovered *me* when I published
the *Diary,* but actually I discovered *you.* When I published it I
thought it was the story of one woman—one often has the impression of being a solitary human being and unique. But I suddenly
found that my diary didn't belong to me, that it was other women's
diaries too. And when the letters began to come, I really discovered a whole segment of women that I didn't know. I had friendships with women before, very close, very long-lasting and endur-
ing ones, but I didn't know about these various lives and the struggles of women in little towns. I discovered literally thousands of
women and became aware that this was a dazzling moment, a marvelous moment for all women.

But the letters I received, because I had exposed myself and because I had shared all my difficulties, came because the diary had
started out as a secret. There was no feeling of censorship, no feeling that someone was looking over my shoulder, so I was truthful.
I wasn't really writing for anyone, even though at first I began the
diary as a letter to my father who had left us. The diary was intended to be a description of the new country that I was coming
to, a description of America, to entice him to come back, as I
didn't believe that he had gone for good. So it began, in a way,

for someone else. It was really written for someone else and, then, because my mother didn't let me mail it, it became a secret. It became something that I did for myself. Also, because I couldn't speak English at the age of eleven, I didn't have any companionship, and the diary became a companion. All through life it changed roles, it became various things: it was a writer's notebook, it was a storage place for dreams, it was a sketchbook of everybody around me.

I made several discoveries when I opened it up and when I let it go, when I shared it. But the major one was that relationship was impossible unless one gave the most secret and the deepest part of oneself. This is what one very rarely gives, and why I could was that I had been able to build it in this shelter, as it were, in this spirit house, where I felt protected from censorship, from criticism, and from vulnerability. And finally this secret self got strong enough so that I reached a certain point in 1966—very late as you can see—where I felt I could face the world with it. And yet I was very afraid. I was afraid of what we all are afraid of. I was afraid of being condemned, misjudged, criticized, misunderstood.

To show you the extent of my fear, just before I published the diary I had a frightening dream. I dreamt that I opened my front door and was struck by lethal radiation. Instead of that, however, I opened my front door and found a sense of union with the world and communication with other women. Instead of finding myself destroyed, I found the beginning of communion with the whole world. (73-I)

Now what had happened was what Ira Progoff describes in his metaphor: going inside of a well and digging down and down in order to find the deepest levels of ourselves. For if we dig deeply enough, he said, we finally reach the water that everybody shares, the universal water, the collective unconscious. We reach the rivers which feed the wells. There is a connection in the depths, the kind of connection you don't get when you have shallow meetings with others. So it was my desire to find my deepest self and my genuine self that was responsible.

R. D. Laing also described this when he said that we could only have authentic meetings if we constantly peel off traditions, what we have been taught, the persona, the false face that we give to the world in an effort to protect ourselves. For in protecting ourselves from harm we build a fortress, and in this fortress we wither, we die; we die of solitude like the women who have been writing these letters from little towns. So that in wanting to protect ourselves, we often really entomb ourselves.

Now when I gave up these protections, when I gave up the persona, and when I shared what I had felt at twenty and thirty and forty, by publishing the diary, then I found that we were able to communicate because we were meeting on that deepest level, which is a feeling level. So that it didn't matter if I came from another culture, it didn't matter if you had a different type of father. The facts didn't matter at all. What mattered was this quest for the self, the emotional evolution, the overcoming of obstacles, the fears that we shared, the timidities, the confusions, the conflicts, and then the step-by-step struggle finally to come out of them into a state of freedom and harmony. So I found that the whole secret of human connection with others was to give the deepest self, for only then would you receive the deepest self of others. (73-F)

When I was writing the diary, however, I felt I was doing a selfish, egocentric, narcissistic work—because I was being told that all the time. I never even knew at the time that there was a tradition of diary writing which came from the year 900 in Japan when women had no other way to express what they felt than by writing diaries. They put their diaries inside their pillows, which is why they were called "pillow books." So diary writing has always played a very important role in womens' development. And mine particularly centered on the obsession with growth. (73-A)

I used to have a garden and plant seeds. And then I would dig the earth from the plant and look at the roots, because I wanted to watch them grow. Of course I ruined the poor plants! But there was an obsession with the desire to see how things grew, and of course the next thing I realized that I could watch grow was myself. (73-D)

And the way I cheated you perhaps, by being a novelist, was in selecting the place at which I would start to open up the diaries. I made a novelist's choice in saying to myself that I would start where my life expanded and became more interesting. I didn't tell you the minor parts, the desert parts, the entrapped parts. So in a way you were deprived of the story of how one can grow from a very narrow form of life with restrictive patterns to an expanded one. Sometimes people have said to me: "Of course, in Paris and with such friends as you had, everything was so easy, so open and rich." But that's not the way it happened. That was really a later part of the journey which began in a very restricted way. (73-N)

I am very much surprised and often very much distressed by some of my opinions and some of my attitudes at the age of twenty. Maybe that's why I didn't start the *Diary* at the age of fifteen. There were things I wished I hadn't thought and hadn't said, but then they were there and I had to accept them, because that is part of this confrontation with the self, with the changing self. It also makes you accept the fact that we do change and can change and that certain rigidities or certain inherited traits or certain things that have been taught can be outgrown. There were things I had been taught by my culture, my Latin culture and religion, that I was sorry I didn't revolt against before, and it bothered me to read what I had written when I was so submissive to them. (73-B)

I was also surprised when I opened the diary of age eleven to find that I was really fictionalizing and saying that I had the most wonderful pianist father in the world, I had the greatest singer mother in the world. I was making everything the way I wanted it to be. Not calculatedly, not knowingly, but it was fiction. And it's only looking back and talking about it as I do now that I could tell the truth. So there is in the writing of a diary the danger of not facing certain truths which we find painful. At eleven I didn't want to see what the true reality of my homelife was. We have that even in maturity, the difficulty of not wanting to write about painful things or wanting to tell them in a different way. But I think the greatest problem we have—and I'm sure you have it too—is the fear of someone reading over our shoulders, of someone passing judgment on our secret selves. (73-K)

Here I had another dream which is very significant. After my mother died, I dreamt that I published the diary, and she read it. Which indicated that the person I was most fearful to confess to was my mother. She had once said: "Since you write about that monster Lawrence, you're no longer the nice little girl who wrote such a funny diary at the age of nine." She passed judgment on me as a writer and never would read me again. So you see that this fear lasts very long, the taboos last so long. (73-N)

For a long time too, as you know, the diary was written because I was afraid to confront the world with a fictional work. I was very much afraid of what I call the formal work, and the idea of sitting before the typewriter and saying, "I am now starting a novel," was enough to freeze me to death. So the diary, as well as being an achievement, was also an act of timidity. (73-D)

This was why I took so much time to listen to the conversation of people and why the diary is so full of what they said. I was observant, but I didn't have faith that I could do a work of my own, until I finally decided that because I loved D. H. Lawrence I would write about him. This is something that every young person does. I found a model. I found someone whose work I wanted to develop further, because he was trying to write very often what woman felt. He wrote very much as a woman. And then I wrote a book made out of dreams, but I was still very afraid of the formal work, of facing the world and saying: "I am a writer, I am a novelist." So I was always hiding in the diary; the diaries served the purpose of a retreat for a shy person who doesn't want to come out into the world. (73-E)

And I was writing obsessionally in the diary until Dr. Rank asked me to stop for a little while so that I wouldn't be, as he put it, possessed by the diary rather than possessing the diary. He thought that it had become compulsive, and he wanted me to feel free of it. So he took it away from me, and I was very restless and very unhappy. I compared myself to an opium smoker who is deprived of his opium. What he thought he was doing at the time was to push me out of the diary into writing fiction, into being more imaginative, more creative, and not devoting so much time to the diary. I was so comfortable with the diary! It was so easy and so free that I was enjoying it, and I wasn't facing the real fiction writing which he thought I should do.

Now what happened is that I did a rather foxy thing. Because when Rank stopped the diary entirely, I spent my time writing a portrait of him. And then I took the portrait to him and he said: "Oh well, go on with the diary." But he did deliver me of the feeling of duty, the sense of obligation, or rather the obsession with writing in the diary. And he was right about that. From then on I was much freer to choose an event that I thought was worthwhile, and I became more and more free with time. I didn't feel I had to record every day. So he was trying to liberate my fictional self because he felt that the writing of the daily thing was antithetical to creation.

However, ultimately I didn't find it so. At first there was a conflict: keeping a day-by-day documentary, like a journalist, was preventing me from fictionalizing. But actually I found later on that they nourished each other, that working at the fiction made me write better in the diary and that writing the diary kept me much closer to basic emotional truth. I didn't want to be a realist in our sense of realistic fiction, but I did take my fiction from reality, from emotional reality, and the two finally lived in harmony. (73-B)

It was, of course, because I suspected the accuracy of memory that from the age of eleven on I made such a careful recording day by day of everything I heard and saw. I really felt that memory interfered and intercepted and distorted experience, that everything was rearranged and reordered in terms of what we are today. And I wanted to see a development of life, the growth and development of experience in terms of a continuous evolution, observing all its transformations. Watching a person grow, watching a writer grow, and watching an artist grow, as I did so carefully and with such minute intensity, made me aware that memory was treacherous and that this instantaneous portrait contained an element which was left out of memoirs and certainly out of fiction. As D. H. Lawrence once said, the greatest problem of fiction was how to transport the living essence, the living quality of experience into a prearranged art form, and the danger in this transposition, this carrying of experience into fiction, was that it might die in the process. Now in the diary, no such death takes place because there is no distance. The living moment is caught, and in catching this by accumulation and by accretion a personality emerges in all its ambivalences, contradictions, and paradoxes, and finally in its most living form. (66-A)

In Europe the diary form was very respected. Every writer had a diary; the diary seemed to be a part of the development of the writer. We never looked on it as a purely subjective occupation; it was part of the literary life, it was a cultural contribution. Amiel, Gide, George Sand, and Virginia Woolf—all our writers kept diaries. But in America we have had very few. American tradition has not encouraged diary writing. But now we are taking it up with a different purpose; we're taking it up as an instrument for knowing ourselves, for creating ourselves. (73-K)

Today, diaries are being taken more seriously. There is a group of young future psychoanalysts who were given diaries to write as part of their training. After six weeks they sent for me, and they said that they were absolutely petrified with fear. I said: "How can you be? You are men who are dealing all the time with all the complexities of human nature; you're psychologists, you're going to deal with all the difficulties and problems of human behavior. How can you be afraid?" They said: "Well, we used to talk about all these problems in groups, but we never sat alone in a room with a blank book and had to face ourselves." They were mature, but they were afraid.

Now this fear is also very natural because we have grown up with the idea of an eye looking over our shoulder. Either it is the eye of the parent, or the eye of the teacher, or even in some cases they said God could see everything that we did. Those terrors of being watched are part of our childhood, and they are certainly based on fact. And this very idea of being watched by the world is what makes it necessary for us to turn to a secret occupation where we can really confront ourselves without the sense of the rest of the world watching. We have lived with too much consciousness of the world watching us. We think it is always a virtue, but it's not a virtue when it prevents us from being truthful or when it prevents us from developing ourselves. (73-E)

Now the value of the secret is that we are never quite sincere if we are writing something which we think someone is going to read. The necessary condition is that it has to be a secret. I matured enough to feel that my diary no longer needed to be a secret, but the very condition of it was the fact that I didn't think anyone would read it, and therefore I was utterly sincere with myself. Also it helped me to make the separation between my real self and the role-playing woman is called upon to do. The roles which were imposed on me as a woman by my culture—from two different cultures, the Latin and then later the American—I fulfilled. I did what I called my duty. But at the same time the diary kept my other self alive, it showed what I really wanted, what I really felt, what I really thought. (73-D)

So the reason I believe in this so much and can talk about it now so fervently is that it was my own discovery. By gradually building up this shelter of the diary, I built a place where I could always tell the truth, where I could paint my friends truthfully, where I could maintain the vacillating phases of relationship which baffle us sometimes and from which we would sometimes like to run away. The diary obliged me to stay there, to stay whole, and to continue to feel. I had to tell the diary everything. I could not afford to drop out; I could not afford to become insensible, because then I would have had nothing to tell to the diary. (73-E)

Humorous things happen too. There is an incentive to make your life interesting, so that your diary will not be dull. We used to talk sometimes about that. There is a period, in the third *Diary*, I recall, when I say: "What is happening? I really haven't anything very interesting to say, and I must do something about it. Really this is my fault, this is my life to create." This creation of expression, you see then, is tied to the creation of one's life itself. (73-B)

So it's very essential, this pursuit of the inner world, and don't let anyone say that it is a selfish occupation or that it is a narcissistic one. One critic, Leon Edel, said that the *Diary* was nothing but a narcissus pool. To which I replied: "I have never seen a narcissus pool in which a thousand characters appeared at the same time." This is absolutely true; as a matter of fact, I counted them! But our culture has a suspicion of what people do when they turn inward. The fear was probably that they would turn inward, as if inside a sea shell and never come out again. Well, sometimes we have good reasons for not coming out. But I found that I did come out the other end, that the sea shell has an opening. (73-E)

I attribute to my diary this faculty for receiving others, for being prepared to receive the face or the voice, the presence, the words of others. It's a form of loving, it's a form of attentiveness. And when sometimes the students say to me: "Of course, you knew so many famous people," I say: "Don't forget they were not famous at all when we first knew each other; we were accidentally thrown together and none of us had done anything; we chose each other finally for genuine reasons, for potentials in each other." We were not finished writers, were not famous writers; we were just like students sitting next to each other. But we paid attention to the one who was sitting next to us. We didn't seek the famous writers in France. We simply encouraged each other and made our own growth. So we learned to live with others, to help others be creative, to help others achieve their work. We were very encouraging, very fraternal. And then, of course, inevitably everything I heard I would put down. It's like those little Japanese flowers that you put in water. I would finally learn to let it come in full bloom. Instead of being hasty about the descriptions, I wanted to go deeper and deeper and deeper.

At this time, when we live such an accelerated life, when we think that contacts are very transient and passing and superficial, then more than ever we have to examine the fears we have about revealing ourselves. Part of this fear found its expression in the novel. Nevertheless, women continued to write diaries and we know that George Sand, even though she produced so many novels, felt it necessary to keep a diary in which she told about her own life.

So the secrecy that I kept for so many years, until the time that

I decided to share the diaries with you, revealed something to me that I think applies to all of us. It revealed the fear we have of exposing our deepest self, and it is this fear which has played a major role in what we call the alienated society. I don't think it comes from the external cause, the transience of American life, the fact that we move about, the fact that we are easily uprooted. For the fact that I was uprooted is exactly what made me turn once more to writing.

When I came to America I couldn't speak the language, and I had no friends. So the diary became the friend and the father confessor. It was also the substitute for the absent father. And it was in this way that I learned the vital quality of what seemed to be a monologue, an interior monologue. For it wasn't only that. It was the way I was going to rebuild the bridge that was broken by the separation of my parents and by the uprooting to a foreign country. So the writing began to have a living, vital meaning which had nothing to do with literature. The diary became not only a companion, so that I wouldn't be lost in a foreign country with a language I couldn't speak, but also a source of contact with myself. It was a place where I could tell the truth and where I felt that nobody would look.

Now this habit which I acquired accidentally as the result of a psychic trauma—became a guiding element in my life and took on a different color after awhile. It was not only the story of myself but of the adventure of coming to a new country. It became the diary of an adventurer. It made me look at my life, at sorrowful moments, at moments of great disintegrating experiences, and constantly reminded me that it was an adventure, that it was a tale. Somehow the transference into writing gave it just that little bit of space which I needed to sustain the painful part of the experience. So there were always those two guiding objectives. One was growth, watching my own growth; and then, in watching my own growth it naturally follows that I watched and observed the growth of others around me. So your attentiveness, your care for what is happening, your watchfulness, your meditation on what happens, your examination of what happens, the fact that you are observing others and that you are not only writing down your life but that you are also naturally concerned with the growth of people around you, make that a necessary part of our existence. Because what we don't write down often remains rather nebulous in our feelings. And at this moment, particularly when women are trying really to find their identity, I found that the thing most lacking was this power of expression of what you feel in a certain situation, what you think, what you believe, which you want to impart to others.

Tonight I was asked to talk about writing, not writing as literature but writing as intimately connected with our lives—I would even say as necessary to our lives. . . . And now I want to tell you, from the very beginning, how this writing happened to become for me so linked with life and how it was a necessary part of living. When I was nine years old a doctor made an erroneous diagnosis and said I would never walk again. My first reaction then was to ask for pencil and paper and to start making portraits of the members of my family. Then this continued in the form of notes which I gathered in a little notebook and even wrote on it "Member of the French Academy." Quite obviously there was then a turning to writing as a way of life because I thought I was going to be deprived of the normal activities of a child or an adolescent. But I'm trying to use this as an example of the importance of writing as a way of learning to live; for when I was able to walk again and there was no question of that impediment, the writing remained a source of contact with myself and with others. (73-B)

It's also very symbolic that when I was asked once to go to a masquerade in which we had to dress as our madness I put my head in a bird cage. And coming out of the bird cage was a sort of ticker tape of the unconscious, long strips of paper on which I had copied a great deal of writing. This was, of course, a very clear symbol of how I hoped to escape from my cage. (72-J)

You might say, however, when you are reading the *Diary* now: "Oh well, it was easy for you, you could write well." But I want you to know that at twenty I wrote very badly, and I purposely gave my first novel to the library of Northwestern University so that students could see the difference between the writing I did at twenty and the writing I do now. The mistake we make when we choose a model is that we choose the point of arrival. We are unaware of the things that have been overcome, like shyness, or not being able to speak in public (I couldn't even speak to the people I knew). The final achievements are what we notice and then say: "Well it's no use modelling ourselves after this or that writer because we don't have these particular gifts." I didn't have any particular gift in my twenties. I didn't have any exceptional qualities. It was the persistence and the great love of my craft which finally became a discipline, which finally made me a craftsman and a writer. (73-D)

The only reason I finally was able to say exactly what I felt was because, like a pianist practising, I wrote every day. There was no more than that. There was no studying of writing, there was no literary discipline, there was only the reading and receiving of experience. And I had to be open because I had to write it in the diary.

So I would like to remove from everyone the feeling that writing is something that is only done by a few gifted people. I want to eliminate this instantly. . . . You shouldn't think that someone who achieves fulfillment in writing and a certain art in writing is necessarily a person with unusual gifts. I always said that it was an unusual stubbornness. Nothing prevented me from doing it every night, after every day's happenings.

It's not only the people with unusual gifts who will write their life in an interesting way. It has nothing to do really with the literary value of the work. What is important is that in the doing of it you begin to penetrate much deeper into the layers of consciousness and the unconscious. I registered everything. I registered intuitions, prophesies; I would be looking into the future or looking back and re-examining the past. (73-B)

I don't want to make writers of all of you, but I *do* want you to become very aware of your orientation. First of all, of how much contact you have with yourself. If you remember, in the early diaries I spoke of my feeling that I was playing all the roles demanded of woman, which I had been programmed to play. But I knew also that there was a part of myself that stood apart from that and wanted some other kind of life, some other kind of authenticity. R. D. Laing describes this authenticity as a process of constant peeling off the false selves. You can do this in many ways, but you can begin by looking at it, for there is so much that we *don't* want to look at. I didn't want to see exactly where I was in Louveciennes before I made friends, before I entered the literary life, before I wrote my first book. I didn't want to see that I was nowhere, but wanting to see is terribly important to our direction. And to find this direction I used every possible means. Not only friendship and psychology and therapy, but also a tremendous amount of reading, exploration, listening to others—all these things contributed to my discovering who I really was. It wasn't as final or definite as it might sound now, because it doesn't happen in one day and it doesn't happen finally. It's a continuum, it's something that goes on all of your life. But once I was at least on the track of what I could do, then the obstacles began to move away. It was not something that anybody could give me, it was something that I had to find inside myself. (72-J)

So I'm speaking now of the diary not as a work of literature but as something necessary to living, as a way of orienting ourselves to our inner lives. It doesn't matter in what form you do it, whether it's meditation, whether it's writing or whether it's just a moment of thoughtfulness about the trend, the current, of your life. It's a moment of stopping life in order to become aware of it. And it's this kind of awareness which is threatened in our world today, with its acceleration and with its mechanization. (73-F)

In his introduction to the first volume of the *Diary,* Gunther Stuhlmann says that my real life as a writer and a woman is contained in the pages of the journal. I should add to this that what I meant by my real life was that, as many people do, I had two roles to play; one in the world, in which I sought to please everyone, in which I sought to inspire, in which I wanted only to give the best of myself; and then the other truth contained in the journal of how I felt about these people I met, how I felt about what was happening. And in some respects this split originated in the philosophy that truth is destructive. At least I believed that certain kinds of truth were destructive, and these demons were going to be kept secret within the journal. What changed my attitude was the realization that these things that I had condemned were actually the most valuable, that the secret and intimate portraits I made of people, as well as of myself, were far deeper and more revealing than these roles that we all play in life. Those who misunderstood the *Diary* were the ones who were so obsessed with the idea that any introspection, any regard for individual growth, any concern with one's personal conflicts was narcissistic. We saw a great deal of these hysterical, mass, unthinking movements in our period because we did give up the self. The self has to merge with collective interests or general humanity, but first of all it has to *exist* in order to be able to make a choice and to make a contribution. The loss of personal identity, this depersonalization, led to a most dangerous state of dehumanization as we have seen from some of the phenomena of American life. The people who turned to the diary in this period turned in order to find the core of themselves or something they could create with, something they could cling to, a basic understanding, a capacity for evaluation, a knowledge of distinction of quality, these things which had been lost in a kind of anonymous mass unthinkingness.

The diary was not published out of nostalgia for the past. I realized at a certain moment that it connected very strongly with contemporary life. I don't think I would have published it if it simply had been memoirs of people who had died and disappeared and vanished and played no role in the present. But I found that the thinking of Rank, the work of Henry Miller, and the very strong influence of Artaud were active in contemporary life. So that the *Diary* is not a *Recherche du Temps Perdu*. It is actually a seeking to unite the past, the present, and the future. My life today is just as it was when I was writing the diary; it is always very full and very rich. I'm always exploring new realms of experience, I'm always curious, I'm always ready for adventure.

I did not wish to recapture the past. But I was elated to find that the things and the people and the places I had loved could remain alive forever. I was pleased to realize that I had awakened to life permanently. This was a discovery which really pushed me into editing the diary. I felt humble about it because I felt that it was not really a biography as much as a portrait of others. Of course it's necessary to be an individual, to be the proper mirror for others. If you have a small mirror you cannot reflect big personalities. In my great effort to perfect myself as a sensitive instrument with a wide range I made a comparison always to the mirror. The mirror has to have identity and an existence and intelligence in what it records. And of this I am proud in the diary; I did record essential things. (66-A)

The personal life, deeply lived, takes you beyond the personal. This was the discovery that I made when I relinquished the diary, which was my secret. I discovered that it belonged to everybody, and not only to me. (72-H)

Instead of being discovered when the *Diary* appeared, it was I who made a discovery, of thousands and thousands of women I didn't know, of a whole segment of American life I didn't know. But that is perhaps the only important thing that fame brings, that it helps you to connect with a wider world. And so I am the one who made a discovery, who discovered you. (72-L)

* * *

Q. Did the publication of the *Diary* change your feeling towards the diary—having once let us read it, from then on did you feel differently when you sat down and wrote the diary?

A. N. I started so young, don't forget. That is very important. I started at eleven. It was such a strong habit, I kept it secret for so long that I have faith in my own capacity to keep secrets. So that when I write about today or yesterday and the day before yesterday I tell myself this will never be read, and I believe it! I can believe it since I was able to keep a secret that long.

Q. The *Diary* is such a personal thing, that I wonder why I read it without a sense of separation but rather with a sense of identification. How is it that so many women could identify with it?

A. N. I think it has nothing to do with literature, it has nothing to do with my having been a fiction writer. It has to do with the point I was trying to make, which is that when we go deeply into the personal, we go beyond the personal. We achieve something that is collective. In other words, by going deeply into my personal life I described not a unique experience or a special kind of woman, but rather I have touched a collective emotional identity. So women would say that even though their fathers were not like my father and though they were not born in Europe—even though the facts were not quite the same, certainly the emotional reactions were. When women write to me, they don't say: "I like the way you wrote the diary"; they say: "It's like *my* diary." Or else they say: "I feel as if you were a friend and I can tell you everything." In other words, it is what Jung said: if we go deep enough into the individual we do not individuate exclusively. I'm not a special or unique phenomenon. I thought I was when I was twenty. Because nobody else thought or read the same things I did, I thought I was eccentric. But you see what I found out is that if you go deeply enough, the personal life really goes beyond that and reaches universality. (73-D)

Q. I'm not presently keeping a diary, but sometimes I do feel the need to sit down and write down my feelings. So I decide I will write a diary; I get everything ready, open the book, and then comes the question: where do I start?

A. N. Put yourself right in the present. This was my principle when I wrote the diary—to write the thing I felt most strongly about that day. Start there and that starts the whole unravelling, because that has roots in the past and it has branches into the future. The main thing is that what you feel strongly about today is where you're *at* today, and that is what the purpose of the diary *is*. Otherwise you would write a memoir; I would be writing about my past now. The importance is *now,* taking it *now,* where you are now, how you feel today, what is the strongest feeling. I used to choose that way; that's why not everything is in the diary. I chose the event of the day that I felt most strongly about, the most vivid one, the warmest one, the nearest one, the strongest one. That was my method of selection. You can't do a whole day, and I certainly couldn't put down what I thought in a whole day. Because actually we think universes in one day. The important thing is *today*. Then one day you may have a recollection. Occasionally in the diary something would come out of the past and I would pick it up. Or a dream may throw you back just as it may throw you forward.

Q. That doesn't seem to fall into the pattern of what a diary usually is. You know, all teenagers are supposed to keep diaries and lock them away from their mother.

A. N. Those are calendars.

Q. In my journal writing I try to work out the negative feelings that I can't work out directly. But I find that it isn't always working, that it doesn't release me. Sometimes it seems that I have to take it further, and I'm really frightened of that. How do I separate what I can work out in my journal and what I must go and work out with the person?

A. N. Well, what happens, I think, is that if we do the first clearing up of our blind anger, what happens is that we then realize what we are really genuinely angry about. So then by the time we bring it to the person it is more articulate and it is more clarified. The whole journal emphasizes the clarification process. Instead of striking out at my younger brothers for what they did, I would clear up what had made me angry and by the time that had passed, the blind anger, I could talk to them and improve the situation, whatever it was.

But I know that we can also use the diary for negative reasons. And I remember every time I used to hear a fire engine, I used to think: "The diaries are burning!" I didn't know why until I was talking to a doctor and remembered that my friends had asked me the day before where my demon was. Obviously my demon self was in the diary—if my diary burned, part of my real self was gone. I haven't that feeling anymore. My real self is not in the diaries, it's here! But this is all part of the process. We tend to complain and lament and wail, as I did in the diary, which I really didn't want to give to the world. But then you begin to make a synthesis.

What's so wonderful about the journal is that it helps you to make that inner journey and then finally to make a synthesis between all the parts of yourself, so that they become unified. The diary does help us to do that. Otherwise we experience negative feelings without sorting them out.

Q. I have a very difficult time writing about my husband and being honest. I write only the good things, and I'm sure it's connected with the fear of his reading it.

A. N. Of course. It's your fear even of *thinking* it. But the fact that you write it already means you are thinking it more clearly and completely.

Q. Yet I would like him to be able to read it. So far, our relationship has been one of complete honesty, and you know, I fear to tread upon that by keeping secrets.

A. N. That's very difficult. It may seem to us, in terms of our conventional idea of loyalty, that it is disloyalty to look with complete honesty at a person we love. But I found that it is much less damaging than not being honest. Because the thoughts are there, and the impressions are there. They are only being repressed. So they come out in hostile form. As I told you, when I was very angry with my two brothers, expressing in the diary what I was angry about would often show me how foolish my anger was or how unjustified. It actually cleared the relationships. So instead of doing damage, it did the opposite. You might have thought I was doing damage by writing my complaints or describing whatever they did to me that was harmful, but actually it did good. It's a different kind of loyalty. If you are true to how you feel, then you don't have these hidden, destructive tendencies that we sometimes acquire by putting them away.

Q. Did you hide your diary?

A. N. Yes I did. As soon as I found my brothers were reading it and having a great deal of fun over it. Because whenever I was angry with them I would put the anger in the diary. I didn't want to lash out at them because they were younger. So of course they read it with great delight. Then I began to hide it.

Q. It makes me feel strange, though, to hide it.

A. N. It is necessary. I have heard of young diary writers who say that they want to share everything and open everything. They're trying to relate, to be open and trusting, and at the same time to write a secret document. But I think for self-creation, in order really to visualize ourselves and create an identity and a personality, first there must be secrecy. I certainly felt that I had to do that alone, because otherwise either I would be taking my parents' view of the world or that of the book I was reading. I felt I really had to have a separate place where I could create myself, and that there should not be any interference. So I would say, at the beginning, at the vulnerable stage, that I think it's dangerous to share, it's dangerous to write for another. Later on, of course, it's different. Now I'm glad to make relationships in terms of the *Diary*, because now you know me, and I will ultimately know you better than I would know other people. But at the beginning it's dangerous because we still have an unformed concept of how we feel. (73-K)

Q. When you look at something you have written in the past do you find it irrelevant or unimportant?

A. N. Not if you look at it in terms of organic cellular growth. It's not irrelevant if you think of it in terms of growth. I used to make fun of things that I wrote in the diary when I was twenty. I didn't really like anything I found in it. But I know it was part of the process of growth—the arrogant age or the shy age or all the awkward stages of our growth. I never found it irrelevant. I found it humanly pathetic sometimes, and I didn't approve of it. But you see it's part of a whole, and one step leads you to the next. It's your willingness to see the step-by-step progression, your concern with developing.

Q. Do you have to step out of yourself a little bit and look back?

A. N. Yes. And the fact that it's written is what enables you to look back on it. (73-H)

Q. Did you ever get the feeling as you undertook the responsibility of keeping the diary in secret, that you were becoming sort of vulnerable, that you might betray yourself—not necessarily by having to keep up the diary, but by the way you were going to act towards people?

A. N. No. There was not such a great separation between my thoughts and my behavior, there was only a separation between what I thought and felt and what I said openly—or didn't say! But, you know, as you do that, strangely enough you begin to confide in people too. You teach yourself to talk. I often speak of writing not as an art but as something which has a vital influence on our life, because it teaches us to articulate and to tell others what we want to tell them. So I really learned to talk to my friends because I was writing, and the writing was training me to express my feelings.

But I was still, at one period, afraid of opening certain things up or of confiding, because I felt very strongly that I had to live up to an image, a persona. I was usually expected to be the confessor, the one to whom others confessed. Nobody expected me to confess. That seemed to be my role in life, so therefore my confessing to the diary was a natural balance to that. And I do remember a psychologist who impressed me very much by saying: "How do you feel when people open up and tell you everything about themselves." I said: "I love them because then I really know them and I don't judge them." And then he said: "Why don't you feel that you can do the same?" In other words, when other people opened up to me it made me love them, to know them intimately. My difficulty at the time was not to realize that others might feel the same way about me.

Q. My own experience was that I felt it was futile, because I was withdrawing from people to keep up this journal and by keeping the journal I was at the same time keeping my true self hidden.

A. N. Well, I think you didn't wait long enough for the two to come together. The journal first helps you to create the real self. When you feel that you can really show this real self and act it out, then in a way a use of the diary disappears. If you had waited long enough there probably would have come a synthesis between the persona in the world and the you in the diary. Most people cannot make this fusion. It never happens. But then you might as well keep your secret self somewhere. And someday that you in the diary is going to run into the other, make you act in life or talk the way you do in the diary. That's why Ira Progoff asks you to have a dialogue with a dead writer or a parent that is no longer there or somebody you have never met—to have a dialogue with them in order to advance further into what you wish. This incites you to bring those two things together, so that finally the diary and you make one completed person.

Q. In the process of watching the growth of yourself, researching yourself, have you ever had the experience of renouncing, repudiating, or criticizing what you thought earlier, thought was your true self?

A. N. The process of creation *is* a criticism of yourself. There isn't such a thing as growing without criticizing. You wouldn't grow unless you really thought that yesterday's self wasn't good enough. It's implied in the process. When you're shedding something, it's because you really think that you can grow further. The process of criticism is a part of it. There is plenty of that in the diaries. (73-E)

Q. I have been having a lot of trouble because people tell me that I'm selfish and anti-social, that I'm cutting myself off from others and life because I'm thinking about myself a lot, and I worry a lot about it.

A. N. *Don't* worry. Because when you isolate yourself not only do your personal goals become clear but it goes beyond the personal. It is true that some people remain in their little subjective personal world. Some will always remain. But I found that having solved the personal world, having solved the things that prevented me from relating to others—fears, anxieties, mistrust (as when I first said in the diary that because my father left I would never love anybody again)—when you solve these things, then you come out to others and you grow beyond the personal.

Q. That makes sense. But now I feel that I'm so occupied with myself that there is no room for anybody else.

A. N. If your intention is true—which my intention was, to rebuild the bridge that my father broke—then you really do want to go towards others and you shouldn't feel guilty. But, of course, when people tell you that you begin to believe them. I didn't know at the time what I was doing. I wasn't strong enough to think:

"Well, I'm doing something that is beyond the personal." However, every now and then I would have an inkling that I might be speaking for other women too. If you are really reaching for something beyond, you do emerge finally. But you can't come out while you're troubled by your neurosis, for if you don't deal with it, with your personal difficulties, then you have nothing to come out with. The pain of trauma is like physical pain. Somebody who has a physical wound can't pay attention to others because he is so bothered by physical pain. So you see my attention was freed, could be turned towards others the minute I had solved whatever was troubling my soul. The abscesses of the soul are the same as any other physical pain, and you know very well a person who is ill turns in upon himself and usually pays no attention to others. So in a way if we have a problem of the soul, it is the same thing. We have to solve that first before we become truly collective or communal, giving and outgoing.

Q. I get the impression from a lot of people I talk to who are writing diaries and reading yours that they think diary writing consists in the abandonment of all critical attitudes and faculties, whereas I feel your critical attitude and training were essential to your development of clarity of thought and clarity of prose.

A. N. Yes, I see your point. But my critical clarity did not come from training. Because, in the first place, the diary started when I was eleven so it was a spontaneous act, it was an emotional act. People are right when they say the mainspring of the diary is an emotional flow. The critical thing was quite different from what you are thinking of, academic criticism.

Q. Yes, but I'm not talking about academic criticism. I'm talking about a really subjective criticism of the aesthetic quality and nature of the experience.

A.N. When you begin you're afraid to lose your oneness with things by standing away and criticizing. Before the Millers came into my life, I remember thinking that I was getting too clairvoyant, too clear—that that faculty was working too much without much experience underneath to feed it. So I was glad of what I call this moonlight and chaos. I was glad of the people who lived like nature, very irrationally, and who didn't have that faculty. But I was always ambivalent about it: about seeing clearly but then living passionately. If you live passionately, you're bound to get into confused states. There is always that. But then I did also have a need to sort out and understand this. You're right about the need to understand, to clarify. Because that takes you to the next step. In confusion and ambivalence there is stasis. If you are caught in ambivalence, you really stay there. The ambivalence of deciding whether I was going to go to the diary or going to write a novel, for instance. Then you don't move.

Q. What I really mean is that if the diary simply becomes a tool for finding yourself it can become as much of a trap as a lot of other predicaments. You have to be able to critically separate and evaluate yourself, or else you will never be able to put yourself into a different artistic mode.

A. N. You're quite right. There is a method of synthesis made in the diary for which I feel indebted to psychology. Experience shatters us, but psychology helps to integrate those seemingly irreconcilable elements. Psychology shows you that they don't need to become hopelessly "either/or" wars going on inside oneself, as in the choice between whether I would be a diarist or write fiction. I found I could do both, one was feeding the other, one was helping the other. Writing fiction made me write the diary better, writing the diary made me write fiction from more spontaneous sources. What we regard as conflicts can be resolved—to mutual enrichment.

Q. When I started pulling away from my family to go up to my room and write, they got quite distressed with me, and I think were worried probably about the introspection. I was wondering how your mother reacted when you started writing in your diary.

A. N. Oh very badly, very badly. First of all she said what the Latins always say—that woman shouldn't be intellectual. Then she said I was ruining my eyes, and I would never find a husband. I should be learning to sew and I should be learning to cook—which I didn't like—I should be learning all the domestic things, preparing myself to be a wife and mother. So my mother thought that too, that the writing was a threat to my future, to my life as a woman. I don't know about my father because I wasn't living with him. I don't know what his reaction would have been, but I do know when I told him I was interested in dancing he said: "Women in our family never danced!" So there were a lot of taboos, regular taboos. The Spaniards, you know, have a saying that the woman must make up for being intelligent; she must be extra charming so that people will forgive her. (73-K)

Q. What was the proportion of your life that you gave to journal writing?

A. N. Always in the evening after the day was done. Just what was left over from the day. I used the day for my fiction or for my duties or my home life. It was always only when the day was over that that little part of the evening belonged to me. So it wasn't a big proportion. It wasn't hours and hours of writing in the diary. (73-B)

Q. You speak of spontaneity, and I think that this would be absolutely necessary to get down your thoughts this way. But your books are so beautifully written that I can't help but wonder if you don't go back later and do some rewriting and polishing.

A. N. No, not in the diary. In the novels, yes.

Q. Not in the diary? Because you seem to have the precise word each time, you give the exact shade of meaning you want. It doesn't seem possible that you could do this right off without going back and polishing.

A. N. Well, I would compare that to belly dancers who begin dancing when they are three years old. Their technique becomes such a part of them that they aren't conscious of it. I think it's really the fact that I began *so soon* to tie words to experience and to think in terms of words or in terms of images. I think that spontaneity has entirely to do with the fact that writing became a habit.

Q. Is it possible that if you had gone back and polished you would have changed some parts and would have started to rationalize about what you had written?

A. N. Yes, it would have acquired a different quality. I don't know why I did that really, why I wanted to preserve authenticity.

Sometimes I felt it had a little to do with being a great deal with artists and being with writers. I saw them fictionalize almost instantly, making up stories, making up the present, making up your personality. As a woman, for some reason, I felt I wanted to keep the authenticity of awareness for others; I wanted insight rather than the imagination. I saw a lot of imagination in the artists around me and I wanted somehow to have basic truths recorded. I don't know why exactly, but that became an end in itself, a feminine attitude which I've often discussed with psychologists. Rank used to say that the reason man created was that he was not afraid to cut the umbilical cord and use his imagination, but that woman was afraid of separation. So I turned that into a creative thing. Not wanting to be separated from human life became the basis of my art. (72-W)

Q. Did you go back over the diaries at all then?

A. N. No, I didn't do that. I couldn't go back over the diaries because then their spontaneous quality would have been spoiled. It would have spoiled the fact that there was a change in the writing as I was growing. You can see that the first *Diary* is not as well written as the second or the third. There is a progression in the craft. But I couldn't tamper with that because I would then have changed the character of it.

Q. What about just going back over them at the time you were writing? I was wondering if you would write something and then go over it or did you just try to get something down right away without worrying about the style of writing or typing?

A. N. Yes, I had no erasures. In the original nothing is erased, nothing is polished really. That's where I learned spontaneity. I think most of our inability to create is timidity. Just as children create spontaneously until they are told they are not doing it well, or something like that. They dance, they write poems, they draw. So the diary was my way of maintaining contact with spontaneity: nobody was going to see it. I thought and believed that for many years. Or if I showed it to a friend it would only be a fragment. So that helped me to overcome the censor. (72-I)

Q. Did you speak quite freely of the fact that you were writing a diary over the course of the years, and were your friends aware of their role?

A. N. Oh yes, I used to talk about it. And always, you know, when you have a secret you would like it to be found out! There were times when friends would say: "Don't put this in your diary." And there were other times when I had to learn to lock it up because my brothers would steal it and of course have a great deal of fun with it. The secrecy didn't come at the beginning. At the beginning I thought my family would know everything I was writing down. But then as you go into your teens you begin to have secrets from the family and I began to lock it up. Now with friends, what I used to do when they felt anxious was to read them their portrait, as I did with Henry Miller who worried about it, and then didn't worry anymore. (73-E)

Q. I would like to know whether the act of writing about an event in the diary changed you in a way that just experiencing the event without writing about it would not do.

A. N. I think it depends on whether the writing is spontaneous, and connected with the subconscious part of your life or whether it is a self-conscious, intellectual, analytical process. There is a distinction. Now when I analyze in the diaries because I'm confused, I'm lost, I'm troubled, and I'm in conflict, then my writing is a way of getting myself out of that. But when I describe an experience and immerse myself in it, let's say the description of Fez, Morocco, a city which I felt immersed in, the writing is not an act of self-consciousness—provided your skill has been perfected, become spontaneous. Then it is as much a part of me as, say, somebody's singing. It's like someone singing after something has happened. Then, as I said, it is a natural form of expression, a way of living, really. (73-B)

Q. You mentioned that in doing the diary you felt held back because of people's opinion that it was a selfish occupation. Were there any other fears that you had in relation to this introspection aspect of the diary?

A. N. We have always a conflict because we would like to be different from others but we also want to be near others. So that

as you work at your individuality, you have anxiety about separating yourself from others and creating a distance. You try to
be at one with others and to keep your friends and at the same
time you're trying to be different—which is the problem of the
teenager usually. So my problem was, for instance, I loved to
read and my companions in school didn't. So whatever differen-
tiated me from them caused me anxiety, because it caused separation. I wanted to find the things that I liked which they liked, that
we could do together. We would skate together, we would dance
together, but we didn't read together. So there was always some
part of me that was left out of things. I think all of us share this
double fear: we know we would like to be ourselves, we know we
would like to be different, but we also would like to be near others
and have people think as we do and read the book we are reading.
(73-E)

Q. Would you advise all young people to write?

A. N. I don't see why not, for even if they don't become great at
least I think their lives would be enormously enriched. We don't
have to look at everything as an achievement. I never thought of
my writing really as working towards some achievement. I never
imagined the situation today, for example. It wasn't what I particularly wanted. I simply wanted the bridge to be remade towards
the world which my father had broken, a bridge towards the world.
Since I was traumatized, timid, or whatever it was, or a foreigner
in a foreign country, I wanted this bridge to be created, and it was
created by my work. But I didn't do it for a literary reason. (73-D)

Q. Do you feel that this inner search can only be done through
writing a journal, or do you think there might be other ways?

A. N. Oh yes. This inner journey can be made in other ways beside writing. Writing helps because it encourages us to be articulate, and it functions as a mirror of our life. It's not a matter of sitting down and doing beautiful writing. I don't think we should
think of it in terms of literature. If we're using it as a means of an
interior journey, I think it's very valuable. There are other ways,
of course. There are some people who have found it through medi-

tation, there are people who make their inner journey in religious ways, or by going to other cultures even. (73-F)

Q. Your diary really is both diary and journal, which I think of as a sort of super-diary. Because most diaries or many diaries simply list facts, what happened, but you also list what you are thinking.

A. N. Yes, it should really be called a "journal." The French word —*journal*. I don't know how it got translated into "diary." (72-A)

Q. How much editing did you do to your diary?

A. N. Well, the editing was done with two things in mind. One was ethical, because, while I can share my life, I had no right to reveal the lives of those who didn't want theirs shared. There were some things that were confidential, which therefore I could not give. Then another reason I had to edit the diary is that there are repetitions. It's very much like a painter who makes many sketches of a person before he makes the final portrait. So in the original I recorded every day my impressions of a person as he was today, tomorrow; again and again. Finally I would hit the real portrait. So there would be fumblings, and that kind of editing I had to do for your sake. And there are repetitions in the diary because you begin anew each day. But some day you'll see it in its entirety. (73-F)

Q. Are the novels an extension of the diary?

A. N. They are. They're reality pushed to its mythical other dimension—the further dimension. When you are faithful to a portrait, you cannot go beyond that portrait, and faithfulness is part of the diary. But in the novel you can push this discovery to many more dimensions. It doesn't matter, you're free. This freedom is what the artist takes and what I learned not to fear anymore because the experience in itself was grounded in the diary. I think if I hadn't had the feeling of being grounded in my human reality I still would have been afraid of that imaginary, mythical world. (73-H)

Q. Do you still write novels?

A. N. I really don't like the novel anymore. Because the novel is too indirect. It's the mythology of woman; it has composite characters. But I think today we need to know people better than we do in fiction. We're interested in that unmasking. Part of the novel always remains to be interpreted and that's a hazardous thing. Whereas I don't think there can be many misunderstandings about the diary's function. We need that direct expression, that's the only explanation I have. We don't read literature objectively, we read it for what we need. And right now we need the knowledge that growth is sometimes slow but organic. (71-B)

Q. Do you use a different artistic yardstick or measure for the diary?

A. N. In writing the diary, I tried to overlook, to forget all procedures of writing. I wanted to make no demands on myself as to whether I'd written it well or not well. I wanted to shed all that, and I succeeded because I felt it would never be read. (73-M)

Q. Weren't the first English novels written as diaries written by women, in a novel like *Pamela?*

A. N. Oh yes, I forgot that. Another interesting thing: Did you know D. H. Lawrence got his knowledge of women, in spite of Millett, from a woman? His first sweetheart kept a diary, and he read it. And of course we know Fitzgerald stole quite a bit of Zelda's diary. (72-D)

Q. How do the people you portray in the *Diary* feel about having their portraits published?

A. N. I have to show it to them. The rule of the *Diary* is that the portraits have to be shown. The major portraits, not the minor characters, but the major portraits, have to be released by the person who is portrayed. Every character in my *Diary* has had to give me permission to publish the portrait I made. And since my intentions were never destructive, most of my portraits were hardly changed by the people themselves. They felt that at least if I told the whole thing then readers could balance and not judge. I had very few important things taken out. (73-D)

Q. Many women identify with you when they read the *Diary.* Some even change the course of their lives, like the young lady I met who left home with her lover after having read the *Diary.*

Others begin to write diaries. How do you account for this?

A. N. I'm doing for them what was done for me by books. They awakened me. As a teenager, I read voraciously. I still do.

Q. Don't you feel hesitant about revealing so many of your thoughts and experiences to the scrutiny of the whole world?

A. N. No, because I think that the personal ceases to be personal at a certain point, and becomes the diary of everyone. The diary reveals growth, a quest for meaning. Thus it speaks to and for everyone, and identification becomes possible.

Q. Some readers were disappointed because your *Diary* did not reveal intimacies and scandal. What determined your editing?

A. N. Certain intimate aspects of one's life and that of others should be preserved. Scandal obscures rather than enhances the deeper meaning of experience.

Q. How do the incidents in the Diary become transmuted in the alchemy of art?

A. N. The answer lies in the function of art which is to seek essence and meaning. In doing so, you depart from the realistic to gain profounder and more universal perception through skill, craft, experience, technique. (69-A)

Q. In the *Diary* you go by month. In your original writing of the diary did you go by day or did you also go by month?

A. N. At the beginning it was every day. At the age of eleven, if I skipped a day I had to make an apology to the diary. I felt I had neglected it. There was an obsessional quality about the dating then, not losing anything. But after that I became much freer, and then I only wrote when I had something to write, and there would be periods where I didn't write for several days. It wasn't a faithfully kept diary.

Q. In the diary—the original volume you kept—did you write the day or did you have it like the public volume where you just have the month and don't differentiate the days?

A. N. Yes, because it would have been very tiresome always to say the sixth of October, the eighth of October. Very heavy. So I didn't bother with that when it wasn't important. Now when the dates were important, such as the publication of someone's book or a certain meeting with someone, then I would put in the date. But if I had always put in the date it would have been highly over-loaded. If you saw the biography of Stravinsky, you will see what I mean by strict recording and overloading with footnotes. (73-B)

Q. You mentioned that before you published your diary you didn't realize how much you had in common with other women and that you had a great fear of revealing yourself. So what at that time was your reason for publishing it?

A. N. Because I suddenly realized that the diary was not nostalgic, but that it was full of things which were now becoming very central, very present in the young, in the new generation. The things I have wanted for America were happening now, the people I had described were playing a dynamic role in the present. Artaud was having an effect on the theater, for example; there is a renais-sance of interest in Otto Rank. All the things that I had gone into were contemporary. What had happened was that I was really writing some years back of things which are now contemporary. I saw this connection between the past and the present. I realized that the past which we usually throw away, saying what happened in the thirties has nothing to do with us, suddenly was all intercon-nected with the present. Then I realized the diary was a dynamic thing, something that was alive. That's when I decided I wanted to publish it because there was a connection with the present. If it had been nostalgic, I wouldn't have done it, and I would have waited for it to happen after my death. (73-E)

Q. Do you feel there is a great discrepancy between your audience, which is mostly women, and your private life, which is mostly con-cerned with relationships to men?

A. N. You mean that in the *Diary* the relationship to man is very important. I'm not so concerned about the fact that women have outnumbered men in response to the *Diary*. I think it's because women are trying to find themselves now. The men are not so much concerned with that; I think that's not their great concern. But to have a story of growth, more or less organic and fairly com-plete, is very important to women. I think that's why the stress is on women because the women are trying to find out what they feel. (72-D)

Q. In the process of writing your diary and in preparing it for publication have you ever edited or revised it especially to make it more trendy or stylish?

A. N. That is a question I shouldn't even be asked! If you've read it, you wouldn't ask that question. It is self-evident. It is quite evident that the diary is not an artificial creation.

Q. No, but I just thought perhaps that today you found some of the things you had said irrelevant, and that as you were writing there were perhaps some things you didn't want to be exposed.

A. N. It wouldn't be a diary then. I had to be true to things even if I didn't like what I had written or thought.

Q. You sort of act like your present diary is being held up. But if it's all diary, couldn't you just toss it all in the publisher's lap?

A. N. No. It has to be edited. There are some ethical reasons for editing a diary—there are some people whose lives I am not at liberty to disclose—and there are some repetitions in the diary that are very tiresome. The diary has to be edited, but edited only in leaving *out* certain things but not in *changing* anything. You have to leave out some things because certain people are still alive who would like their lives not to be disturbed. (73-E)

Q. Would you give us a preview of the things we will read in the next volume of your diary?

A. N. You're rushing me, and I really don't know! Because I never read ahead or back. I want to surprise myself, I want to have something new to look forward to. I never really read ahead of time, I read only as I'm going along. So I don't really know what I'm going to find in the next volume. (73-H)

Q. Are you still writing in the diaries?

A. N. No, and it's your fault. I'm answering letters. But I think that that may be the natural outcome of a diary. I'm not concerned about it because I have received other diaries; I have received letters that are like diaries; I have received very personal confessions and I have answered them. Perhaps that's the ultimate *raison* *d'être* of the diary: that it ceases to be a solitary occupation and becomes a universal work. Perhaps that's the way it should end. I still make entries but I don't write in it as much as I used to. Would you rather I didn't answer letters? (73-F)

I have talked about the continuity of the diary even though it takes different forms. At twenty it's different from thirty and at thirty it's different from at forty. And now it has changed again; this year it has become a correspondence with the world, and probably that is the right ending for a diary, that it would start as a river and then flow into an ocean and become an exchange of our more secret and private lives, which is what the letters which I answer are. So I'm not worried about the metamorphosis of the diary which has now become universal, in other words, which has become *our* diary. (72-G)

VII
The Artist as Magician

Sooner or later a magician is always asked the source of the magic which he practices. By what formulas, what words, what means did I acquire not only a sense of magic about life that nothing could destroy but also how was I able to impart it? How was it that when Goethe's *Werther* was published there was a rash of suicides, whereas when my diaries came out there was a rash of anti-suicides? How did all this happen? (73-K)

I remember that as children we were very unhappy because of great dissension between the parents. My father was a pianist and my mother was a singer. The quarrels would overwhelm and frighten us. But then suddenly there would be a quiet time. The piano would begin, my mother would begin to sing, and there would be peace again. And there would be great joy in the house, and the children felt free and they began to dance. This became for me a symbol and established a tremendous indebtedness and love for what I call the art spirits which we are celebrating today. That no matter what the human condition, no matter what kinds of infernos and destructive wars our dictators plunged us into, there was always this escape, this power to transfigure, transform, and transmute. (72-N)

I learned from this that in order to resist the sorrows of human experience we needed another world. Unfortunately our culture kept calling that world an escape, making it a most unvirtuous thing to do, to escape from the present. To escape from everything was really not taking part and not being involved in life. I don't understand how it happened but it was part of our ideology, and there was a great taboo on anybody who was able to move away from catastrophe. It wasn't realized that the moving away from catastrophe or trauma or ugliness or whatever monsters we encounter was *necessary* as an *anti-toxin*. We need anti-toxins, we need a place in which to recover our vision, we need a place in which to reconstruct ourselves after shattering experiences. I discovered that very early, and my magic was simply the power to move away from paralyzing, destructive experience.

First of all it took the form of reading. While my mother rented rooms, and I was running around with towels and doing all the things that I had to do, I always had a book, because that was a place where I really wanted to be. I learned to move, and the first process of growth is this movement away and towards something. But in our culture we made moving away a crime; we must stay put where we are. And therefore we created also a literature that said that things will remain as they are and nothing is changeable.

So this brings me to a whole set of magic words that I would like you to write down and to keep forever as formulas: the magic words are all in the dictionary under the prefix *trans* which means change or movement—transforming, transposing, transcending, translucent, transfiguring, transmitting. All the words that have the prefix *trans* are words which lead us out of the present, away from the painful, paralyzed spot in our lives. This is why when people say that I am favoring the artist, I respond that it is not that I favor the artist above other human beings, but that it is from artists that I learned to transmute. It was from musicians that I learned that in the midst of sorrows and war and dissidence, divorce and separation, music could carry you and sustain you and nourish you. This is what we must not forget, and which we did when we disparaged the necessity, the indispensable quality of art in our lives.

I don't know what happened, but we began to say that reading didn't help us to live, and music didn't help us to live, that the painter didn't help us to live. For a long time we really disparaged the artist. I know you haven't; this whole generation is trying to restore all those beliefs. I was speaking of the past, and we are entering a new period. But if you think of it, the real reasons for the suicide of Sylvia Plath are not the reasons that we are given when we study her life or her poetry. It was because she lacked the power to transcend the present and to see further than the moment of sorrow.

So this *trans—trans*mission, *trans*position, *trans*cendence—is vitally necessary not only to our human life, but also to our creativity. And creativity is so necessary to our human life because it shows us the capacity for change. At a certain moment in politics, when we feel hopeless and incapable of changing our outer realities, we must remember that; and it will in time produce human beings who will not create this infernal outer reality that we are traversing at this moment. But for that we have to believe that there is a transcendental truth, that our life is not composed of simply a crisis or a trauma or a terrible moment which makes us feel that we might have to disappear or drop out or forget everything. We have to believe that there is a continuity, that life has a continuance. And the artist is the one who taught me that. First of all the musicians taught me how to be consoled, how to be released from the present, so that you can gather your strength again or maintain the spiritual strength which is going to carry you through the inner journey. (73-K)

There is also the power of story-telling, and the whole magic of story-telling, which sustains your life so that you never succumb to the terrible despair of someone who cannot see beyond today's happenings. The magic of story-telling lies in the enjoyment of a flight of language that takes you into another realm. We enter the realm of poetry or art and discover the pleasure of possessing the skill to fly. Because I say the poet teaches us levitation, to fly a little above and transcend the things which usually drag us down into the completely pedestrian, completely entrapped life of everyday, or life completely trapped in history.

We have this marvelous power to escape, but it is not escape in the negative sense of the word. It is an escape similar to that of Olivier Messiaen, who while he was in a concentration camp, composed the wonderful piece for clarinet called "The Soul of a Bird." That's the kind of escape I mean. This composition probably helped him to survive that experience, and I can't imagine one more terrible than that. Whereas when people cannot look over the walls and do not have this story-telling power and perspective, have no separation from events, then disintegration takes place and we despair. We drop out or even commit suicide, like Sylvia Plath. When we have no capacity to look beyond the sorrow or the experience which strikes us, we give up and die. (73-B)

If you're negative, you're going to find causes for negativity. You will yourself build a case. Because we're very clever. We're much cleverer than we think we are. We build cases for our own moods. If you are convinced that you can't make it, and you want to drop out, you're going to find reasons for it. You can always build a case. There are all kinds of things lying around. But if you want to build a case for life being worth living then you build that too. (73-K)

It wasn't enough for me to weep every day because there was war. I felt that you had to create an antidote, you had to create another world, which was called escapism because those who escaped were hated. But you couldn't call "The Soul of a Bird" escape, yet that is what it was, the most beautiful poem of escape. It was proof that you cannot kill the spirit. In the midst of war and horror it was creating something in opposition to the horrors and monstrosities.

I have a friend, a painter, who often used to call me and say: "I've just read the papers and I can't paint anymore today; there are such horrible things happening in the world." And I would say to her: "Paint first and read the papers afterward." (72-N)

I always used art to put myself together again, and that is why I favored the artist, because I learned from him this creating out of nothing. I learned from Varda, who made collages out of bits of cloth. In fact, once he made me cut up the lining of my coat to make a collage, and it was certainly more beautiful as a collage than as just the lining of my coat. I learned from Tinguely who went to a junkyard and made a satire of the machine. I think you probably saw "The Machine that Committed Suicide" in the Museum of Modern Art. He took junk and made it into a parody of the machine: instead of putting the tops on bottles, it would break the bottle or it would commit suicide. Or he would create another satire of the machine and make us laugh at it. Varda also went to the junkyard, and from discarded boats made himself a beautiful Greek sailboat. This is the power to create out of nothing which we need to restore ourselves. On depressed days in New York I could go to the Metropolitan Museum of Art and look at the *Sun* by Lippold. Some of you must have seen this; it takes the whole room; it is actually more radiant than our natural sun. And, just sitting there and looking at the Lippold *Sun,* my melancholy would be dissipated. That is why I call the artist the magician, because he holds the anti-toxins to cure us when we are shattered, or when we are in a state of despair or sorrow about what is happening outside. Being able to create something out of clay, out of glass, out of bits of material, out of junkyards, out of anything is the proof of the creativity of man and the magic of art. (73-L)

I saw a book recently which greatly reinforced my faith in human nature and our innate creativity. It's called *Handmade Houses: A Guide To The Woodbutcher's Art,* by Art Boericke and Barry Shapiro, and it's a book with photographs about all the people who have built their own houses without the help of architects. The houses are perfectly beautiful and have all kinds of imaginative and natural shapes. Some of them are like fairytale houses and some fantastically original. The builders did everything they wanted and anything they wanted. One of them built a tea house suspended over a river in Oregon. The book is really worthwhile and shows the wonderful capacity to create which is in almost anyone. These people just took wood and built beautiful houses. (73-N)

So when we throw out the concept of aesthetics as not being democratic we're really depriving ourselves of the consolation and heightening of our lives, a healing power. If you are in a state of sorrow and a state of despondency or cut off, for example, and you suddenly see someone who is wearing something aesthetic, it does help. That is why it is a shame that we have cast this off as a luxury, as a symbol of some class distinction, for actually it doesn't cost money. It isn't a question of luxury, and I'm writing now in *Diary* V about artists that I have admired who created the most beautiful lives without money or with very little money. It isn't luxury, and it shouldn't be associated with class or privilege. I think it's something we have to create with our own hands, which a lot of the new generation are doing. Beautifying everything they can, touching everything with some work of the hand.

I think in that we are very close, this generation and I, close in the feeling I always had of wanting to transform rooms, trying to make them beautiful. Once I even wanted to take a parachute and design on the parachute the kind of surrounding I like to have and carry it around the world, to put in these ugly hotel rooms, hang it from the middle light. Just to have something beautiful around me, as with paintings. It was really the idea of beautifying the environment—in a very "kooky" way—but it was certainly the idea of carrying my environment with me so as to modify it and take away the sting and the corroding influence of ugliness. I really think of ugliness as a threat to our happiness. It depresses us, it diminishes us and makes us despondent.

It's so ironic, such a contradiction, that we're always looking for highs when the highs are right there in the things that delight the eyes. If a girl is wearing a dress that we enjoy looking at, then we are elated or if we see anything beautiful we are elated. We gave up all the natural ways of getting high and began to look for other ways of achieving it. But it is all possible and available to us right here in reality, even when our circumstances are difficult.

Of course the magician has to start very young and has to start practicing on himself. He has to have many failures and many experiments. As soon as I read Dumas, when I was about nine years old, I wanted to grow a black tulip. You remember in Dumas there is a black tulip. So I kept pouring ink and dyes on the roots. I finally achieved a dark tulip, not exactly black. Unfortunately, I didn't keep the formula. (73-K)

Children do that. Children are true to their creative instincts. They dance, they sing, they write poems. And then something happens in our education which shuts that off. I always had a feeling that it's there in all of us but that we have managed somehow to shut it off and that's why we had a whole generation addicted to drugs. (72-M)

If you've ever watched children as I have, you have seen what extraordinary things they can do, how spontaneous they are. Afterwards somehow this quality disappears, and it must be our culture that does it, because we don't encourage it. I remember a little girl who used to paint extraordinary things at the age of six and then was sent to a school where she was told to trace animals. She *traced* drawings instead of doing them freely. So I think we're all born with a lot of gifts that really disappear. (72-G)

I think some of us are deprived of the original gifts of books in the house which help us to discover creativity. But if a child has it anyway, even without cultured parents or artistic parents or helpful parents, then it must be innate.

I think the artist keeps that child in himself. And you can tell the childlike quality of a Picasso or a Varda, or many artists I've known. As Wallace Fowlie said: "The artist is the one who maintains the innocence of vision of a child, within his maturity." So in a way there is another answer to why we need the artist, why he's really indispensable. Because he does perpetuate this quality we have as children. But also he completes it. (73-N)

For through maturity, we gain something that the child never has, which is consciousness of *others'* struggles. We know when the other person is in trouble, and the child doesn't know that. The child is spontaneous, and he is free-associating, and he has all the freedoms that he wants but he really can't put himself in another's place. But after we have gone through all those struggles we begin to understand the people who haven't made it. And that comes with maturity. So we have something besides what the child has. We have the freedom and yet the sense of what other persons need. We have compassion for others, which is so important. We have a sense of where we've been, and we know our own history.

The first fraternity I knew was in the Bohemian life among the artists in France. If somebody couldn't pay his rent, the others helped him to move; if somebody was ill then everyone else would help; if someone sold a painting then everybody celebrated. It was the first fraternity I knew, and I've retained a kind of faith in it. Also it was universal: our fraternity in Paris consisted of a black Cuban artist who was a protegé of Picasso, a Japanese poet, an Armenian—every possible race, every possible nationality. And yet the tie was extraordinary. The bond was that we were writing, painting, composing, and that established a commune all by itself, a mutual sense of responsibility. That became an ideal for me, the fact that it was creativity that held us together. (72-D)

As a writer I wanted simply to take all the various expressions of art into writing, for I believed that each art must nourish the other, each one can add to the other. And I would take into writing what I learned from dancing, what I learned from music, what I learned from design, what I learned from architecture. In every form of art there is something that I wanted to include, and I wanted writing, poetic writing, to include them all. Because I thought always of art not only as a balm, as a consolation, but I thought of art, as I said, as a supreme act of magic. (73-L)

It's partly language, for language to me is like the discovery of a new world, really a new state of consciousness. A new word to me was a new sensation. Reading the dictionary, anything at all, can add not only to your knowledge but also to your perceptions. When I read about seals, I discovered a new color, which is a different color from the colors we know. The knowledge of flowers can generate a sensation or produce an extra sense. And language in itself can do a great deal to stimulate new perceptions.

I remember I used the word "rutilant," and the American critics all fell on me and said: "Why do you use such fancy words. Why not just say gold?" Well, rutilant isn't gold. It's red and gold mixed. So you see, you discover a word and that gives you a new perception too. We mustn't disparage the language and say: "Don't use the fancy words." That word meant exactly what I meant: gold and red mixed. Of course, that's a foreigner's advantage. As a foreigner, you explore the language because you don't take it for granted. You have to study it. So I made more discoveries, because it was new and I was driven on to find all the new words. And then you're amazed that people don't use them all. (72-I)

We forget that language can be used for many things, that it was used by primitive people as magic. It was used to enchant, it was used to seduce, it was used to make others feel what you feel. It was used for a million transmissions far more subtle than explicit direct statements. (72-M)

That's why I was so worried at one time about American literature, because we were one-dimensional and we were saying that the only way to communicate was to use clichés, to talk about the weather, to simplify our language, to make it plainer and homelier. You know that period, don't you, of stripping language of all shadings and rhythm and inspirational power. We really took the whole magic out of American literature because we were saying that we were getting closer to reality that way. But we were getting further and further away from it, and there was no rhythm. You remember that it took Jack Kerouac to restore jazz rhythm to writing. All the things that affect the senses, which we receive from writing at its best, were really put down at that moment when we were trying to simplify language so that we could understand each other. As if we were simple, assuming that we were that simple! (72-I)

Gaston Bachelard, the French philosopher, said something very touching. He said sometimes he thinks that what we have suffered from most is *silence*. The silence which surrounds our acts; the silence which surrounds our relationships; the things we cannot say, that we cannot tell others. There was a moment in America when I was afraid that people had decided never to read again, never to depend on literature, and never even to talk again. I was very troubled until I realized that what they objected to was babble and not talking together; what they objected to was a literature that didn't bring them life but abstractions. And therefore, for the novel not to die—for writing not to die—we had to return to the sources of life, which meant biography, which meant basing all happenings on truth, but not forgetting that art would then transform this truth into poetry. (73-L)

We have two distinct needs. One is a human need to be intimate with experience, to be very close to experience, to be as directly related to events as possible. And we think we satisfy that need through the media. I think that is an illusion, but there are people who do write letters and documents and the kind of journalism which gives that illusion of participation. Then there's a second need in human nature which is to create something that has more permanence, which is the myth of our lives, the symbolic, spiritual significance of our lives. And this we can only do with a word that I know you don't like to use but which is *art,* which is literature. The second step is to transform our experience through a well-crafted medium into something that has permanence for all times, articulateness for more than ourselves—so that it becomes timeless. Those are our two fundamental basic human needs. We need to corroborate the reality of our existence through intimacy, and we need also the myth because, as Malraux said, art was given to us so we could escape the human condition, so that we could see beyond it. (72-G)

We need the documentary; we need the psychological story; we need the knowledge of our daily life, the inner journey, which the diary can accomplish; but we also need the fiction because the fiction is the myth. And the one example I can give you where the diary has its limitations, and then the story takes over and tells you more is the incident of the rag-pickers. In the diary I described as a journalist would the rag-pickers who live on the outskirts of Paris. I told exactly what I saw—the shacks and the bags and the things laid out on the floor and how they lived, the children and the broken-down things, the objects they collected. But that is all

I could say. I could say exactly what I saw, but in the diary I couldn't go into what I saw later, when I started to write the short story. I saw the metaphor. I saw that the rag-pickers could be used as a metaphor for our wanting to throw out objects from the past and not being able to get rid of them, because the rag-picker picks them up and brings them back again. The rag-pickers symbolized the fact that we really can't throw out the past. So you see the fiction can reveal the myth behind experience and we need both. We need the myth, the poem, and then we also need this human document from which we get our contact with the self and with our inner life. (73-B)

Both expressions are necessary: the direct one which we call the documentary, the historical documentary of our lives, and the other, the transformation of that which gives us a perception which really helps us not to be *always* caught in our given condition, in the present, which gives us a perspective in history, the perspective of literature. That's a very consoling thing, and I think the loss of that, the fact that in American culture the literary or the artistic person was not valued, was the reason we got into trouble. Because there was nobody to tell us that our life had a transcendental meaning and a definite significance, that it wasn't just the daily routine we received on television. That other perception was missing because we wouldn't let the artist play his role. For that is his role: to lead us beyond the rather despairing and deadening routine of daily life. That's a role that our culture really denied for a long time. The poet didn't have prestige; a writer was not a prestigious person; literature was not valued. And even now the word "artist" is denigrated. (72-G)

For instance, when I mentioned the word at the Art Institute of Chicago, they objected to it; they have a prejudice against the word "artist." They say: "We are craftsmen." They don't want to say: "We're writers." I don't know where it comes from. I don't know its history, but I know that in this culture there is a disparaging and devaluation of the role of the artist in society, the artist as a useful member of society. (73-H)

We forget that in the ancient community of the Indians in Peru, the Incas, the poet had a very unusual position. He was half-prophet; he was the one who made them see beyond the daily burdens of existence. We lost that, we gave that up. It was only the political routine, the immediate, the so-called relevant that we thought was important, forgetting that in order to exist we really need another concept of existence or else we really do begin to despair. (72-G)

So I saw that the artist had to be a dedicated person, that he was not sure of worldly rewards, that he would have to wait, that he had the most difficult task of all, which is (as Otto Rank put it) to balance our two wishes: one, to stay close to others, and two, to create something which may alienate us from our culture. The artist is the one who has to risk the alienation, as I did for many years because what I was writing was not in the trend of that moment. I had to wait for many years for synchronicity between myself and the feelings, attitudes, and values of this generation. This waiting is difficult, but most writers will have to go through it. They have to separate themselves and, at the same time, understand and reflect their culture. They have to be contemporary and yet to see beyond. For it's in this moment that they begin to shape the future for us, the future of architecture or the future of music. This is the difficult moment when we sometimes repudiate them or disregard them or treat them with great indifference. But the artist persists because he has the will to create, and this is the magic power which can transform and transfigure and transpose and which will ultimately be transmitted to others. (73-L)

The writer, the artist, is *driven* in a way. As Rank said: The neurotic is the one who hides his dream from himself; the average man is the one who hides his dreams from others; the artist is the one who feels compelled to make his dreams public. He feels that somehow or other this is a self-justification for his creation, that he has to give it away. And that is why just writing my diary wasn't enough. It had to be given. (72-M)

Bachelard also said that what the artist has done is to make it possible for us to believe in the world, to love the world, and to create a world. And I really believe this because when I began the creation of the diaries, I never knew that I was creating a world which was an antithesis to the world around me which was full of sorrows, full of wars, full of difficulties. I was creating the world I wanted, and into this world, once it is created, you invite others and then you attract those who have affinities and this becomes a universe, this becomes not a private world at all but something which transcends the personal and creates the link. Bachelard says we suffer from silence; what the diaries did was to speak, and then you spoke to me in return. I receive diaries, I receive confessions, I receive letters, and then the dialogue is established, the exchanging of secret selves. So the universal link can be created by each artist when he really turns to his individual creation and is not afraid of ignoring the current fashion.

Each artist has to struggle not to conform to the culture but to add to the culture, to create the future. And if you read the life of da Vinci, you see how at each frustration, instead of becoming embittered, he would look for something else to study, another thing to develop. If he was frustrated in developing his revolving stage, which we still use today, then he would take up the study of birds and of flying. So he would move, and he learned and taught us to be ready to shift our ground, but always to go forward, never to despair.

When the artist starts out on his road it seems a lonely one, but he dares to follow it. And this daring is so important, this sense of adventure. Even by beginning a diary I was already conceding that life would be more bearable if I looked at it as an *adventure* and a tale. I was telling myself the story of a life, and this transmutes into an adventure the things which can shatter you. It becomes the mythical voyage which we all have to undertake—the inner voyage, the voyage, as in classical literature, through the labyrinth. And then you begin to look at events as challenges to your courage. I'm not saying that we all have to be heroes, but that we do have to complete the journey and believe that there is a way out of the labyrinth. (73-L)

Now I have a story I want to tell you because we are talking about magic and the necessity of magic. In 1970 I had a touch of cancer and I was given radiation at the Presbyterian Hospital in New York for two weeks—six minutes each day. And I found myself in this dirty yellow room with a huge and very ugly machine in the middle. It was absolutely frightening, like something out of science fiction. You have to lie on the bed and they make a little drawing on your body where the radiation has to strike, and worst of all the machine makes a terrible noise. So how was I going to deal with that? It was not so easy, but I decided that this machine was a projector and that I actually for six minutes was going to see the film of the loveliest, most happy and joyous days of my life. So as soon as the machine went on I closed my eyes and the film began, image after image of every place where I had been happy, every occasion, one after another. It was usually the sea and the beach and Tahiti and the south of France and Mexico. The landscape didn't change so very much but the situations did, and I was always choosing them. After six minutes when the noise stopped, the film would stop, and I would go home.

The only worry I had was that I wouldn't have enough film, but the automatic continuity of the images got so real that at one point I was seeing myself driving down the road in the south of France and I was about to turn to visit Durrell, in my recollection, when I stopped myself and said: "I don't think I want to go that way, because I didn't have a very happy visit; I think I'll go the other way." So it went on, and I did have enough film to last the two weeks, six minutes a day, and I was completely cured. Now I am absolutely convinced that I helped the whole thing psychically. That's what I call magic. Because I haven't had any difficulty since.

So I wanted you to know that there isn't any occasion, there isn't any situation, where the psychic force of life, the love of life, and its joyousness can't somehow transport us and transfigure an event into one which we can recollect with pleasure. Because it showed me that actually what I loved best was a natural life and that nature was the basic thing I wanted, because I never pictured a city and I didn't even picture myself writing. (73-K)

I have had friends who reproached me for my love of the artist, and they said: "Well, don't you love the non-artist too?" I said:

"Yes, but I give to the word artist a very broad meaning. For me an artist is whoever has creative will, whoever creates anything—a garden, or a child, or a friendship, or a life. (72-N)

So these are the anti-toxins; they are the thoughts that help us to take anything at all and create something of value. They can create beautiful cities; they can create, recreate what every child is born with, the capacity to write a poem, to dance or to paint, which somehow we seem to lose later on, but which we may now be finding again. And it is important for us to recognize that favoring the artist is simply favoring creation as against destruction. It is favoring the intention of the artist, the motivation as compared to other people's motivations, which are not always dedicated to something beyond themselves. Creation is something that will ultimately be given, and which needs to be given. For as Dr. Kuntz wrote so beautifully in *Art as Public Dream:* "Only if dreams are made public through art can they affect the nightmares we enact in everyday life." (73-L)

* * *

Q. I wonder if you found any special ingredients in the personalities of artists which are responsible for their becoming as unique and defined as they are and as well known, just as we hear of Jesus Christ more than any other name or we hear of Hitler. Whether it's destructive or creative, what gives these people the force to rise and become that well known all over the world? Is it, do you think, sometimes a narcissistic thing or some inadequacy which gives that person a natural drive to become that way, to think he is destined, to feel that he is a special messenger?

A. N. That is too long a question to answer, but I can say that you are putting the wrong thing first. The artist doesn't strive to be known; he does his work and sometimes he dies unknown and sometimes he dies famous. But that is not his orientation. You're making the fact of fame a voluntary desire or a select drive belonging to the artist. An enormous number of artists have died unknown, obscure and without fame.

Q. That's why I wonder what distinguishes the ones that do become well known from the others.

A. N. This has to do with the unfairness of the media. I don't even want to go into that. We select one artist rather than another, and sometimes we make very poor choices. That's all blindness, I think, and very often it takes us a hundred years to recognize the prophetic qualities of an artist. I would like to answer that question in another way. I always thought of the artist as having the capacity to alchemize and transform ordinary daily living, the human condition, into something else. He has what Rank calls the creative will and which I used to call creative stubbornness. I found in the artist more of the ability to be given dross and to turn it into gold. (73-B)

Q. Do writers then write only for themselves or do they write because they want an audience?

A. N. No, you don't write for yourself or for others. You write out of a deep inner necessity. If you are a writer, you have to write, just as you have to breathe, or if you're a singer you have to sing. But you're not aware of doing it for someone. This need to write was for me as strong as the need to live. I needed to live, but I also needed to record what I lived. It was a second life, it was my way of living in a more heightened way. So there you might say you do it for yourself, but then what difference does that make? You are a part of me and I am a part of you. So you're also doing it for others. (73-I)

Q. What do you think is the function of art for society? You seem to suggest that it is a kind of therapy for the artist.

A. N. No. No, I didn't say that.

Q. Well, what more is it than just the response that the artist has, his personal need to create?

A. N. I don't think the artist creates because he has a need to create in that sense. I think the artist creates because he hopes to communicate with the world, to reach what I call the oceanic level and to achieve a universal communication, in whatever way he can and by whatever skill he has. I don't think that therapy is involved in this. The fact that we do something because we need to doesn't mean that it's therapeutic.

Q. Are we limited to art as a means of perceiving the deeper reality?

A. N. No, we're not. The artist helps because he dedicates his life to the craft that is going to enable him to express the deeper reality for you. Just as the violinist who learns to play the violin is doing it for you, so the writer is always trying to become more articulate. He's dedicating all his time to that. We have other ways too. We have religion, we have philosophy, we have a million ways to give our lives another dimension.

Q. Is there something though in the daily life that could be used as a way of escaping?

A. N. *Not escaping! Not escaping!* That was a word that we used to condemn the process with. That's the word used by the *enemy*. There is a difference between escaping and transcending.

Q. But is there not anything in our daily life itself that would help us transcend what we consider the meaninglessness of that life, other than philosophy or religion or art?

A. N. If we had no sense of its meaning at all? One of the terrible problems that the students had—not in your generation but in the generation before—was saying that life had no meaning at all. That it was absurd, that what was happening in the world was meaningless, that their personal life was meaningless. But that was because they could not see beyond the facts of daily life. In other words, we need something that gives life its meaning or rather reveals its meaning. The meaning is there, in human life, but we need the revelation of that meaning.

Q. Is its meaning absolute or universal or is it individual?

A. N. I think it's individual, and in the end the individual becomes the collective. It's the same thing. You are both collective and the individual. The two merge. Now the role of the artist is a difficult one because he is supposed to stay close and intimate with his time but he's also obliged to see beyond it, and sometimes he will create something that we're not ready for. His vision is long-sighted; and we've had trouble with him because sometimes he has seen a little further than we have, into the future as in science fiction. I was brought up on Jules Verne, and I thought his was merely a world of imagination but he was always inventing things that came true. So sometimes we get into trouble with the artist because he lives counter to the current, to the average current.

Q. But then we're also very often confronted with the artist whose long-sighted views don't materialize.

A. N. That's a negative point of view. The scientist has made errors too, you know. Sometimes he doesn't foresee what will happen in the future and doesn't plan for it. We have all made errors. We all have our blind spots, not only the artist. And it is more difficult for the artist sometimes because he *does* have a vision. For example, suppose I had submitted to the culture and the thinking of the forties, which I was tremendously against. Suppose I had given in and yielded and become the kind of writer that they were shaping then. I wouldn't have had to wait twenty years for recognition, I could have gone along with the stream. But then I would not have forecast in some way what your consciousness is today. We wouldn't have met at some point or other. The fact that it is twenty years later doesn't really matter. You see if all the writers give in to their period and become absolutely like their period then we would never have the writer that we need, the one who provides another state of consciousness. (72-G)

Q. You emphasize the subjective character of art. But do you think it's possible to create something objectively?

A. N. What do I think about the artist who does not put himself into his creation? We have found that's often true; I mean in abstract art, for example. But the self is still there. Even the creation of an abstraction is a quintessence of some kind of vision, which is individual. So we always come back really to the vision of the artist being personal. That it doesn't show in the final work doesn't mean anything. The fact is that there is still a person behind the abstraction. The artist is the one who makes his dream public, and whether it takes an abstract form as in science or in painting doesn't matter. It still comes from a personal vision. And if the vision is poor he won't see anything at all.

Q. What I mean is that your diary, for example, I would regard as a direct expression of yourself, and what I'm wondering is if it's just as possible to create something without putting your personal self into it?

A. N. Oh yes, I'm not saying everybody should produce only diaries—I don't mean that. I mean that the diary can serve as a contact with yourself and ultimately with others. It can be a useful thing apart from its literary value, its art value. It depends on what you are seeking. If you're seeking an objective expression, that's fine too. We have objective expression by people in science, we have it in all kinds of occupations and professions, and certainly in the abstract arts.

Q. I'm thinking that you can learn about yourself and achieve the same product by not expressing yourself.

A. N. Now you're questioning the value of the personal experience as against the objective experience. Is that what you're saying? You didn't quite see what I meant. I said that we needed the personal experience because our world has become too objective, too scientific, and too technological, and that we're swimming in abstractions. What I said, and evidently you didn't quite feel it, was that it is necessary to have a personal life. Whether you express it in your art or not doesn't matter. It's necessary to have it because we live in too abstract a world.

Q. I agree with that. I was thinking that it is possible to create from an objective rather than a subjective self.

A. N. I don't think you're making your question very clear. Do you mean a separation from the self and a purely objective self who refuses to look in? Is that what you mean?

Q. No, I mean that you can make something which is an artistically, a creatively valuable object, which does not contain your inner self.

A. N. Well, let's leave that to the art critics, the value and possibility of purely objective art. (73-E)

Q. Presently we seem to want to make such a distinction between the novel as a strictly fictional form and autobiography as strictly a personal form. Do you think that in the novel of the future we will overcome this distinction?

A. N. Yes, I hope so. I hope that they will weld so that our fiction won't be so unbelievable, so one-dimensional, so psychologically unreal. I make such a distinction also between the reality of the realistic novel and the psychological reality of certain novels or certain films. If they come a little closer, then we will be able to read fiction again, if we know that fiction is rooted in psychological reality. So many of our so-called realistic novels are absolutely impossible, because they are simply not believable. They are psychologically *unrealistic*. (72-W)

Q. What made you transfer from writing the diary to novels?

A. N. There was always a writer there who wanted to face the world with her craft, and the diary, I thought, was something which had to be kept secret forever and not something I could give. Whereas the neurotic is the one who wants to keep his dreams hidden from himself and the normal person is the one who wants to keep his dreams hidden from others, the artist is the one who is driven to make his dreams public. So somewhere I had to find a way of speaking to you, which was fiction, because I felt the diary could not be given. I didn't know how to solve the problem of keeping the secrets that people had confided in me and how not to break through ethical rules. I didn't know at the time how to solve that and so I thought it would only be published after my death. (73-F)

Q. When you read now, are you attracted to novels, to fiction, or to journals or diaries?

A. N. I am more attracted to biography. But I think there is a trend in the novel now which is trying to approximate the diary, trying to get back to the basic reality of experience. The novel is imitating the diary, is trying to come nearer to biography in order to be revitalized. It had gotten so far away from life that it didn't mean anything.

Q. That's interesting. Your critics accuse you of being romantic, of living in an ivory tower, of being removed from life, and yet you are saying that you are attracted to those novels which resemble biography because they really do get close to life.

A. N. The apparent contradiction comes from the critics who labeled me as very far away from life. I wasn't far away at all. I was like Cousteau, at a level like the bottom of the sea, where they couldn't follow.

Q. In the *Diary* you refer to Dali appearing at a lecture in a diver's suit.

A. N. I was very amused by that. He did not explain it, and I interpreted it to mean that the artist had to live in another atmosphere which very often the critics couldn't enter.

Q. This is similar to Varda's saying that the artist essentially wants to recreate water. Going into that watery existence, then, whether it is Dali or Varda or yourself, is an important act.

A. N. Yes, water is the origin of birth and water has always symbolized the unconscious. The artist must always find his roots in that. And it is this which has created the misunderstanding, with critics calling my work far away from life because these depths do not resemble the reality in which they live. (72-Y)

Q. Do you think types of novels are related to cultural values and attitudes?

A. N. Yes. At some point in our culture the individual became almost taboo. Europe went the other way. When the war came they had psychological writers like Proust, but they had no writers for violence, no writers for action, no writers to face the mystery of war. And so they turned to American literature. Sartre wrote an essay on the subject—at what point France became dependent on American literature because American literature could deal with action and war. That's the time when they began to read Hemingway. They turned to American literature. The French read more of it because they reached as far as you could go in subjectivity. We reached as far as one could go in the novel of action, up to the point where there is no pause for reflection, because action is a speeded-up thing. Neither one is right, neither extreme is right. We couldn't live with Proust today. We couldn't read or live by Proust. Neither the rhythm nor the completely subjective aspect of his writing would appeal to us.

Q. What about a writer such as Céline who is said to have influenced several American contemporary writers. What is your opinion of him? Has he influenced American writers or is this just a myth?

A. N. No, he has influenced American writers. He influenced

Henry Miller, and he was almost the first of the down-to-earth French writers. He was a doctor among the poor, but Céline was not as strong even in his own way as the American novelists. He was still more an intellectual than a man of action. (72-W)

Q. In the third *Diary* you talked about your feeling that American poetry was becoming very dry and prose-like, in contrast to the poetry of France and Spain. I was wondering if you still feel that way?

A. N. I can't deny what I said, but I can say that's no longer true. That was a one-dimensional period, and I felt that the poets were trying to be prose writers. We always made a distinction: that prose was pedestrian and poetry was levitation. I didn't feel that poetry at that time was levitating. Today that is changing again.

Q. I know you don't want to hurt any of your friends' feelings, but are there any poets that you remember reading in, say, the last ten years who are levitating?

A. N. I really cannot speak for poetry because my specialty was trying to win the poets over into prose and trying to win the novel over to poetry. I became almost a specialist on prose poems. I was really moving away from poetry because I wanted the poets to write the novels. In *The Novel of the Future* I mentioned all the writers that I thought were combining the two dimensions: the levitation of poetry and imagery of the unconscious and also the other, the action and consciousness of prose. I mentioned William Goyen, who for years has been out of print. All the writers I mentioned, everybody complained, were out of print. But they're all in print again, which is very significant. William Goyen is being reprinted, and Anna Kavan has just been rediscovered. I had found her in the thirties and now she has a recent book called *Ice*. I mentioned Nathanael West, who I didn't know at the time had been in France and had been influenced by the surrealists. He was a writer I always liked, for he had, I think, several dimensions.

Q. Do you think a poet could also bring music into poetry?

A. N. Yes they do. I have no specific poem in mind. I don't read them as much, and I don't study them. But the poet always had music, except when there was a period of making poetry into prose. That is what worried me at the time. They were making poetry very, very pedestrian. Poets were refusing the metamorphosis. They refused to transform, transfigure, transcend, to make their poems symbolic. But that's over.

Q. When you and Henry Miller and some others were writing erotica for the private collectors, and Miller insisted that you should cut out the elaborate poetry, did that produce a kind of mental cramp?

A. N. No. I really didn't succeed in cutting out the poetry, and after a while I wasn't given any more to do.

Q. What ever happened to it?

A. N. Well, it's there, you know. We talked about it in the women's movement because we were saying that erotica written by a woman would be very different from erotic writing by a man. I did about a thousand pages, and they are there. They're unpublished, but I gave a few samples of it away in the *Diary* to show that it was very different from Miller's or from other male writers'. But we may come back to that kind of writing because I make a distinction between erotic writing which is beautiful and which is as poetic as can be and pornography. I think that they should be distinguished, and there is no reason why we shouldn't return to the *art* of erotic writing. The Europeans had a great tradition of it, and it was their best writers who did it. In our culture it was the worst writers who did it. Here it was a degraded thing, whereas in France very good writers enjoyed doing it. They always did that as a part of the game. So we had some very good erotic literature, beautifully written, and really wonderful to read.

Q. I think that might be because you didn't have that Puritan ethic and taboo against sexuality.

A. N. Right. There was no taboo on it. The culture didn't look down on erotic literature, and so there was no shame involved. But here there was always that derogatory downgrading of the sexual. So when writers wrote about sex they did it in that sense too. It was something that they themselves looked down on. (72-G)

Q. Do you think that in the novel of the future the novelist will be a character rather than the outside observer or objective narrator?

A. N. Like *Rashomon,* you remember *Rashomon,* the Japanese film? Well, if you look at it very honestly, there is no objective point of view; there's always only one person's point of view. The historian and the philosopher can make the links between various perspectives and in that way objectify them, but the experience is subjective. That is what we have not been willing really to admit, that each one of us does see the world differently, and that if we cared more about what makes the individual lens, what causes the differences of lens, we really could understand each other much better. But we don't want to do that. We want to pretend that there is one objective story. There isn't. The historian and the philosopher can take these elements and say in such a period, at such an age, individuals had certain interests in common and it meant this and that—the psychology of movements and the philosophy of ideas and currents. But they come from basically subjective experiences. I think we read subjectively, we judge films subjectively. If we are really honest there is no objectivity. (72-W)

Q. What do you think of the writing of James Joyce?

A. N. I never enjoyed James Joyce very much, even though I know it was multi-language. It was a tour de force and it was skillful, but I thought it was a sort of cerebral unconscious. It didn't give me the feeling of an authentic, oceanic, free association of images. It was a scholar's fantasy, and it didn't appeal to me as much as what I call a genuine flow. It was an intellectual and scholarly work, but somehow it didn't seem to me like the real flow of the unconscious. I also felt that way about the surrealists, that many of the things they did were consciously and self-consciously surrealistic. We were always trying to figure out whether Dali was a genuine madman or a simulated one. It was part of the theory of dadaism, you know, to do absurd things. But I think Rousseau provides a much more authentic depiction of unconscious things than Dali, much closer to our dreams than a Dali dream. (72-D)

Q. How do you feel about the absurd playwrights, who just show

the futility of life and depict the dreams people will have, and how
they try to rebuild them but that they never can?
A. N. Well, there are a lot of writers like that, and I don't enjoy
them. I know Beckett is a very talented man, but I don't enjoy
reading him because he is always writing about death. He is always
writing about death and the negative side of life. No, I can't say
that I'm attracted to them. I know some of them are great, very
great geniuses. Ionesco is less negative than Beckett in a way, although he has the same kind of lack of faith. (73-K)
Q. In 1947, in your essay *On Writing,* you wrote about what you
called the collective neurosis of society and expressed your fear
that the authors of your time would not be able to transcend it. Do
you still feel that way?
A. N. I think we're still struggling with that, yes. But we're very
aware of it now. We weren't so aware at that time. Any artist of
that time who even wrote about neurosis would be taught as a psy-
chotic instead of as an interpreter who was reflecting what was
happening to society. Today we know that the neurotic type which
kept coming up in literature was a forewarning, was prophetic of
what we finally suffered, which was a collective neurosis. The difference is that we now are aware of it. I think we are fully aware
of it, and that's why we have made a sort of philosophy of psychology, the broad use of psychology in order to get ourselves out of
this. We had to come out of the collective neurosis, but we also
had to recognize that when a writer defined these things it wasn't
because he himself was necessarily very sick, as people felt about
Tennessee Williams. As he himself said: "Whenever you touch on
their illness, they turn against you." When a writer like that was
trying to forewarn and tell us about the anxieties we would have,
the fears with the bomb, with all the things that were happening,
he was trying to prepare us, but we really didn't listen. We didn't
think of reinforcing the center. We thought of having bomb shel-
ters! It was always outside, we always believed that the danger was
outside. We never thought of the danger of being psychically
shattered. (72-M)
Q. Earlier you were speaking of the interest the young have taken

in Hermann Hesse. Did he have any influence on your own work?
A. N. I must confess I read him very late, and that he did not
have an influence. It was a recognition of a similar route, if you
wish, if you eliminate the interest in the East, which I didn't have,
or the interest in Eastern philosophy. But he is not the one who influenced my work directly and vitally. I read him very, very late—
only a few years ago.
Q. Could you say something more about your relationship to
Artaud and how you felt about him and his art?
A. N. I felt an understanding of Artaud's visions, hallucinations,
his moments of madness as well as his moments of genius. Unfortunately you don't know enough about his work because the seven
volumes which he did intermittently between madness—just as
Virginia Woolf did her work intermittently—are not translated
into English. I'm afraid you have received a rather one-sided impression of Artaud even though he has had a great influence on the
theater, and had very prophetic things to say about the theater,
about films. Also about poetry. His correspondence is interesting,
his whole life. And there is a book by Bettina Knapp which will
give you the total life of Artaud and an understanding of him.

Now, I had an ambivalent feeling in the diary about the artists
who went beyond the margin of human life, who lost their contact
with human life. He says in the diary at one point, "There's a moment when I feel absolute loss of contact with human beings." This
kind of madness always gave me anxiety, because it's something
we're always very near to; it could happen to any of us. And so I
had a confused mixture of compassion and fear of what had happened to him. I didn't want that. I didn't want to lose my footing.
I didn't want to become a mad genius. And when I see an artist
who does not link his art with humanity, I'm very troubled. (73-G)
Q. Do you have any opinion concerning what it was that created
the atmosphere in Paris in the thirties which was so conducive to
artistic achievement and collaboration?
A. N. France had a great freedom of expression, encouraged orig-
inality, the individual creations. It had extremely literate and intelligent critics, an absence of commercial competitiveness, and a

tradition of fraternity among artists. Thus it attracted artists from all over the world, and created a magnetic center for them.

Q. The surrealists were active in Paris at that time.

A. N. I know many of the surrealists: Breton, Artaud, Ernst. But I do not subscribe to it as dogma. I have used surrealist techniques whenever I have tried to describe subtle reveries, dreams, states of feeling; in other words, when not describing action. (69-A)

Q. How would you define your relationship to surrealism?

A. N. Even though I never joined the surrealist group in the thirties, surrealism was a part of the very air we breathed. Everything was surrealistic—all the paintings we saw, all the films. In a sense my writing is surrealistic only insofar as it is concerned with superimposition, with life experienced on a multiplicity of levels. I didn't use surrealistic techniques all the time, and the surrealists didn't believe in the novel anyway. But I recognize how important the influence was, above all the emphasis on dreams which inspired *House of Incest,* and the great necessity, as Breton said, of rediscovering love. (73-M)

Q. If you had never heard of surrealism, would you have done the same thing?

A. N. When I was twenty, I was doing it. But surrealism gave me a focus, a certitude. (69-A)

Q. In the *Diary* you frequently mention Marcel Proust. Has his work influenced your writing?

A. N. Proust was very important; he was the first one to show me how to break down chronology (which I never like) and to follow the dictates and intuitions of memory, of feeling memory, so that you only wrote about experience when you *felt* it, not necessarily when it happened. And of course this element became very strong in my work. But there were also other influences. I wanted to write a poetic novel, and for that I chose models like Giraudoux, Pierre Jean-Jouve, and Djuna Barnes, an American writer, author of *Nightwood.* Later on it was D. H. Lawrence. Lawrence showed me the way to find a language for emotion, for instinct, for ambivalence, for intuition. (73-M)

Q. In your writing I notice a particular absence of the sordid or

violent or particularly ugly aspects of life or experiences. I was wondering if this means you feel there are less magical possibilities in these aspects and whether you have deliberately left them out?
A. N. In this case it depends what our destiny has been, where we we were put as a child, what kind of childhood we had. It just happened that I was not given very much of the sordid and ugly experience. I did have a few ugly experiences connected with poverty, being a foreigner in America, my mother not knowing how to earn a living—problems of that kind. But I didn't have the experience of a Dahlberg or a Henry Miller, or a Mailer. I didn't experience violence. So they are not *left out* of the diary, they just weren't there. It wasn't any deliberate selection of experience.

Many students have told me about being born into terribly difficult childhoods and one of my best friends in the *Diary,* if you remember, was Frances whose father was a taxi driver. There were six children, and they were always hungry. She was my closest friend, and we were always amazed at the difference in our backgrounds and yet how we arrived at the same place. She turned out to be a very fine and very sensitive artist, and we're still very close friends. I think we do have terribly toxic and destructive experiences but the main thing we have to focus on is how are we going to transform them so that they don't damage us.

Any experience can be damaging; if you want to take it that way, things like the separation of parents and the uprooting of a child's life can be fatal experiences. You're thrown forcibly into yourself and sometimes you stay there, you can't come out. So while there wasn't any selection of experiences, there was a constant effort to transform what had been destructive into something else. In other words, I wrote the novel about my father to exorcise him because that was a bad influence on me. I would have spent my whole life looking for surrogate fathers, and I would have been very much enslaved by the educator or the professor or the psychiatrist or whoever represented the figure of the father.

Some of us have had very terrible and violent experiences, but I don't think that's a reason for becoming destructive and paying society back with the same coin. I think we have to go through this process of alchemy so that even the horrible things we have experienced are transformed into creative experiences. I think we can transform almost anything, but some writers in America have felt that, since that was their experience of childhood, all of us must *remain there* and not evolve from it. I wanted always to get out of it; if there was something sordid and something difficult, I wanted out of it.

Q. The birth story certainly is about an awful experience, but it's beautifully written.

A. N. Yes, that's why a friend of mine almost lost her job as a teacher in a high school in New York, a school of industrial design for children who cannot go to college but who are especially gifted and will go from there to professions. She almost lost her job because she taught the birth story, and the parents came and protested. But she said: "Well, it's a shame that you should object to the birth story told by an artist when your children are going to go around the corner and read about the same thing in some vulgar magazine. You should be happy that they should receive it in this form, which is with a spiritual meaning attached to it, which, even if tragic, is not ugly, which is made part of our experience and given a meaning." So finally they did see that. It is the expression of it that is important. That could be *made ugly*. If you want to make it ugly with no meaning, then you emphasize only the physical details, the horror and all. You could make it ugly. You can make anything ugly. (73-K)

Q. What is your attitude toward the modern novel of violence and the so-called "cult of ugliness"?

A. N. This is part of the negative, destructive experience of our times. But there is a duality at work. Some of the new and middle generation of artists are working to defeat this through a new awareness.

Q. The use of "gutter language," as you called it, how do you feel about that?

A. N. In some instances, when it's natural, organic and part of the experience, it may be justified. But often it is a deliberately offensive and aggressive act. And it is insincere. I do not believe it will take the place of articulate speech. It is a limited form of expression.

Q. How do you account for the prevalence of this phenomenon in so much writing today?

A. N. Commercialism, for one thing; then catering to the illiterate. Among certain poets, it's a rebellion against traditional literature which used language removed from the people. It's a perversion of the democratic idea.

Q. In your *Diary,* you wrote that your teacher sent you to buy popular magazines in the candy store so you might study so-called colloquial speech because your use of words was too eloquent, and that this led to your decision to quit school altogether.

A. N. From the very first, I waged war against the impoverishment of language. I refused to adopt colloquialisms when they were not part of the work or unnatural to me. (69-A)

Q. Do you think the film is going to influence the novel?

A. N. I think there is a mutual influence. A lot of writers have become worried about writing disappearing altogether and having films in the libraries instead of writing. But what will happen, I think, is that the novel will come closer to the film. It will have less space-filling descriptions and reduce dialogue to essential talk, not talk just to fill time as there is in many novels but talk that is essentially important to the relationship. Also the films have brought us back to the importance of the image and the study of dreams, which is also now being done by scientists and is being treated with great respect by them. Before, it was limited to the psychological, and was regarded as esoteric.

But today scientists are saying that dreams have achieved respectability. They said, at U.C.L.A., that we needed to dream to be healthy human beings, and they now are admitting that this is a very natural activity.

Now the dream and the film resemble each other very strongly, and I think they are already mutually influencing each other. I think Fellini's *8½* is like one long dream, and also some of the films of Bergman. We are admitting now that we do think unconsciously in terms of images and that symbolism and images were not only part of the romantic movement but are a part of our makeup, since we are still dreaming in symbols despite our scientific period. So I think novels will join the film. They will be shorter like the integrated circuits. They will be much smaller and contain only the essential, I hope, in contrast to the method in the old novel, of putting in all the furniture whether you need it or not. They will compare to the modern theater which gives you only the elements that are part of the drama, instead of recording everything that was said. For, most of the time, what we say is to mask our feelings rather than to reveal something. When we are making a film we are forced to reduce dialogue to its essential, and that's what I hope will happen with the novel. (72-W)

Q. What might be some of the problems in translating your work into film?

A. N. I think my work is very well suited to film as we had intended film to be, which is to picture the inner life, the fantasy, the dream. But until they actually handle films in that way, it would be very difficult to do my books.

Q. Are there any contemporary films which correspond to your idea of cinema as an art form?

A. N. Yes. There is a film called *A Safe Place* by Henry Jaglom in which all levels are exposed simultaneously; it wasn't easy to understand but I loved it. It had a magical quality. I also felt the recent film of *Women In Love* was faithful to the ambiguities and ambivalences of Lawrence. (73-M)

Q. I would like to hear you discuss some of the more practical aspects of plotting, planning, and structuring novels, the process you go through.

A. N. I always answer that by saying that I was *born modern*. Because I left school very early, I had very little initial training. I became self-taught and I read a great deal, but I didn't know the discipline of the novel. I never learned about the form of anything. So I went my own way. My own way happened to be the way of the poet. My novels would begin always the way a poem starts for you, one line which was an image, and I wouldn't even know where I was going from there. The only concrete roots I would have for a novel were that I would take a character that I knew, usually someone from the diary, who would then, in the process of fictionalizing, become composite and would change and would no longer be the person I started with. (73-B)

Q. You often use psychological rather than chronological time. Do you do this consciously?

A. N. I am aware of this but I do not do it consciously, in the sense of "intellectually." It is the *rêve éveillé*. Selectivity, evaluation—these are secondary steps. There is a difference between consciousness and awareness. Awareness is a welding of intuition, observation, enlightenment arrived at through years of work, through discipline of the spirit.

Q. Which other writers deal with time in that way?

A. N. It was Proust who made a tremendous contribution here. He said that reality was in what we felt rather than in exterior events. A good example of this is in the sequence in which he does not feel the death of his grandmother until a long time after the event. There is a chronology of emotion, of memory. Giraudoux also was aware of this breaking down of chronology.

Q. You seem to have an affinity for French writers. Do you consider yourself an American writer, or what?

A. N. No. I consider myself an international writer. I like to think of myself as among those who transcend region, nation—who are universal.

Q. Has anyone but me ever told you that your style sometimes resembles the Poe of "A Dream Within A Dream" or "Eleanor"?

A. N. No. But it's interesting because the symbolists, Mallarmé and Baudelaire, translated Poe into French long before Americans began to appreciate him. Rimbaud knew his work and was influenced by it, as were other forerunners of surrealism. Rimbaud's *Illuminations* influenced what I did in *House of Incest.*

Q. Henry Miller was writing *Into The Night Life* at the time you wrote *House of Incest,* was he not?

A. N. Yes. We were in Paris. A certain similarity exists between these works. (69-A)

Q. I don't know if this is a question, but it's about two things that you said. One about imagery first coming from the unconscious and everyone having it, but that you then had to put that in perspective. You said you had an obsession with words and with language and that pushed you to make yourself a tool with which you could make something out of your unconscious. I wonder if you could tell me more about that.

A. N. Well, the two are necessary. For instance, the only thing I have against the great many students who write poetry today is the feeling they have that everything that comes from the unconscious is interesting, indiscriminately, that it doesn't need to be polished, that it doesn't need to be disciplined, that it doesn't need to be edited. This is what I call the slovenly school, for I really don't believe that. I do think that the craftsman must come in at a certain moment. There has to be a freedom of flow absolutely unimpeded by the critical mind, but the second stage is the disciplined craftsman who says: this part is unfocused, this is trivial, this is unimportant, this hasn't been finally said; no, this is not born yet. It's like some of the questions last night which had no clarity and no focus.

So I think that the two processes are necessary, letting the unconscious flow but then knowing how to select what is significant, important, or meaningful. I have a friend who dictated into a tape recorder for days and days and days and days and came out with six hundred pages of everything that went through his mind, and he thought that this was authentic stream of consciousness. But it was both meaningless and valueless many times. It needed a form. It needed editing. That is really where the craftsman, where the artist comes in. And then sometimes by editing, the pattern which isn't clear becomes clear, just as in editing a film. It's very much the process of editing a film, where the editing *is* the emphasis. Without that you would just have a lot of formless, absolutely meaningless material. We need the focus, and the focus of course can be very faithful or sincere. That is, when you follow the unconscious, the unconscious forms patterns, very very rigid patterns, itself. So when you finish writing a spontaneous poem or a spontaneous novel you see a pattern. It emerges at the end. You don't see it at the beginning but at the end. There it is. So then you can edit with integrity to maintain this pattern, this thing that came through.

Q. Can you see the pattern when you're half-way through it at all?

A. N. No, you really don't, you really don't see it until it's all there. It's almost like doing a collage, the way Varda said he made his collages. He cut little pieces of material and then he pinned them here and there; he didn't know quite what it was going to turn out to be. But then suddenly he would see a woman and a house and a castle or a flag. You don't know quite where you're going, but at the end you see it does form a pattern.

Q. Then when you get to the end do you have to go back and edit all the way through?

A. N. Then you have to edit, yes. Then you find the parts that don't belong or that are foggy, where the language failed.

Q. When the pattern becomes obvious is that the end then, like looking at a book of collages?

A. N. Yes. When I finished *Seduction of the Minotaur*, I ended with a definition of "tropic," which was change, and then I realized that there it was, that was the meaning of the book. It's the opposite of control, of imposing a meaning. Of course we don't know what went into my imagination, memory, what programming went into my writing the novel. We don't know what subterranean nourishment created that particular pattern. That's too much for us to track down. I could say, in the case of *Seduction,* that trips to Mexico led to the creation of Lillian, and the association of the character with a place, but I didn't know what the theme of the book was going to be.

Q. Is there a time when the thing jells and you know you're ready to write it? Is that how you pace yourself?

A. N. Yes, for example, let's take the book *Collages* which is typical of that. *Collages* was inspired by seeing Varda work with his little bits of material. I began to think about the people that I knew in Los Angeles and they suddenly formed a pattern of dreamers. They were all absolutely possessed by some myth or some dream so I put them all together with others not from Los

Angeles, like Nina de la Primavera who was a sort of Ophelia and a woman who fabulated. I put them all together and that formed a collage of dreamers who couldn't possibly talk to each other because each one was pursuing his own fantasy. So they were like little pieces in a collage. They never absolutely could meet each other, but each one was completely possessed by a different kind of fantasy. I had the Japanese woman, and Varda also was one of the characters, creating his own world. When I started I couldn't see any design or pattern or anything. But then I suddenly realized that the pattern and theme was a collage. (72-D)

Q. What do you say to people who say that writing is a lot of hard work? It seems to me you have emphasized the joy of writing and the almost therapeutic effect it has on you as a person. Would you say that your better writing was done under strenuous or under relaxed conditions?

A. N. When I was working on the diary I had the sense that I was free, whereas when I would sit down and say I am starting a novel I would be, like so many others, completely paralyzed by fear, by stage fright. That, I might say, was painful. But after awhile I resolved to allow the novel to nourish the diary and the diary to nourish the novel. To overcome the fear of the formal novel or facing the world with a formal work, I would take characters sometimes out of the diary and start from there and that would help me overcome this fear of starting the novel, and then I would go on. But every craft is difficult. I am not saying that writing is easy. Every craft which becomes a skill you want to improve on, and I did want to improve my writing. Even at the age of eleven when I made my first description of arrival in New York I said: "I must rewrite this; I didn't tell it well enough." So there already was a concern with telling it well which you might say was the beginning of the artist's concern with expression. (73-B)

Q. Do you continue, as before, to support artists?

A. N. In America today it hasn't been so necessary, it isn't so acute. But in me responsibility for the artist is still very strong. The feeling of responsibility is due to what John Pearson said yesterday: "Why don't we pay the poet instead of the analyst twenty-five dollars an hour?" In Europe the artist was more trusted, and there was always the café form of life he could turn to. The café was always the life-saving thing. An artist knew that if he turned up at the café in the evening he would find a friend who would pay for a dinner. There was always a place where he could go to if he was down. And yet in spite of that many artists in France died of starvation or loneliness. When they got ill and stayed in their little room, nobody knew what was happening to them. Satie was one of them and the Peruvian poet Vallejo was another. His friends didn't know he was ill because he didn't come to the café. We didn't know that he was slowly starving to death. So it happened right among us and we didn't know it. My sense of responsibility for the artist derives from the fact that my father was an artist, and somehow I feel that terrible sense of responsibility for the one who is creating—as long as he is creating. When I find someone struggling to create it arouses my protectiveness. (72-D)

Q. I have found that you have always been more than generous to young writers. You've always been terribly excited and supportive of them, young writers, young painters. Have you ever encountered people who say to you: "We don't know if they're artists yet, they're not seasoned; there aren't any standards to judge them"?

A. N. Yes. But my response may come from the feminine feeling for something which is *being* born, the care for something which is in the process of growing, whether or not it may prove successful. You know many of my "children" did not become the greatest artists, the greatest writers in the world. But then greater critics have also made mistakes.

Q. How do you think you know when something is a fine work of art?

A. N. That's difficult. I've made mistakes.

Q. Well, of course. But what I'm really asking is, what moves you or what is it that you look for, that you respond to? What are the qualities that seem important to you, though I know that you are not going to impose them on someone else?

A. N. Usually with young writers, I am less concerned with the craft than I am with their attitude, their humanism, their humanity. I prefer that to the slick cerebral writing because I find that those have more of a chance to contribute something to human experience. So I am not so severe with craft because I think that the craft gets molded by the meaning and the intention after a while. If I were a teacher I would not be concerned immediately with craft. I would be more concerned about their attitude, whether they listen, whether they pay attention, whether they are vulnerable, receptive, all kinds of things which have to do with relationship. I feel this will make a good writer.

Q. Today when a book is picked up which has craft, which is slick, is well done, that book even if it says absolutely nothing, is given some serious attention. Do you find that you can be interested in a book which has content but has no craft?

A. N. Well, I am sad if that is the case, but I think that with time the craft gets refined by the content. I am interested in a book now by a young man who is trying to find a new language for the rock and roll life, for the drug experience, as Kerouac found a new language for his generation. Sometimes it is awkward, but I am more interested in that manuscript than I am in some books brought out which are supposedly about the subculture but which are cruel, cold, and really caricatures. Those I find will lead nowhere. They are very slick and have all those things which the publishers associate with the subculture, but I think the real manuscript of the subculture is this one where the writer is trying to find the language for this particular kind of experience which the rock and roll musicians have.

Q. Have your ever fantasized yourself as head of a publishing firm?

A. N. That would be wonderful. It really would be wonderful, because I would allow for this kind of innovation and experiment which has not yet reached perfection, but which needs to be nurtured. You see, in science, for example, we have research, and sometimes scientists research something which leads nowhere. We don't have that in writing, but we should. Sometimes the first book is not all that it should be, but is showing some kind of intuitive or emotional futurism.

Q. In science it is the questions not the answers, which are important. The one who formulates a new question is really considered terribly important.

A. N. In writing it should be respected too.

Q. It should be, but we are looking so much for answers.

A. N. And also publishers are operating according to outdated standards. Remember the time when they asked me why I couldn't write something like *The Good Earth*. In other words there was no possibility for any research, any experiment in another direction. There was no possibility of getting that done. And today, there is more or less the same thing.

Q. Of course it is astonishing—why would they want you to write *The Good Earth* if it had already been written?

A. N. They do that in film too. There is always a second *Women in Love*. There will always be a second *Bloody Sunday*. There is always a second and a third. There will be other *Easy Riders*. And in the book world that is very strong, very, very strong.

Q. You've always been terribly attracted to film. Perhaps after the novel, you have been most interested in film. Have you thought about why that is?

A. N. That's the part of my life that has not been fulfilled. I love films, love dealing in imagery. We were talking a little while ago about Bergman. I love the expression of the film itself. When I read my novels, I get a film impression. I get a visual impression and I have a visual impression of people when I see scenes taking place. So I feel very film-oriented. But the problem of turning my novels into a structured script baffles everybody.

Q. You have never been able to find a film-maker who could work with the flow and the distillations and the images?

A. N. They exist but I haven't been able to contact them.

Q. In *Diary* IV you do get involved with film-making to some extent.

A. N. Yes, I worked with Maya Deren and then later acted in a film based on *House of Incest*. I enjoyed making that film and acting in it . But, for example, several people have wanted to make a film of *A Spy in the House of Love,* though it has not happened yet. I have met people who have the sensitivity to make a film which will correspond to the book, which will be in the same style, but when the film must be translated into a commercial venture then it no longer exists. I would, or someone would, have to fight for the film the same way I had to fight for the *Diary* and the novels. (72-Y)

Q. Do you identify yourself now as an American writer?

A. N. I'm really writing for America and in English, but I would like to go beyond that. I can't say I'm an American writer, although I'm identified with the new consciousness. I prefer to think of myself in more universal or international terms, particularly as I partake of two cultures. (73-M)

Q. Mallarmé spoke of the agony of facing the blank page. Some writers have felt they "dried up," as they call it. Do you ever have these periods of dearth? Of gestation, perhaps?

A. N. Never! The white page for me is like a ski slope; I go absolutely mad. I go mad in stationery stores. Just to see beautiful paper gives me a desire to write.

Q. From what source do you draw?

A. N. What do you mean?

Q. Well, some writers draw on some belief in the divine; others from personal emotional experiences. From what source do you derive your desire to create?

A. N. From joy! From enjoyment. The way the birds sing. I write when I'm in love with something—a scene, a character, a book, a country. "To paint is to love again," Henry said. For me, to write is to love again—to love twice. (69-A)

VIII

Furrawn

The first time I was asked what I wanted to make of my life—I think I was about fourteen years old speaking to a group of people who were French—I said I wanted to have lots of adventures. And that caused quite a gasp because, to the French, adventures are tied strictly to love affairs. But I really meant it in its widest sense, and I think that sense of adventure always carried me through my troubles and difficulties and tragedies and all the things that we share in common, whatever human loss or grief. Back of all these things there must have been a conviction in my mind that this was a mythological adventure and that one could look beyond the sorrow because the sorrow was only a part of that journey. I never for one moment had the feeling of a Sylvia Plath—that there would be no tomorrow. The sense of adventure is tremendously necessary to our vital continuity so that we can transcend the tragedy, the sense of tragedy and losses as we go along the way. (73-J)

Once we accept the fact that experience can be painful and that there is an end to relationships and that there are things with which we will be challenged, as long as we have a place that says this is our life and it's going to go on, then we won't have any of this tremendous pessimism or suicidal impulses. If we considered our lives as a whole, if we could just see that they're not all just happening today, that there is always a tomorrow and that there is always something to overcome, this gives us elation and courage for the continuous struggle, and prepares us for the second birth with its great delights and compensations. (73-E)

As you know from mythology, the outer journey was full of dangers and full of monsters. And we do have to remember that the image of the outer journey is the same as the image of our inner journey. It is a labyrinth, it is sometimes dark, we can't see around the corners, we sometimes feel blindfolded. But we have to continue. (73-K)

We cannot forget that every one of our lives is an adventure. In every one of our lives there is a possibility of escape, of expansion, of growth, of sublimation, of transcending the obstacles which seem absolutely impossible to move. Now the obstacle I thought I could never move was my link with the world which had been broken traumatically. But I really did believe what Joseph Campbell describes as the mythological journey of the hero, and I never took the word "hero" as literally meaning somebody with exceptional gifts or exceptional courage. I simply took it to mean one who was very persistent in his quest. Joseph Campbell, in *Myths To Live By,* talks about this mythological journey, and the same one that's taken by the heroes is also taken, as we know, by the schizophrenic. At a certain moment there is a break in the life, something happens which breaks the connection with life, as many of the students have felt that there is a breaking away from one culture or one group or the people you are close to. So it happens to the artist, it happens to the mythological hero, and it happens also in madness. The difference is that in mythology the hero completes the journey and comes out of the labyrinth.

There is an emphasis today upon not having heroes and not having models, and I think it came out of the feeling that the hero had special qualifications and special privileges that we could not possibly possess. But when I was fourteen or fifteen I immediately adopted heroines who helped me to live, and I want to emphasize the fact that in mythology we have all recognized that the hero is not the one who has special gifts or special skills. He is just a very stubborn person who decides to complete the journey, whether it is climbing the highest mountain in the world, whether it is taking the outward journey or the inward one. (73-J)

The myth helped me, you see. It helped me to realize that, to make that transposition, and regard my life not just as a simple human life with troubles but as a part of a mythological journey which we are all engaged in. You see the whole idea of the hero I took seriously. The myth was really helpful to me because it showed me that the journey was a long one, was an arduous one, was a complex one, whether it was the adventures of Odysseus or the interior adventure. This helped me to consider my life not only as a personal and emotional thing but also as a tale. My salvation was always to say: "Well, this is an adventure." Putting it on the mythological level would rescue me from disaster, from feeling that I just couldn't cope with it all. (73-K)

I consider it very sad that you made a symbol out of someone like Sylvia Plath because even if her poetry was beautiful her life was not. She collapsed at the first challenge to her courage. And I am sorry to see that you make a symbol of her and love her despair, as in the romantic days people loved Werther who committed suicide. I'm sorry about that because I don't think our first challenge and our first sorrow should really cause this kind of inner disintegration. It wouldn't if we were prepared for it, if we did not make the demands of a smooth and happy life without obstacles. If there was growth without difficulties, we wouldn't grow into anything. Part of the growing process is really this aspiration towards life and art and towards the other, which demands strength from you, which demands the inner journey. And this is where we come to the inner journey. How did I build a resistance which made me not put my head in the oven whenever anything came that destroyed me?

The first catastrophe that hit me and which hits many children was the separation of the parents and then the uprooting from the country where I felt at home to a new country. Usually that has been enough to cause what we call alienation. But how did I fight that? How do you fight that? I made a little island for myself and that was the diary. I was going to tell about the journey to America, and I was going to look at it as an adventure, as in all the adventure books I had read. In other words, the fictionalizing of my life was helping my sorrow, was helping the uprooting. To look at it as an adventure was the answer. It was painful to leave my Spanish grandmother; it was very painful to leave Spain which was very joyous and full of music and where the woman who washed dishes sang all day. All kinds of things like that I missed. But the other way was to look at coming to America as an adventure, and so the diary starts. (73-A)

Later on it became more obvious that my struggle was against every trap, every entrapment of experience, every limitation, every restriction, either by the poverty which I experienced in my childhood or by being uprooted and not speaking the language of my new country. I had to find immediately the way out, and, though I only discovered it recently, the etymology of the word education is *the way out.*

We all feel overwhelmed sometimes, and what happens sometimes drowns us. But two or three things might help. One is to consider that no matter how tragic, this is a journey that has continuity and continuance, and therefore you won't always be in this spot. You will move. Another is that we do heal up, and another is that it we maintain feelings—if we continue to feel, then the range and the kind of experience you will have will change too. If you can traverse this moment, if you can just transcend this moment. Write the word transcend hundreds of times. It meant a lot to me. I used actually to write it and put it up on my wall. Write all those words because they help you to move. What happens if we are trapped in a human sorrow is that we in a way die for awhile, or when someone that we love dies we die for awhile. So what we have to do is to maintain this continuity of organic life. (73-K)

Life is an adventure, and you're going to find very great difficulties, great obstacles and monsters and minotaurs. But if you are prepared for that you are also prepared to look at it as part of the adventure. It starts with sorrow and it starts with loss, but you don't surrender. What I did was to create a little spirit house which was the diary, which was my companion when I couldn't speak English very well. I could write there everything that happened: and the first word I learned—this is very symbolic—was *you*. I thought *you* was a beautiful word, it sounded beautiful.

So the diary became a companion, a solace, replacing things that I had lost, and it also made me look at what was happening as really a saving grace, as an adventure, and adventure means sometimes many dangers and many obstacles. So everything that happened became part of the adventure. It was painful, it was difficult. I would be stranded on a desert island called Richmond Hill, Long Island, which was as much a desert island as you can imagine. But I had to get out of it. And how did I get out of it? It becomes a game, it becomes a game by challenging your wits. How do you escape? Symbolically enough, I remember once in France some- body locked the gate. They had these big locks and big keys for the garden gates in France, and I was locked in the house and couldn't get out. Of course what I did was to take a ladder and go over the wall. I mean there was always this quest, this search for ways to come out of whatever trap life sets us. Because it does set us some traps. (73-A)

I got very upset recently when after giving some very affirmative talks in two colleges, both times at the end of the talk they asked me about Hemingway's and Sylvia Plath's suicides. My reaction was: "What a failure my talk was, when here I am talking about life and affirmation, about everything going forward and the future and then people asked me about suicide." I felt very badly. Then I turned to Ira Progoff and said: "What does that mean?" Of course he, as a more objective person, said to me: "Whenever one is very affirmative, people feel the need of affirming the negative. There is some cussed thing in all of us that when someone is too affirmative we feel that we have to remind ourselves of the negative." (73-K)

I once found myself, like many young women in their twenties, trapped in a suburban life, and a suburb of Paris is no different than a suburb of New York or Chicago. It is the same loneliness, it's the same isolation. There aren't books enough in the library, and there aren't many people to talk to. When I found myself there I had a dream. The dream was that I was writing words on my hair and that with this hair I made a braid, a long, long braid with writing on it, and I threw this braid over the high wall of my garden and I escaped from my life in the suburbs. Now this was a dream, and the reality was that the first book I wrote then connected me with the vivacious literary life of Paris. It was the writing which was the way out.

Now there is always a way out, there is always a way out through the creative will. It's just that we have become very passive because our culture has made us so. We have been fed by television and by passive entertainment to such a degree that the idea of the creative will is almost unknown now. When the young write me, they write to me as if the place of despair in which they are has absolutely no opening. And yet today when I heard the "Soul of a Bird," I thought that if one can escape from the concentration camp he certainly can escape from the narrowness of any life. (72-N)

And this is what I want to restore. This is what I have been able to restore to a great degree with the *Diary*, by saying, first of all, as a writer you may have to wait twenty years for recognition. It doesn't matter. The struggle itself is beautiful. The sorrows are beautiful, the disappointments are beautiful, everything is right. You may be angry, you may be despairing, you may be depressed, but ultimately these are battles that can be won. And the battle over one's self-confidence and the battle to achieve an integrated image of yourself is a very wonderful one. It's a great adventure; it is the adventure of the inner journey. (73-G)

As soon as the *Diary* came out, I received letters from women (and men too, but more women than men), and I discovered many things. I discovered the loneliness of women in little towns; I discovered their hesitancies, their timidities, their lack of confidence, all the difficulties of seeking to create in an environment which was not helpful, without the encouragement perhaps of friends, which we had, a fraternity of artists in Paris. It was a strange discovery. It made me aware of the isolation in which we live, geographically. It made me aware of how difficult it is to make one's inner journey alone. (72-L)

So I would like to call this evening by a word that a friend of mine, Bebe Herring, found embedded in James Joyce. It's the word "furrawn," and she used it as the title of her novel. "Furrawn" means the kind of talk that leads to intimacy. I think we have needed that so much. I think the only reason why the response to the *Diary* was so much greater than I had ever expected was because we suddenly realized that we didn't know each other very well. People would say to me: "I knew the same people that you are describing but I didn't know them as well." It's because we never took the trouble to look deeply into each other, whereas I was always much more concerned with the secret self, with the hidden self, with the deepest part of the self. I would give a great deal of time to my friendships because I found the other really not very interesting, the one-dimensional gift that we usually make of ourselves. (73-I)

Now I would like you to talk with me, and to ask me questions, whatever questions you feel like asking. The only one I won't answer is—I know you want to ask me—what is not in the *Diary*. Ultimately you will read the whole thing, a few years from now. Ultimately you will know the whole story. But you must remember that if I have the right to share my life, I don't have the right to impose that on others. The writer and the artist feel that their lives are necessarily to be made public, that their lives belong to you. This is an artist's conviction, that what he is doing is not for himself; it has to be given away. The painter feels that, the film-maker. So the artist is conditioned to say: "Whatever I do, even if it's a work that I kept secret for years, ultimately it has to be given away." Our dream has to be made public because that's our role. But I can't impose that on people who are not artists or who do not wish to share their life in that way and who are not convinced—as I am—that their life belongs to you. (73-G)

* * *

Q. How does it feel to have achieved recognition as a major literary figure?

A. N. Well, I never imagined that it would happen. It's a lovely feeling; you lose your sense of isolation. And you can live out your universal life. You're in contact with the whole world, which is probably the wish of every writer. I have a feeling of being in touch with the whole world. (73-M)

Q. Do you feel that the experience you had in the thirties in Paris is substantially different from that of other artists and writers?

A. N. No. You see that's why I published the diary. I think that those are essential and deep enough experiences so that they continue and they exist today—the conflict about war, about working, about committing ourselves, about male and female creation, and the relation of men and women. All those were basic things which continued to be very very important, and today the problems are the same. So the matter of years doesn't make any difference. Because if you touch a certain level, despite the historical period, certain basic things continue to be relevant. (68-A)

Q. When you assisted Carlos Castaneda in getting published, how familiar were you with his manuscript and what was your reason for helping him? Why did you feel he should be published?

A. N. Well, because I felt that he went into the world of hallucination and drugs with a great awareness and that he was half what you might call Western Man—he was educated at U.C.L.A.—but he was half Indian. When he came to see me he had just finished a book which U.C.L.A. had turned down as a master's project because they thought it was not anthropological enough, not enough an objective study. So then I brought the book to New York. I was really indirectly responsible. I believed in his sincerity and I believed he was trying to take us into a different dimension, beyond cultural objectivity. And then, when I took his book to New York, U.C.L.A became worried and so decided that they would publish it. That's the only thing that happened. But I found the first book very interesting, didn't you? (73-H)

Q. What effect do you think working with your press had on the writing? Did that give you a sense of the public dimension of writing? Did it perhaps take you away from the diary, push you into another area?

A. N. Of course at first the energy that was put into the press was taken away from the diary. That is the human element. But there is another aspect to printing. When you live with a page, a single page for four or five days, when you set it, which takes a day, and then you print it, look at it so many times that you become an extremely severe critic, then you begin to look at the book as something outside. You must have had that experience when you saw something you've written printed. It's another way of looking at it, which the press promoted, that is as a book in the world. And I would see the books come out in the world, and I would have a party at the Gotham Book Mart, and I would become more aware of the connection with the world. Because before the press, you remember, I spoke of being deprived of publication, as being deprived of connecting with the world. I couldn't think of any other way of connecting the writing with the world.

Q. A book is for the world. So how does the artist deal with the situation where he finishes a book and puts it in a drawer?

A. N. It is a very devestating thing for young writers to write one book, two books, and then have nothing published. It is as if communications are cut off. They can't go on working. And that is why I am helpful, because I realize that can be death to a writer. It can stop one. I got a letter the other day from a young man who wrote a history, a novel, who wrote many things and nothing, somehow, came through. It really does kill them. So for me the press was symbolically important, and I wanted everyone to work at the press. I wanted each one of us to work at the other's book. We could have done a lot of books that way. I wanted to do *The Black Book* by Durrell. But nobody wanted to work. It was very hard work. It could have been a wonderful press at that time, because there were a lot of books which were out of print.

So this is the importance of doing your own printing, which is now being done by so many young people. Some women in Connecticut have set up their own press; I can think of about four or five, including Rochelle Holt who set up her own printing press. I think it is a very fulfilling thing to do at first. (72-Y)

Q. There were—was it three hundred copies of your first book done?

A. N. Yes. And the Gotham Book Mart, Miss Steloff, whose history you probably know, was the one who took them and sold them. And they disappeared right away. I met a publisher once who said: "How did you manage to get known with only three hundred copies of a book?"

Q. Do you have one of those three hundred still?

A. N. I have some, yes, but they are very rare now. They are collectors' items. I used to make mistakes in the division of words. You know foreigners never learn how to divide English words. So I was teased by the critics for many years because of the way I divided the word love. I had "lo-ve." (72-A)

Q. Miss Nin, Edmund Wilson said in his review of one of your books that you deal with conflicts created for women by living half in a man-controlled world against which they cannot help rebelling and half in a world which they have made for themselves but which they cannot find completely satisfactory.

A. N. That's one of the themes of *Diary* IV. I think it's run through all the volumes really. I wasn't as conscious as we are now of the evolution of woman. I wasn't as conscious of the difficulties I had in expanding and growing. I think Wilson was right in saying I had not yet created my own world in which I felt that I could move independently, and at the same time I wanted to move in relation to man and believed in relationship so that I had to bring everything with me, involve the man in my own expansions. And it was difficult, it was difficult to do that.

Q. But you seem to be saying that you weren't as aware of the difficulties *then* as you are in looking back on them.

A. N. Not so conscious, I suppose. I express them spontaneously in the diary, almost subconsciously. I wasn't so aware that it was happening to so many women. I knew that there were difficulties; my women friends were in difficulties—when they wanted to paint, the devotion to the man came first, the devotion to the family and to personal relationships. I became much more aware the last few years, more conscious, of something that was then more subconscious.

Q. Has that anything to do with the fact that nowadays many of these things have labels? Women's liberation has put labels on the difficulties and so they are more recognized than they were?

A. N. Yes. Today women's problems are more organized. The women in the movement have brought up the things that I didn't know about—the laws, inequalities in work. They're more conscious of the situation as a whole, historically and politically. (72-F)

Q. In *The Four-Chambered Heart* you dramatize one of the recurrent themes of the *Diary*; the complexity of woman's "goodness," her habit—inborn or learned—of placing others' needs and desires before her own. How does this "goodness" relate to woman's search for her own psychology?

A. N. I think it was imposed on woman. This idea was taught to her by the Judaeo-Christian morality. Woman was supposed to be unselfish, devoted, helpful, nourishing. And if she departed from this sort of behavior for one moment, she felt burdened by guilt. But Djuna begins to question it. "Am I really good," she asks, "or am I trying to fit a form, a structure, a pattern that was given to me?" She asks herself why she's always involved in relationships with rebels, with people who aren't bound in the ways that she is, irresponsible people who do whatever they want. Eventually she understands that she tried to cast out her own imperfections by putting them onto others. When we do this, we feel responsible for those "bad" people, because we know they're doing something for us. They're living the dark side of ourselves. Meanwhile, we can go right on believing that we're "good." But Djuna discovers that these other people are more honest than she is, that she's cheating by refusing to act out her dark desires. This is a difficult admission, but it has its compensations. If you cast your shadow, or your double, onto another, you will experience great anxiety. You're responsible for that person's life, and you know it takes a destructive form, yet you have no control over it. On the other hand, if it's your own destructive drive, you can become aware of it and control it. That's why Djuna felt that she was a victim of Rango and Zora. She had to combat their destructiveness all the time with her creativeness. They were playing an exhausting and unnatural game. (72-X)

Q. What made you choose the name, Djuna? Was it your attachment to Djuna Barnes?

A. N. My admiration for Djuna Barnes must have had something to do with it. Actually, I found the name in an anthology of Welsh names. It happens to be a man's name. Djuna Barnes never forgave me for this. She wrote me an angry letter saying that her father had made up that name for her, and now, in *Winter of Artifice,* I had stolen her name, her father, and her life. I answered that the name was Welsh, the father was mine, and the women were those I knew. But I love her and her work. (69-A)

Q. Suddenly I have just been struck by the fact that in your early years you were in contact with incredibly dynamic people like Miller, Artaud, Rank, and Gonzalo, and that as you came to the States there is a kind of paling and lessening of energy. Was that difficult for you?

A. N. Part of that was the usual withering that comes from uprooting. You must find your world again. The other was that the young came to me and the mature writers didn't. That was not my choice really, as you can see from the *Diary.* I longed to be with people like James Agee, people of my own age, but it didn't happen. They didn't come to me.

Q. And you could not seek them out?

A. N. No, I was not the type of person who could do that. That was a mystery to me, why the young came to me and formed my world. Of course, later on that stopped and I had more relationships with people who matched my maturity. (72-Y)

Q. You say that it's when we trust others that we achieve intimacy. But if that is so why are there so many holes in the *Diary,* things you don't talk about or leave out?

A. N. You have forgotten that I have a right to share *my* life, but I do not have the right to impose that on people who do not wish to be shared. All that I could give you, I gave you, and if you feel that there is more left out than I gave, that is something I can't help. You have to take me as I am, and I am a person who is very concerned not to destroy others. What you call the holes in the *Diary* are there because I did not wish to be destructive of other human beings. (72-H)

Q. In the first *Diary* you make allusions to "my childhood diary," and I have a sense of what you might call jealousy about that. It's as if everybody else is enjoying that diary but I'm not getting to look at it.

A. N. Well, to tell you the truth, when I had to make a choice, a decision about where I was going to start, for *your* sake, like the novelist that I was, I decided to start where my life became more interesting. I left out all the bad times, the little towns in America where there weren't enough books for me to read, for instance. I just didn't think it was interesting. But I can see now that if, like a scientist, you're studying a life organically, then of course you want to know the past. I wasn't aware of that. I was being a novelist and saying "Now this is where it becomes really interesting," and the result is, of course, that you get the feeling of a miracle. I arrive in Paris. It's so easy. But it wasn't like that at all. There were periods when I felt like Sylvia Plath, and periods when I lived in Richmond Hill—you can't imagine a more terrible little town, or Queens. Leaving that out makes a distortion, I know. So I will publish it now, I have to.

Q. That's really good, because I have this feeling that I want to know what your experience was of growing up, what you were like as a teenager.

A. N. You'll be bored.

Q. I don't think so. I think it will be good because it will humanize you.

A. N. Possibly yes. The struggle, even poverty, which nobody believes I experienced. When we came to America we came as immigrants really, with nothing at all. Then the struggle with the language, the struggle with the culture which was foreign to me. Yes, everything should be there, if you're studying an evolution.

Q. It's like I sort of need for my own struggle to identify with yours.

A. N. I do flash back to a few episodes, but they're not all there. I guess I was thinking more as a novelist. But I will do the child diary now, which will go up to teenage. I realize now it is necessary because we need to know how a woman develops, and we need to know the obstacles. We really need to know what the difficulties are as well as the achievements. (72-I)

Q. You used Sylvia Plath as an example of a woman who was not able to go beyond destructive experience. My question is what kind of a realization of yourself does it take to be able to transcend?

A. N. Well, that's a very good question. There is always the question of what makes one person able to sustain a destructive experience, and it's a very complex question. I would say it depends on how much of an inner resistance, an inner spiritual core you have. Now why she lacked that inner resistance to catastrophe, I don't know enough about her life to say.

Q. But you see she was using that process of inward journey that you talked about. So I suppose I'm asking what realization does it take to come out, to come out at the other end of the journey?

A. N. I think it's a combination of many things. I think it's a recognition that life is going to deal us blows and that experience can be destructive. I think it's being prepared for that. I would say it's almost a philosophical attitude, and it's something that psychology can give, and that therapy, in spite of all the attacks it has been undergoing, can give us. It's an objectivity, a certain realization that the ideal and romantic, the perfect experiences we are always demanding or expecting are sometimes not given us. (73-B)

Q. Miss Nin, I read somewhere that you have one hundred and fifty volumes of your diary. Does this mean a hundred and fifty notebooks?

A. N. Yes. They are not quite volumes. They are like school notebooks or those diaries that they sell, you know, some that are small, sometimes they are big. It's not as impressive as it sounds. But there are more than a hundred and fifty now. I've lost count.

Q. How many more will there be?

A. N. I don't know how far I can go, because I find that the mature artists I write about are very generous about their lives. They don't mind what you write. But the young artists, who aren't yet known, are very touchy. So as I get closer and closer to the younger writers, I find it more difficult to publish their portraits.

Q. I see; in other words you might get a complaint from, say, Gore Vidal. I don't know if you did, but you mentioned him. Or someone who is younger than, for example, Henry Miller or Edmund Wilson.

A. N. Yes, because the older artists are used to sharing their whole lives. I mean their life is known, and they have a sense of humor about it. They are detached from it. But if you take someone who is twenty years old and has just written a novel, he is very vulnerable and very touchy. Also, of course, I'm making portraits of many kinds of people now. Not always artists, not always writers. But I don't know how far I can go without getting in trouble. (72-A)

Q. What happened finally to Gonzalo?

A. N. I am often asked what happened to the characters in my *Diary*—and notice that I am calling them characters myself. I should have footnotes sometimes, but I don't want to betray the diary. The end of the history of Gonzalo comes many years later. In the volumes you have I didn't know yet what happened. He went back to Paris, but I only heard much later about his death from cancer. So I can't very well put in Volume IV a footnote and say: "Gonzalo ten years *from now* died." You see it would be a falsification of chronology. So I'm obliged to make you wait to find out what happened to the characters, instead of as in Proust, who skipped a few chapters and said: "Twenty years later. . . ." (72-H)

Q. Do you have a sense of destiny, or "calling"? I mean, did you choose writing or did it choose you?

A. N. I never thought about that. It began so early. As far back as I remember, I knew I was going to be a writer. Very early it became an *"idée fixe."* (69-A)

Q. You've always had a fascination for the very young. I mean teenagers and young men or young women in their twenties. Is it because they aren't yet molded, and they're less predictable and more fun to be with?

A. N. I'll tell you one thing. The situation was quite different in France. My companions were older than I was in France. Miller was, and Durrell was only a little younger. I didn't have this in France at all. What happened was that when I came to America the kind of writing I was doing appealed to the young, and it was the young who came to me. So it wasn't a matter of choice; I didn't really select. But I found friendship more possible with the young and the students and it's continued to be somewhat that way. My relation to them was closer during the period of neglect which I had when I was writing the novels, from 1946 until the *Diary* began to be published.

Q. What's happened to some of those young ones whom no one ever heard of until your *Diary* and possibly not since? Did some of them simply fail to live up to their promise?

A. N. Some yes. Some gave up half way. Others became famous. For instance, there's James Leo Herlihy. And others just disappeared. They gave up writing, they got discouraged, they felt defeated. So I lose track of them, I lose sight of them. They go to another country.

Q. And Gore Vidal was another young man, or rather he was a young man when you first met him? "Troubadour Vidal" he called himself, didn't he?

A. N. Yes. But he changed a great deal. He became another person from the one I described in the *Diary*.

Q. But even when he was young, he refused to think of himself on the same level with the other young people. Didn't you say he once called and said: "Get the kids out of there, I'm coming over"?

A. N. He was very arrogant, very arrogant, and very sure of himself. And later on he lost the quality that I did like in the young which is that they are not rigid yet, they're not formed yet, that they're of the future, and you always have a feeling of hope, of what they're going to accomplish, the fascination with their potential. Probably also because I didn't have childen myself I focused on the young this love of what they might become. (72-A)

Q. As I read your *Diary*, I felt very disturbed and uncomfortable about when you are giving money. These artists and people are receiving their sustenance from you, and even one surly character just comes in and growls and looks in your handbag. Could you talk more about your experience with that whole thing. I find that a very difficult area—being a woman and having some maternal impulses toward almost anyone who needs something and at the same time wanting to protect myself from being ripped off.

A. N. I understand how you felt. There were many issues when I was editing which I had scruples about including. But then I realized that I had to include it because I had to make people realize that the writer and the poet are always in financial trouble. This is a reality I accepted. And then I had known poverty from the age of ten to the age of twenty, the extreme poverty that foreign people will have when they come to a strange country. My mother didn't know how to manage; my father had left. So I knew poverty. And so then when I had an income of some kind, even moderate, it seemed to me that I was richer than everybody else and I couldn't bear it. I mean I could rent a house and I had something, while all my friends were Bohemians who really had nothing at all. And the sense of responsibility for them was very strong.

The fact that it took the commercial or practical aspect—bringing an electric heater along or money—didn't mean anything to me because it was symbolic of aesthetic neglect. I had always seen the artist, especially in Europe, in need, and my father was a very modest teacher of music in France when I was born. It was a moderate if not quite a starving situation. So it seemed to me that the artist always was in those desperate straits. And I tried to help until it became too much, until as in the case of Patchen there wasn't even the beauty of a friendship given in return. Then I rebelled. I rebelled very much against that type of patronage. The other was simply protection because of friendship and love and mutual work. Miller, for example, was a very generous man in his own realm, in his own way. He was giving his life in the stories, and with most of the others each one had brought gifts, and it was an exchange of gifts. But with Patchen it wasn't that way.

Q. Did Duncan and Patchen read those parts of the *Diary* before it was published?

A. N. Yes, of course.

Q. What kind of weird ego to want to have that in there!

A. N. Yes, I gave Duncan the chance to have it out (I have to do that you know). But he didn't. He questioned only one inaccuracy: the car he slept in was not in New Yok. It was in Long Island. (72-D)

Q. Did you ever find when writing in your diary that sometimes it was easier to express yourself in another language, say in French or in Spanish rather than English. Or did you always write in English?

A. N. Well, no. The early diaries are in French, and I only began English at sixteen. I must say, though, I didn't ever go back to French or Spanish, and I really had a love affair with the English language from the first time I began to study it. I loved the language, and I found that it was sufficient, in fact, very rich and just right for what I wanted to do. So I never did go back. In fact, I can't write any longer in French or in Spanish. So there was really an adoption of English as a permanent language. And you know they say that when you begin to dream in a language that means you are of that nationality. So I guess I have really become American, for I dream in English. (73-B)

Q. Is there anything in your experience like Joseph Conrad who said he would probably never have written had he not stumbled upon English?

A. N. Yes, I felt that way. Maybe if I had never come here I wouldn't have written the way I did. Yes, I discovered the English language and I loved it. But also I seemed to have had a great affinity for it. (72-I)

Q. Do you intend to write any more fiction?

A. N. I can't answer that. Perhaps short stories. It is a challenging form. In the short stories I have written I feel I can't change a word. I can change the novels here and there, but not the short stories.

Q. Which are your most popular books?

A. N. Well, people seem to care a great deal for the *Diary.* Perhaps through them they will discover the novels. Of the novels, *Spy In The House Of Love* has had the widest reading audience so far.

Q. In your book, *The Novel of the Future,* you mention a play you wrote at the age of eleven which prefigured your life philosophy. In what way?

A. N. The story was of a blind father whose daughter described the world for him. Then he was cured of his blindness, and instead of being shocked by the discrepancy between the real world and that which she had created in such marvelous colors, his reaction was: "That doesn't matter; now I can create the world as you saw it; you gave me a dream which I can now realize."(69-A)

Q. How would you define your philosophy of life and from where is it derived?

A. N. It doesn't have a name. I mean it doesn't belong to any one person. I think we all make an adaptation of things that we have learned on the way. I learned a great deal from psychology. If that is philosophy, I would say that is my basic touchstone. (73-F)

Q. Speaking of the unconscious and other dimensions, I once told some therapists that insanity was simply a unique place rather than a place of disease. "You should try going there sometime," I said. "Oh no," they said. And then I understood that they were treating insane people because they were terrified of that.

A. N. They wanted to keep it in control. There is a wonderful woman now, the woman who wrote the book *Diary of a Schizophrenic Girl,* who did the opposite. She decided she was going to learn this girl's language, what she meant by her behavior and gestures. Instead of trying to bring the girl immediately into our world, she went into hers, and by doing that she did bring the girl into our world.

Q. These men that I met couldn't have done that. In addition, what I had asked them to do was to contemplate staying with someone as they went through their agony, sitting it through, being a companion to someone in that state.

A. N. R. D. Laing does that. Laing is the only one that I know, as a professional man, who is willing to go through periods of disturbance with a patient.

Q. I haven't noticed that he has a great reputation with the professional medical men in our society.

A. N. No.

Q. Students read him, of course.

A. N. Because he is willing to go into uncharted lands and then to come back and write about it. He has overcome that fear.

Q. Let me ask you a question which you may not want to answer, perhaps, because it may seem too divisive. Do you think that it is easier for you to go into that uncharted place because you are a woman?

A. N. I almost foresaw your question. I don't know what the answer is. I was going to try to answer it for myself. Instead of fear, I had a need for knowing what things meant. I was convinced that if I knew what things meant in the world, things which frightened me, all the irrational behavior, war, everything else, I felt that if I examined it, I would be in less danger. I had the opposite instinct. I wanted to know the meaning. I didn't want experiences that I didn't understand, that I feared. So I was pushed into that realm as far as I could go. If I had an anxiety, I wanted to get to the bottom of it. That drive was very strong. Now I don't know if I felt that because I was a woman, because woman lives a little closer to her non-rational, emotional self, or because I was trying to rescue myself from being emotional, from getting into chaotic situations, from being deceived or betrayed or any of the things which happen to us. But I did want to know what things meant. (72-Y)

Q. Talking about the second birth, is there any particular time when one knows that this process is taking place, or does it happen imperceptibly and gradually and organically?

A. N. I would say it happens organically and imperceptibly, that you are not quite aware of it, until suddenly you encounter a challenge and find out that you have changed. An example of this is the fear I used to have, my not being able to talk to others when I was twenty, my fear of speaking in public when I was thirty. And then one day, much later, I found myself forced to speak. A friend of mine, who was a professor, said: "Will you come and talk to fifteen students of mine?" So, of course, I went, as I was, without notes or anything at all. And then he pushed me into an auditorium with three hundred persons. I had to talk for an hour, and I found out I could! So that was a sign of the second birth for me, overcoming a difficulty accidentally. It made me find out I could do it, that the fear was not justified. But we don't usually have such clear landmarks of our second birth. We are aware of lows and highs; we are awfully aware when we fall backwards and when we slip backwards, and we are sometimes very severe on ourselves. (73-E)

Q. I was once into psychology very much, and it was sort of like in Dante: it took me to a gateway and from there I went on alone.

A. N. I did the same thing. I took what I needed to overcome a traumatic knot about a conflict that paralyzed me and took all my energy, which we all have at a certain moment. I took that, and then I wouldn't have anything to do with it. As I said, I'd take my submarine and go back into the depths. I don't want to live in an analytical world. You're quite right. But we need it because we *are* modern. We don't seem to have been born into a tradition which helps us through other means. (72-G)

Q. Do you think it's possible to teach and be creative, to be a creative teacher, or is there a basic incompatibility there?

A. N. Creativity and teaching? No, I never had that kind of conflict. But then I wasn't part of a university! I kept very free, on the periphery. I'm interested now in teaching because there is an international community college started in Los Angeles where each one in his field—mythology, or architecture, or philosophy—will only take five or six or, at the most, ten students and they will get individual supervision. It's going back to the idea of the master and disciple; it's a struggle against the idea of mass production in education. You choose the person who is the best in the field you want to develop, and then you stay with that person eight months. You develop a kind of concentrated contact with the writer or the philosopher or the mythologist or whoever you have chosen to work with. They're trying to do that all over the world, so that if you want to you can go and study in Italy or in England or in France. They are trying to get people all over the world and in all types of fields. There will even be a medicine man who will teach American Indian lore.

The conflict between teaching and creativity comes from two things. Teaching is sometimes dangerous, because as you teach you tend to make formulations and these formulations have sometimes enclosed the students in a set pattern and discouraged them from seeking change. Then sometimes if the teacher comes to the students and says one thing today, and tomorrow he has changed, he might find it a little difficult to carry the students along with his change. But there are plenty of teachers who do change and do carry the students with them into change. That I suppose is what you would call a creative teacher. (73-N)

Q. Does a knowledge of the *Diary* change one's interpretation of the fiction? Do I need the *Diary* to understand the fiction?

A. N. Well, this is hard for me to answer. Many people who have gone through the *Diary* have understood the fiction better. Yes, I think that's true. Because the fiction was poetic novel, which is a sort of mythology, and then the *Diary* gave the human key. For even though the character changed in the process of fictionalizing and became composite and mythic, in the *Diary* you do have the key. And having the real human beings from which the characters were developed seems to have made them more understandable. That's true. But I don't think the *Diary* changes the interpretation or that the fiction is dependent upon it. (73-D)

Q. If you were doing a seminar in your own writing, which would you start with, the fiction or the *Diary*?

A. N. I would relate the two in terms of the process of creative transformation. I would try to show you how you could make poetry out of any situation and how you can find a meaning in any situation. (72-K)

Q. How does it feel to see your works translated into so many languages?

A. N. In Japanese I can't even recognize the names of the characters. And I sign the book at the wrong end. It's always very interesting to be translated. You have a feeling somehow that you're beginning to occupy a new country. (73-M)

Q. Having overcome your fear of sharing your life and having established your identity, what problems, if any, do you have now?

A. N. I'm now in another cycle. I have other demons to worry about. The major one now is: once you become articulate for something that is happening to others, the danger then is that by multiplication the thing becomes dissolved or distorted. How do you retain its integrity? In wanting to share with all, there comes a point where many things begin to threaten the integrity of that sharing. I have the drama now of multiplicity versus integrity. Since the thing I believe in is so intimate, there is the danger of trying to communicate and being faced with addressing the uninitiated.

Q. It sounds like a third fear of losing *your* identity in the people that you're sharing with.

A. N. It's a new kind of danger. It's not the fear of loss of identity, it's the fear of the thing itself becoming distorted as it reaches the outer rim. You see, *here* we are with a certain integrity, with a certain synthesis; there is a certain rapport between us as a group. There is no destructive element, but there is a destructive element outside in the world which can take a thing and distort it as it spreads, as it tries to reach more people, and that's the new cycle that I have to overcome. I don't know whether I've expressed it very well because it is so new.

Q. What is the difference between the cycle you're in and the one you left?

A. N. In the cycle I left there was really a greater dominance of the intimate life, the personal life, very little public life. I was called out by the woman's movement to be a public figure. But before this, I never took part in the public life. My only public life was with the students in the colleges. I was not a public figure.

Q. What has it done to you?

A. N. I'm meditating on that. I want to see whether it's dangerous to the things I believe in. My cycle isn't very clear yet. It's something that has happened to artists and it's happened to many people. I think it happened with figures like Huxley. Whoever becomes a public figure is also in danger of betraying himself. I'm very careful of that, and I know I'm not going to change, but I have to decide how I'm going to be in tune with this, or what it is I'm going to eliminate. The problem is how to grow with integrity, relate to others, but not become again part of another dogma, another mass movement or another blind sort of activity. I think D. H. Lawrence put it awfully well when the war problem came up, about going to war or not going to war. He says it's harder sometimes to hang onto your soul than to go along with the crowd. It was much easier to go to war than it was to hold out. I have to do a certain kind of hold-out in order to preserve the things that I'm talking about.

Q. Tillich said once: "It's very difficult not to become my own follower."

A. N. I don't think that can happen. It's too late for that. I know I'm very stubborn about change. But let's not talk about where I'm at, let's talk about where you are at.

Q. There are a lot of people in your audience who did want to become your followers and make you into an idol or a cult figure or therapist or whatever was their need, and you refused.

A. N. I refused that.

Q. And you did it by putting it back on themselves. It was like saying, long after I'm gone and I'm not here you have to find something in yourselves. It's like what you said about your writing, that maybe someday you will not make personal appearances because we will all know your writing so well. I think that would be a mistake, but I know what you meant.

A. N. Yes, because you see I'm aware. It's not modesty. I'm fully aware that as a craftsman who loved language and loved to articulate what was happening to me, that the only difference really is that I spent my whole life articulating something for you. I'm only a spokesman, I don't think of it as a thing that came out of *me*. But something made me concentrate on the idea of being able to articulate this, whatever was happening to me, and that's all. That is why my work speaks to you and is yours.

Q. I think that's really rare. Most people who are not that secure with themselves or haven't really resolved things in themselves will latch on to the possibility of making themselves into an idol.

A. N. Yes, but that must be if you think that you have particular gifts. Now I don't think that I have particular gifts. I had certain obsessions which made a craftsman out of me or made me need articulation. I think the artist is no more than a hypersensitive instrument of receptivity. I really think of it that way. That he's open and he's receptive and sometimes he becomes prophetic because he has a sense of what is coming. I really don't think that's a personal achievement, an ego thing. I don't feel responsible for that. I disclaim any personal responsibility for having particular gifts. I don't think I did. I think I was a mute child who needed to speak and who needed to write and who was lonely. Whatever the reasons were—and they were many and they're very complex—something made me concentrate on that craft which became vital to all of us, which was to write how we felt.

Q. It's as if you act as a channel.

A. N. Yes, I really believe that. I really believe that. I spoke about the integrated circuits. I think it's just simply because I am a tuned-in, receptive instrument. That sensitivity in the artist is strange. We don't know the origin of it, and we don't know how it's preserved. But I don't think one can say: "*I've* done this." Also, all that I've done I've been helped to do. I was taught by the philosophers, I was taught by books. How can I say: "*I* am a special kind of woman"?

Q. I feel that some people who come to hear you have very high expectations of you, almost as if you were a demi-god.

A. N. A demi-god! How could they expect that after reading me?

Q. That's the problem now. At least before, when you weren't

published and nobody had read your *Diary,* at least you could
have small audiences of really intense understanding. Now you're
going to probably have to develop something to deal with it.
A. N. I don't think I want to do that. I want to have a dialogue
with somebody who has read the work and has questions about the
work, since I have been using my life as a story told you about
how you encounter obstacles and how you transcend these obstacles. Every kind, every sort of obstacle turns up in the diary sooner
or later, and it's that story that I'm telling or that I'm using. I have
really nothing to say or to exchange with those who haven't come
to the work. I don't understand why they come.
Q. It seems to me that you're very consciously trying to achieve
this intimacy or openness with an incredible number of very different people, and I'm very curious as to how that feels, because
that's hard to do even with one person.
A. N. I never intended to do that; it was never my intention. My
intention was to dialogue with the students who were studying the
work. That's how it began. So the curiosity seekers or the name
seekers or the dogmatic feminists who came were not *asked* to
come, were not expected by me. As I saw it, we were getting together in order to discuss some kind of study or growth development of woman. We now have a record of it, and I'm like a scientist who studies a kind of insect. I never thought that they would
come, that this kind of person would come. Why should they
come?
Q. I felt you were making a very conscious effort to not close off
even though that was happening.
A. N. No, I'm not very happy about that because I think that it
has been a curse. The curse has been the multiplication of those
who haven't yet made their individual selection of reading the work
before coming to talk to me. They come out of some kind of contagion. And this is where I find the danger of mass thinking or
mass media or whatever it is: that people come without having any
relation to the thing they come to. I would have liked better meeting those who really wanted to have some kind of dialogue with
that particular attitude in life. I do worry about the outsiders, for

as Tennessee Williams said: "If you communicate with others on an unconscious level, some will want to hurt you because they refuse that kind of communication." That's why when you asked me how I feel, I said the only time I really feel very good is when those who want to approach me or the work really come up.

Q. I am amazed, though, at the way you are able to generate intimacy in a large group.

A. N. How do you keep a thing intimate in America where everything is always multiplied by people who have not really approached it sincerely, organically, individually, but just because they heard the name or because they saw you on T.V. This is a vicious kind of thing; it's the non-relationship to things. They come and they're not related to it. It's a dangerous thing, it's a thing that I have usually fought, what I call the mass movements which don't have an orientation; they don't have a focus, and they haven't approached the ideas organically. Because the one thing really about the *Diary* and the way we are using it now for our life is that it's an organic construction; it's something which evolved cell by cell and day by day without a conscious pattern. So those who approach it have to approach it unconsciously and relate to it, and then argue and then question as we were questioning yesterday. (72-D)

Q. You were suppressed in your desire to publish for so long, and then finally the recognition came. But do you ever feel that you were used, that the publishing companies chose you and then created things around you in order to sell books?

A. N. Oh, they try, but I think probably it is only a young writer who is susceptible to that or a victim to that. I'm too mature to be taken in by the things that are built up by the newspapers or the media. Oh, they try. But I don't pay attention to it, I don't live up to it, and I don't believe it. And that's the main thing. I suppose when you're twenty and the newspaper writes something about you, you believe it. But I don't. And interestingly enough, the letters I receive are not flattering, not that kind of letter. They are not letters saying that I wrote the *Diary* well or that I'm a good writer. The letters are in answer to my giving my life, and say: "Here is *my* life." So it's not that kind of idolizing. It's simply saying: "The way you have written, I feel I can write to you and I can talk to you about myself." I'm a present. I have never received a flattering letter, which is interesting and significant. So there is for me no danger. I think that happens only to people who don't know really what their world means or how they intend to use it.

Q. I suppose I've just developed a cynicism, because so many people have let the publicity element move in on them, even if they were innocent of it. You wish that they would have had the faculty to put it aside, to ignore it.

A. N. I know. It's a very dangerous thing, a very, very dangerous thing because it interferes with your knowing me and my work. Actually it's really an obstacle most of the time. I don't think that it brings the genuine person to your door. (72-G)

Q. Are you still keeping a diary?

A. N. No. I said last night that correspondence has taken the place of the diary this year, and I don't question that for a moment because it may have been the logical outcome of the diary. Because the diary was, as a Russian poet said, in some ways a solitary chant, but nevertheless a chant intended to be shared with others. So what's happened now is that I am in communication by letter. And I'm answering these letters because they're very highly personal, because they deserve an answer. That's taken the place of writing the diary, and maybe it is really the purpose of the diary. Instead of being a secret or something withheld, now it is something that is flowing back and forth. So that now I'm receiving diaries. What I'm receiving really are confessional letters and open letters. They're never frivolous letters, or about whether I have written well. It has nothing to do with that at all. It has to do with the life flow, whether the *Diary* set the life flow going.

Q. Do you find your writing is similar in your letters to what you were putting into your diaries?

A. N. Yes. Except that it is with another, as we are talking now. I mean it's not the story of what is happening to me, which in a way I have outgrown. Now it is a talk *with* others. But it's a talk with others on the assumption that there is some exchange going on, that there is some knowledge of the work, and that we're on equal transmission. That's why I don't know how to shut out the people who are outside of it, the outsiders. I don't know what they want, I don't know what they're seeking. I feel that really the ones that come for organic reasons should have come because of my writing. I feel that's important.

Q. I haven't read very much, I must confess. But I came because I was interested in you.

A. N. In other words you put the value on the person rather than on the artist, and that's very dangerous. The work of many artists may be much deeper and larger and greater than themselves.

Q. But isn't that O.K. too? Because in a way some of the things you're saying go beyond your written work. And just the things you talk about and the way you relate, your ability last night to relate so straightforwardly and truthfully to people when they were talking, that's the thing that people are relating to in you, and I think that's just as exciting and intensely personal.

A. N. But suppose I couldn't do that. The *work* would still be the same. There are artists who are terribly reticent, terribly shy. You see I wanted a kind of synchronization between everything, between what one is, what one lives. That was a sort of an ideal of mine, but many artists have remained very shy within their work. I'm sure if you wanted to talk to Kafka you couldn't, and I'm sure if you had talked to me when I was thirty, I couldn't have said a word.

Q. But then you're saying that your identity in all this is primarily the artist.

A. N. Yes. The artist taught me to speak to you. It was the writing, the feeling for reading, the feeling for language, which enabled me to talk to you. I don't think that that can be done mutely. That's a child's dream, that we communicate sometimes without words. To be sure, *after* you have read something and after I see you, there might be some transmission of sympathy or empathy. But originally we do need the articulateness; we do need to convey to others certain things that need to be said.

Q. Sometimes I think people come out of a sort of aggressive curiosity. They come to test you, to see if you can break down their resistance.

A. N. The reason I stress the reading of the *Diary* first is that the *Diary* breaks that barrier, so that I am trusted after the *Diary*. That's why I say I would rather you have approached me through the *Diary*. Because I'm saying that whatever you approach with hostility you'll never get to know, you can never come close to it. It's distorting. And also if you approach it with hostility or if you are testing something, it will not yield its transmission.

Q. I think most people come to be entertained; they are consumers.

A. N. How do we screen that out? I really feel its very important to screen that out, if we want to have vital talks. I'm only here in this city for a few days; this may be the only talk we have, and for this talk to be meaningful we can't possibly have this other element around. That would be like going into enemy country.

Q. Sometimes also I think it's a matter of testing your expectation. I came here and I've read different ones of your books, and I can't help but have expectations.

A. N. Yes, but you have a right to them. You have entered through the work, and you have a right to your expectations. And if I disappoint them, you have a right to say the work and the person don't coincide, don't synchronize, that they don't represent the same thing. That's all right because you have entered the work, and in the work you have made a demand of the person who did it. But the person who doesn't know the work and who doesn't know the artist is really the hostile element that I find so strong in the American culture, so dangerous, so negative, so difficult to deal with. It's the thing that makes us fearful; it's around us, let's put it that way; it's not necessarily in this room, but it still exists.

Q. I think that this sort of group is about as big as it can be, though the thing you did on television, where you are interacting with a small group and people got to see that, accommodated a larger situation. Maybe it has something to do with numbers.

A. N. I didn't like that television thing. I'm ready now to give up what I call the interference of the media, which I think is creating a distorted picture. When we face ourselves like this, this is genuine. But I find the other thing is false to begin with, the situation is false; the person who is sitting next to me has no relation to me nor I to him. And I find that a waste of energy. (72-D)

Q. You and Edmund Wilson knew each other for many, many years.

A. N. I still know him. I still see him.

Q. Occasionally he wrote very negative reviews of your books, but it never upset you too much, did it? I mean you were enough of a pro so that you—

A. N. Well, the second review did upset me, yes. That's why we had the argument that I described in *Diary* IV.

Q. That was after he was separated from Mary McCarthy.

A. N. Yes, when I wrote my first novel. He thought I should write like Jane Austen. So he sent me a set of Jane Austen, but I didn't take very well to the hint. And I said no, I wasn't going to write as we wrote in the past, that I thought women had different things to say, new things to say. So we disagreed. We were friends, but we disagreed a lot.

Q. Well, he wanted to—I think he said—absorb you and become your mentor more or less and teach you how to write. But you didn't want that either.

A. N. I was a very independent woman.

Q. You still are, aren't you?

A. N. I still am. (72-A)

Q. It is purported that Somerset Maugham intended to write about his death. Do you have any plans of this nature?

A. N. No, I have never been terribly interested in the feeling of death, I must say. I have never been interested in the writers who are very obsessed with it, like Beckett. It is something that is foreign to my temperament and my nature, and I very rarely think about it. (73-B)

Q. What did you learn on your tour of all these fifty-six colleges, your appearances in public? Why did you do it, and what have you learned from it?

A. N. I was pulled into it really by the women's studies. Every time they opened a women's studies program in colleges they demanded my presence. That was the main thing I did this year, and I felt I should encourage the study of women writers, women artists, because I think we need for the moment that emphasis. It was not because I want to live with that constant emphasis, woman against man, but because we have to equalize things that needed to be equalized. And then I'm also asked and always have to talk to the young writers. I always learn on the way, I always learn something. I learned, for instance, that a lot of the values of the new generation are the values that I believe in, and that gives me hope and the kind of optimism about the future of America. And I also learn a lot about the future. (73-H)

Q. Has your exceptional beauty been an asset or a disadvantage?

A. N. Sometimes it was an asset when you could charm a critic, and sometimes it really stood in the way. For even in women the feeling persists that beauty means there isn't anything inside. I never believed in mine, so that made it very simple. (73-M)

Q. In the diaries, you speak with great attachment of your home in Louveciennes. Do you consider environment an extension of personality in the same way that clothing constitutes a symbolic extension of character in your novels?

A. N. Yes. I also believe we need to change our environment as we evolve. I know the history of Louveciennes ended at a certain time. Looking back on it, it was the right time. Even though it's painful and you are not necessarily aware when you're finished with a certain experience, you do know, something propels you out. I have been propelled out of several homes. When a certain cycle ends, the house itself becomes dead. I think these are reflections of where we are at the moment. (73-M)

Q. Do you still dance?

A. N. I can't dance rock and roll. But I used to do Spanish dancing. And I loved to dance to the real jazz that preceded rock. (73-F)

Q. Please share with us some background which is not in the

Diary. How do you maintain yourself, your weight? Do you do anything to enhance this or is it just natural, were you born with this?

A. N. Not especially; I'm a small eater so I never gain weight. I love swimming, I love walking.

Q. But you don't have direct routines?

A. N. No, I do some of the yoga breathing exercises and I use a slant board sometimes, but I do very little conscious physical exercise. I love swimming, and I love walking. I will never take a bus if I can walk. Then I don't overeat and I don't overdrink, but those are the only things. There's nothing else. (72-D)

Q. Do you have a favorite song and do you play a musical instrument?

A. N. I have favorite songs at different times of my life, and for the moment it's Dore Previn who has written poetry and has set it to music. I'm very fond of her and her voice. I don't play a musical instrument, but I have been a dancer. (73-F)

Q. Do you feel as much affection for Henry Miller as he does for you?

A. N. Yes I do. We're very good friends. The friendship never really broke. I felt very badly when his birthday depressed him, so we brought him the French song that says the best years of your life are twenty and now you're four times twenty so now it must be even better. (72-D)

Q. Henry Miller and you were friends for how many years?

A. N. Oh, we are still friends. Yes, we are still friends.

Q. But you said when you finally left New York and went across the country on that long trip, you got to Los Angeles or to California at least, and met Henry again, and you thought he had changed quite a bit and there wasn't quite the close feeling.

A. N. That is true, that's true. It wasn't quite the same as the life in Paris. We didn't have exactly that same kind of closeness, and I said the friendship from then on would be more general. But there remained certain interests. There were certain things that we always had in common really. His great interest in Japan was one, in Japanese literature.

Q. He was a most generous friend wasn't he, with his money?

A. N. He was very generous with everything, with his ideas, with his stories, with his life. Yes, he was very generous. He always has been and he is generous to other writers too, which is something that we kept from the Paris days. And we never understood, when we came to New York, the absence of fraternity. But then, of course, the New York scene was different. The French writer never made any money; there was something rather uncommercial about being a writer, and we were always helping each other and inspiring each other and encouraging each other. We missed that in New York, but Henry continued to encourage writers and I did too. We always felt that, as somebody once said, the history of art is a history of friendship—or should be. (72-A)

Q. Do you talk about the past a great deal when you get together?

A. N. Never. We spent a good deal of time together while the film of Henry was being made. We talked only of the present. Our presents are so rich.

Q. In what way?

A. N. Well, now I'm tremendously interested in the relation of science to poetry; you know at Stanford University, the electronic laboratory students have a course called "Anais Nin: Integrated Circuits and the Poetics of Science." I'm also interested now in discovering Japanese literature, in particular. I'm interested in travel. (69-A)

Q. What about your film-making? Do you still make films on command?

A. N. No, I never made films.

Q. You and your group, I mean.

A. N. You mean we acted in them. Well, you wouldn't even call it acting. We were very bad actors, but the film-makers that we knew didn't have money for real actors. So we had to make do. Maya Deren was one of the early ones, if you remember.

Q. You were always bitter about that time when she ordered you around and—

A. N. Yes, yes. But I think since then I have more sympathy for the director.

Q. Can you remember the incident in Central Park where she wanted the ballet dancer to jump and you almost walked off.
A. N. Yes, we thought it was a very dangerous thing. His livelihood really depended on his dancing, and Maya Deren thought that it would make a wonderful leap from one rock to another, a ballet leap. But we thought that he was endangering his whole life, that he might break a leg. So we told Maya we didn't think that she should ask that, and she was absolutely adamant. I mean like a good director she insisted that this had to be done.
Q. Also, she promised you that she wouldn't have close-ups, for example, and wouldn't do this and wouldn't do that and completely ignored all the promises.
A. N. Yes. But then today I wouldn't blame her for that. Because I've watched films being made, and I realize that the film was more important than ourselves. We just wanted to see ourselves a certain way. We were not professional. (72-A)
Q. What are you presently working on?
A. N. I'm editing *Diary* VI. Editing Volume VII will bring me to the exchange of letters and diaries with other women. Then I will go back and redo my childhood and adolescence, because readers say I started the *Diary* at the point where my life expanded. They would like to see how it went from the narrow to the expanded part. (73-M)
Q. Do you have in your diaries enough material now for, say, another ten, fifteen, twenty volumes?
A. N. I have too much material. I have more material than I have time.
Q. How many more volumes of diaries will be printed, do you know?
A. N. I don't know how many I can do. Some may have to be done after my death, and some I can do now. But there is so much that I don't really know how long I will be doing it.
Q. Do you hope to issue one a year for maybe the next seven or eight or ten years?
A. N. I really don't know.
Q. What reaction do you get from the people who are in it? You

said that some are hostile, but I mean, overall, is it a very favorable reaction?

A. N. Overall, it's always been very good. I have never had any difficulties. I have had people who asked to be out of it for reasons of reticence, people who don't like to have their lives exposed, which is natural. But I've never had reactions to the portraits, the changes which were requested were insignificant. Even the portrait I made of Gore, he consented to and made only some very trivial changes. So as a whole I think it's because I never wanted my portraits to be cruel or to be destructive. That was never my intention and because I made an effort to make a complete portrait of a person, they were able to accept it. Because the good was there as well as the other.

Q. Do you think if people were as slow-moving and relaxed as turtles they would live to be as old?

A. N. I wonder about that.

Q. Because you seem very relaxed and very young. I know you're not very young.

A. N. I was neither relaxed nor very young when I was young.

Q. But you now are, I think.

A. N. Yes, I think after a long time you do attain a certain serenity or adaptation or harmony with your life. I'm in harmony with my life now. But if you read the *Diary* you can see I wasn't always like that. (72-A)

Q. Do you find conflicts between your own personal morality and artistic fantasies? I'm thinking of *A Spy in the House of Love,* where this woman was very drawn to go out and have affairs but then had guilt feelings about them. How do you handle your fantasies?

A. N. You can't generalize. I studied one woman, Sabina, and I did say that the effort she made to live out all her selves in this direction simply disintegrated her. It was a study of not finding wholeness by just looking for passion. That's all there is in that story, you see. But that has nothing to do with morality itself. She had inherited a cultural concept of morality, and that was the thing that was doing her so much harm.

Q. Do you find a personal conflict sometimes between fantasies and what you feel is morally right?
A. N. Well, everybody has conflicts between their fantasies and their cultural mores.
Q. And how do you handle these?
A. N. Well, you discover where *you* stand. It's up to you. And psychology usually helps you to realize that the guilt is artificial. It's artificially induced by your religion, by your family, by whoever has had prestige over you. And then you learn to transcend that guilt. I had that at a certain time, but I transcended it so that now I have no guilt for being whatever it is that I am. You see, guilt has been instilled in us. It's what D. H. Lawrence put so well when he said religion had made us meditate constantly on the crucifixion and never on the resurrection. And then Varda had another way of putting it. He said: "We are always talking about the inferno, we never talk about paradise." So it's up to us to get rid of the things that are not genuinely us.
Q. Sometimes when you do what you really want to do, you end up hurting people who are very close to you and people you want to remain close to. That can put you in a terrible conflict at times.
A. N. That's a conflict we'll always have. We will always have a conflict between our growth and our fear that that growth will overshadow or injure someone else. And what we have to do is to create our own private morality and our private ethics and our private faith, for that naturally means that if you're a sensitive person you're not going to destroy people around you. (73-I)
Q. What is the source of your inexhaustible energy?
A. N. I haven't thought about that. I guess it's curiosity, the fact that I still feel things as keenly. I suppose that when you feel alive something propels you into new experiences, new friendships, and while you're responding you have this energy. It seems to be a quality of responsiveness, of remaining alive to whatever is happening around you. While you have that feeling, you go on exploring. Then, I'm always curious. I was in an airplane accident once. One side of the wing had caught fire, we had six minutes to get to Los Angeles, and all I was doing was thinking of all the places I

hadn't seen yet. That was my feeling—that it was a shame not to see everything, to hear everything, be everywhere. (73-M)

Q. I'm curious if you have overcome the idea of writing something that would be a culmination of your work. Because reading your *Diary,* it just keeps going, it doesn't seem to crescendo or build up to something.

A. N. We are accustomed to think of fiction as having a denouement, as having resolution. I don't think that the buildup and the climax and the resolution which we find in the novel is really like our life, and the *Diary* takes its form from life. It has its high moments and its low moments, and it goes on like this and doesn't necessarily come to any climax. Why should it come to a peak, to a finality? You see, you're speaking of finality and there is no finality actually in our life. Our relationships go on and friendships are renewed. There is continuity; there is no climax. There is no finality in life except with death. So the *Diary,* taking its form from life, will never have that. Each volume in a way does have its theme and its drama and its development. But it's not like the novel, because the novel generates artificial expectations—that there are resolutions and things that are final, that we complete and finish with experiences. Somebody once asked me if I now felt completed as a woman. I said: "No, we never finish this creation of the self."

Q. Earlier in your life what role did letter-writing fill for you? I know right now I'm feeling a lot of satisfaction from letter-writing and sometimes at the expense of other kinds of writing.

A. N. I was never a great letter-writer. I guess I was being economical or writing to the diary. I'm answering letters now, but correspondence was not a major part of my writing. Somehow, because I gave so much to the diary, I didn't have very much left for long correspondence. Henry Miller was a tremendous letter-writer, and people were always trying to separate him from letter-writing so that he would do his novels. He wrote forty- or eighty-page letters. So in a way you may be doing something that you enjoy more than the formal work, but you have to examine whether that love of letter-writing doesn't conceal a writer too. Are you aware of that? It may be a preparation for becoming an artist or an author. That's good. (73-B)

Q. You have a list of people whom you have never met that you wanted to meet including Isak Dinesen and two or three others. Can you remember who they were?

A. N. One I wanted to know better is Martha Graham, whom I admired a great deal. I wanted to know James Agee better, who lived in the Village then, and whose writing I admired.

Q. But you did meet him several times?

A. N. I did meet him, but we didn't become friends. It seemed harder for me to become friends with the American writers. I don't exactly know why, but one reason was that I didn't drink. It seems like a trivial reason, but it's true that these writers felt more comfortable with drinking companions. That was really a problem and made things very difficult.

Q. You refused to meet Marshall Field because you said he had too much money.

A. N. Yes, I always had that prejudice against the rich.

Q. You said somewhere that if they were really nice people they would give their money away.

A. N. Yes, I've had this idea. I had it from the very beginning of my life, I think, because one part of my family was all artists and they were all poor, and another part of my family was wealthy and they were the selfish ones. Somehow I always kept that prejudice. (72-A)

Q. Have you ever had a child?

A. N. No. I had surgery when I was nine years old which made it impossible. And we didn't find out until the first child I conceived was still-born—was strangled by adhesions. At that time they made a very poor kind of surgery and created adhesions which strangled the child. So nature denied me that. It wasn't by choice. But I don't feel that unless you've had a child you're not fulfilled. I don't feel that I've missed anything. Because I transferred that to other relationships. As Lawrence said, we don't need more children, we need more hope in the world. (72-D)

Q. You talked about having a tragic sense of life, and you said the tragic sense of life means one's obsession with an ideal, not a primitive, natural life, but an ideal, romanticized life. And you asked yourself when it was that you set such ideals for yourself and made your own life so difficult.

A. N. This was during the period of the early diaries where I was a romantic, or neurotic, if you want to put it in modern terms, and expected extraordinary things. This is no longer true. Maturity means that you begin to fuse what is possible with what you wanted and also to see that your demands are often very exaggerated and very inhuman to others.

Q. Was that one of the chief difficulties in your early life?

A. N. No, that was a problem which psychoanalysis dissolved. You see psychoanalysis gives you a sense of reality—and I don't mean in terms of accepting something lower or of less quality than what you wanted—but in terms of how to fulfill it. What I really learned was how to attain these things that I really wanted, and that they were not impossible.

Q. And you managed it without too much of the pain that you went through at the beginning.

A. N. The early diaries have more of the obstacles and the pains than the later ones. In fact, the one I am editing now is a very joyous volume.

Q. Joy is a word that you use even in the earlier diaries. You talk about joy in little things.

A. N. I was seeking that. I think the quest for joy is a very wonderful one, and I always did seek that in the middle of all the troubles. When I say a tragic sense of life it's because I don't like the comic sense of life. I don't think the things we usually laugh at are very funny. But joy is a different thing. There's another kind of playfulness—*play* the way the artist uses it. It's imagination and trying to transpose and improve on reality. That kind of play is a joyous thing. (72-F)

Q. Would you continue to write even if you had no readers?

A. N. Yes. (69-A)

Q. You have gone so far and come so far—what is your dream now?

A. N. I started as a poet with traumas which threw me into myself. When some people have a traumatic experience in life and are thrown into themselves sometimes they stay there. But my dream was to get out, and now I have fulfilled that—the coming out and then having communion with the world and being able to be connected with everything that happens. I can't say that I have another dream beyond that, because I'm living this one fully. My life has expanded, and the growth has never stopped. I can't say that I have a further wish now. I'm just completing these wishes—that I should have a sense of union with the world and a sense of union particularly with womens' growth and development. And I think I have that.

My dream now doesn't concern just me anymore; it has to do with all women. My dream at the moment is to see women really grow and expand to their full, absolutely fullest capacity. I realize all the obstacles, because I not only experienced them myself but because I get so many letters from women. So I think that is my dream now. It is about woman. (73-K)

Q. Do you go to parties often, and if you do go to parties often in New York or L. A. or San Francisco or wherever, do you enjoy the wee hours of the morn? In one of your diaries I gathered you didn't like that sort of—social aggressiveness I could call it. I wanted to know if since 1966 you're physically up to it, if you stay till the end?

A. N. I'm sorry, but as far as my waning energies are concerned, my fifty-six lectures since September prove otherwise. I don't like parties, no, and I don't like to talk all night except with a very few friends. But I don't think I'm bothered by waning energies yet. I think you'd better ask Picasso. (73-H)

Q. Could you speak a little more on death in the physical sense?

A. N. That's a subject I never think about. I'm completely unprepared. I don't think about it. I think our death in life is what should really worry us. I don't want that to happen while we are in life. What happens afterwards somehow has never been my line, and I really am not inclined or quick to talk about it. I never think about it. I'm very preoccupied with remaining in life as alive as possible, and therefore I really don't believe in aging or chronological age. I think the real concern should be whether we stop living or stop feeling or stop thinking or stop exploring, for there is really no end to life, you know. So I don't want death to be a primary interest. It's not my concern.

Q. I think I remember you saying in the early *Diary* that it was at times when you were most involved with life that you thought most about death.

A. N. Yes, I think we do that into our twenties. I think sometimes we are more concerned about that when we are young. Children play death games a lot. But then I think as you feel closer to it, you don't think about it. (72-G)

Q. Once, when Paul Rosenfeld asked your advice concerning how to begin his autobiography, you told him: "Write your wishes and dreams, and ask if they were fulfilled." What were your wishes and dreams? Have they been, are they being fulfilled?

A. N. My obsession was with love and friendship. This has been fulfilled, personally; and love and friendship with the world through my work. I feel fortunate that those are being fulfilled. (69-A)

Q. I have a question that's been bothering me for some time. How do you pronounce your name?

A. N. Oh, I'll have to teach you that because there are little girls being named after me. I have five god-daughters. The name is Anaïs. If you say Anna, it makes it easier, because there are two dots on the "i," and you have to separate the "a" and the "i." There was a fad in France about three hundred years ago, giving children Greek names. And so we have Thaïs of Flaubert and we have an Anaïs in Colette, and I think there's an Anaïs in Simenon. So the children were given those names generation after generation. I was lucky enough to be named Anaïs. And now you're going to have a few more Anaïses. So it's pronounced Anna-eese. (72-G)

Q. If you had to—you know the old question—if you had to do it all again, relive it, and start creating from the beginning, knowing what you do know now, would your writing be very different, would your life have been very different?

A. N. I don't think I would like to change that difficult inner voyage that I made. It was all very rich, and I wouldn't like to erase all the errors I made. I don't think I would change anything really. The only thing I might have liked changed is that I would like to have been accelerated, I would have liked not to have taken so much time. For instance, the acceptance of my writing took so very long, and I can't say that I rejoice over that. It took twenty years.

Q. But isn't it nicer in the end?

A. N. Yes, but I wish it had happened sooner. There are time elements that I would like to have changed; I think mostly it's the acceleration which happened to this generation and which gives me great elation. They're accelerated, their wisdom is accelerated, their experiences are accelerated. It's not such a long struggle. For them the inner journey won't take quite so long. (72-F)

Q. When it became obvious that World War II was inevitable, you wrote in your *Diary* that "the modern hero was the one who would master his own neurosis so that it would not become universal, who would struggle with his myths, who would know that he himself created them, who would enter the labyrinth and fight the monster." Assuming that you still believe this, can you say anything to encourage those who are still too frightened to make "the difficult voyage"?

A. N. Yes. Keep a vision of the ultimate goal, reward. An expanded life, free of anxiety and conflict. Achievement in love and creation. A sense of deep fulfillment. (72-X)

Q. Before you go, I'd like to clarify something I said before. I said that your *Diary* nearly lost one now because it was forever. I said it didn't belong to our time because it was timeless. I hope you understand that I didn't mean that your *Diary* was turned to the past. I meant the opposite.

A. N. No, I knew what you meant and that was the reason I published it. If I had felt it wasn't timeless, as you said—better even than I did—I wouldn't have published it. If it had been just nostalgic, I would have kept it secret. No, I heard what you said and I liked what you said. And so on this note of timelessness and mutual understanding I think I will say goodnight. (73-E)

Acknowledgments

Most of the tapes used in this edition were obtained from Anaïs Nin herself, but Donna Ippolito of The Swallow Press and Judith Citrin provided me with tapes in their possession. Richard Centing, as is usual in any Nin scholarship, was most generous in providing bibliographical information. I should like to express my gratitude to these individuals for their help.

For the financial assistance which freed me from teaching during much of the preparation of the manuscript, I am indebted to the University of Manitoba and to the Killam Foundation whose funds are administered by the Canada Council.

Pat Spakowski was responsible both for the transcription of the tapes and for preparing the typescript of the edition, and to her a most grateful acknowledgement is due.

This edition, finally, owes its inception as well as its completion to John Teunissen. It was through him that I first became aware of and interested in Nin's fiction and it was he who, while we accompanied Anaïs Nin to Bradley Airport after her 1972 commencement address at Hampshire College, suggested to us the idea of this edition. Throughout the preparation of the edition he has generously shared with me his knowledge of editing and his professional insights. In addition, he continually encouraged me by reminding me of the importance of this project and of the urgency of completing it. Anaïs Nin and I have been very fortunate in our men.

263

Index

Index   265